Colorado Rail Annual No. 15

Idaho-Montana Issue

Overleaf: Scene on the Utah & Northern — watercolor by Mike Pearsall.

55
55
55
55
11

Ogden Logan Franklin McCammon Pocatello Eagle Rock

High Bridge Monida Red Rock Dillon Silver Bow Butte Deer Lodge

Logan Franklin McCammon Pocatello Blackfoot Eagle Rock High Bridge

Colorado Rail Annual No. 15

A Journal of Railroad History in the Rocky Mountain West

Idaho Montana Issue

published by the
Colorado Railroad Museum
Box 10, Golden, Colo. 80401

Monida Red Rock Divide Silver Bow Butte Garrison

Oregon Short Line no. 1270 (an 1882 Danforth & Cooke 2-8-0) waiting for a meet near Pocatello about 1890. (C. H. Peake Collection)

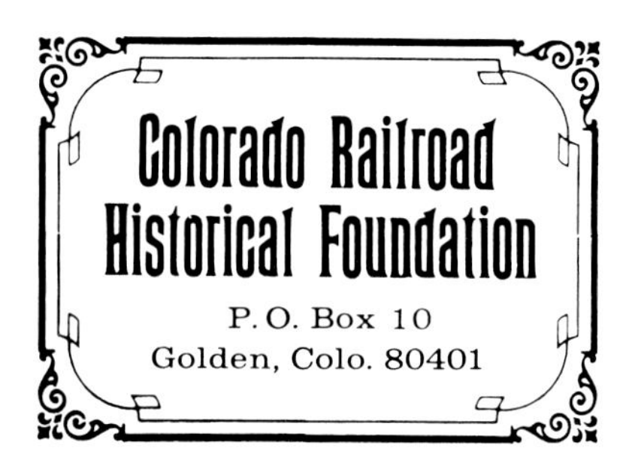

Colorado Rail Annual No. 15
1981

EDITOR AND PUBLISHER
Cornelius W. Hauck
ASSOCIATE EDITORS
Charles Albi
Gordon S. Chappell
Rex C. Myers
Robert W. Richardson

PUBLISHED AND DISTRIBUTED BY
the Colorado Railroad Museum
BOX 10, GOLDEN COLO. 80401

ISBN 0-918654-15-7

Library of Congress Catalog Card Number 70-102682
Printed and Bound in the United States of America
Layout and Production: Cornelius W. Hauck
Typesetting: Quality Typesetting Co.
Printing: Feicke Printing Co. Inc.
Binding: C. J. Krehbiel Co.

Editor's Comments

Although the *Colorado Rail Annual*, as the title implies, has largely been concerned with aspects of Colorado railroad history, our chosen province by definition is the Rocky Mountain West (with emphasis on narrow gauge), and we have been known to stray as far as Nome, Alaska.

In this edition, the fifteenth in the series, we document the story of the first railroad to breach the remote mining frontiers of Idaho and western Montana — the narrow gauge Utah & Northern, a daring and in fact foolhardy venture of the Mormon Church, carried to fruition by the Union Pacific to form a major tributary for its transcontinental line.

Completion of the Union Pacific (and subsequently Kansas Pacific) had brought the realization of low-cost transportation from Colorado and Utah to eastern markets and opened up their mining regions to development. Equally promising mining areas in northern Idaho and western Montana still lay hundreds of miles from dependable transportation, and the arrival of the Northern Pacific from the east was clearly many, many years away. The leaders of the Mormon Church conceived a plan to build a railroad — narrow gauge, for minimum cost — from a connection with the Union Pacific at Ogden for some 400 miles into Montana, to bring the trade of the mining camps to their mercantile establishments. The task proved overwhelming, and the Union Pacific stepped in to complete the project, creating one of the longest and certainly most isolated narrow gauge railroads in the west. The history of this pioneer narrow gauge is set forth in the first part of our book.

The Utah & Northern narrow gauge subsequently became the standard gauge Oregon Short Line & Utah Northern, and in due course was integrated into the Union Pacific System, still serving today as an important division of that railroad. The operations of this standard gauge successor to the Utah & Northern during the first half of the 20th century are also detailed in this edition of the *Colorado Rail Annual*.

Although branch lines to other mining camps and prospects in Montana figured prominently in original plans, none were ever built by the U&N or Union Pacific. It remained for two obscure independent short lines to take this step in the 20th century. One was the narrow gauge Montana Southern, which operated intermittently during the 1920's from Divide southwest into the Wise River country. The other was the standard gauge Gilmore & Pittsburgh, which ran for three decades from Armstead (near Dillon) on the Union Pacific across the Bitterroot Mountains to Salmon, in Idaho's Lemhi Valley. The story of this implausible mountain short line forms the third part of our volume.

Our authors have spent endless hours digging into dusty resources and tracking down elusive oldtimers to compile their respective segments of the book. Many others assisted, and their parts are acknowledged after each of the three main chapters. However, one person was of particular assistance and inspiration — the late Arthur Petersen, of Pocatello, Idaho. For many years Art was an ardent accumulator and keeper of historic memorabilia of Idaho's railroads, and he shared his interest and materials generously. He contributed much of the material that made this book possible, and helped unravel the intertwined threads of fact and fiction that make up the story of the Utah & Northern and Union Pacific. In recognition of his contribution to railroad history preservation, the Editors are dedicating this edition of the *Colorado Rail Annual* in his memory.

Cornelius W. Hauck
Cincinnati

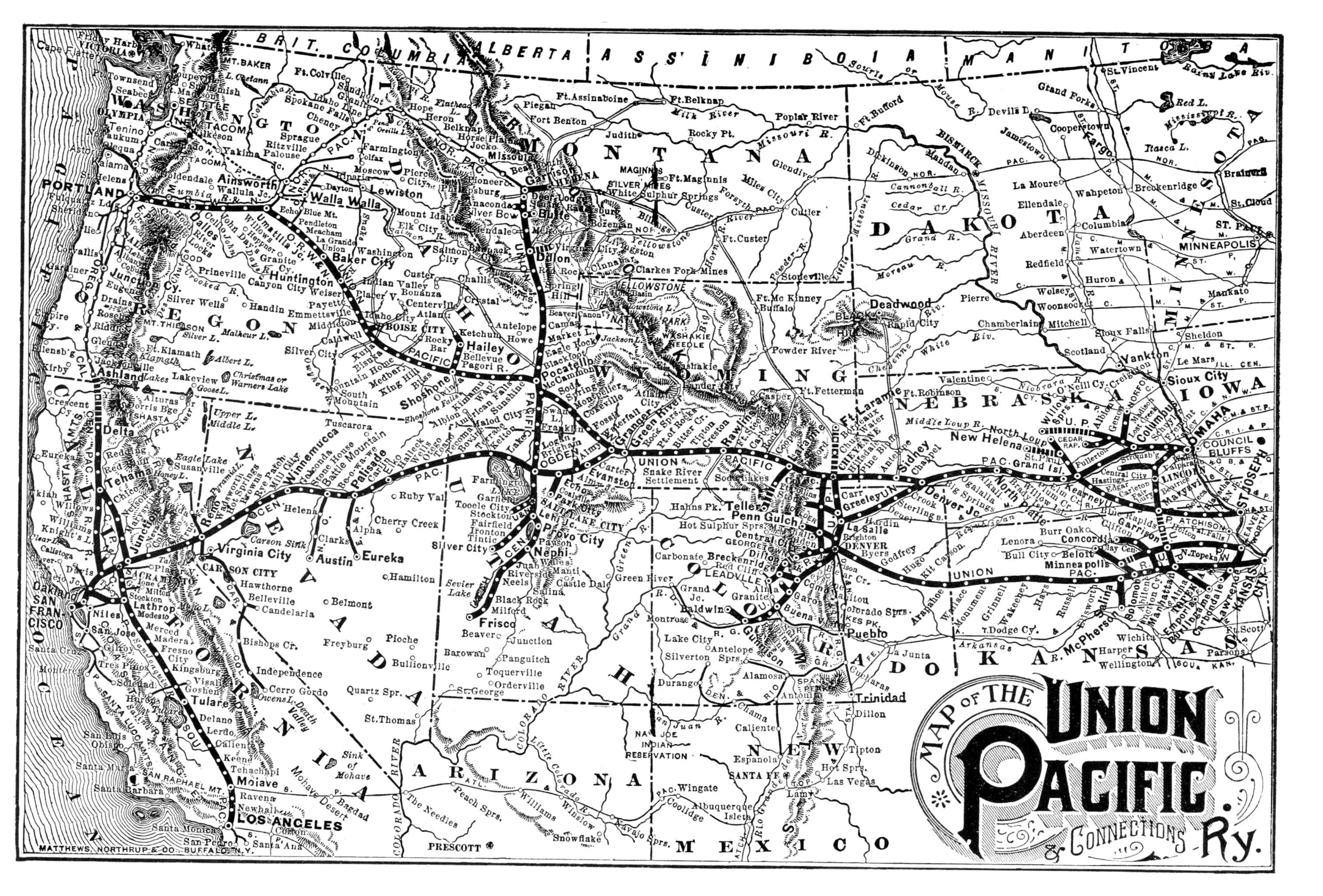
MAP OF THE UNION PACIFIC RY. & CONNECTIONS
MONTANA
DAKOTA
MINNESOTA
IOWA
NEBRASKA
KANSAS
WYOMING
COLORADO
IDAHO
UTAH
NEVADA
CALIFORNIA
OREGON
WASHINGTON
ARIZONA
NEW MEXICO
PACIFIC OCEAN
BRIT. COLUMBIA
ALBERTA
ASSINIBOIA
MANITOBA
MATTHEWS, NORTHRUP & CO., BUFFALO, N.Y.

The Pacific Hotel and, beyond, old Oregon Short Line depots at Pocatello, Idaho, in the 1890's. (Museum Collection)

Contents

Utah & Northern
The Narrow Gauge that Opened a Frontier
by Mallory Hope Ferrell 9

OSL&UN:
the Oregon Short Line Era
by Cornelius W. Hauck 82

Union Pacific, Montana Division
by Cornelius W. Hauck 93

Gilmore & Pittsburgh
Northern Pacific Subsidiary, Union Pacific Tributary
by Rex C. Myers 161

Maps:

Union Pacific System . . 6
Utah Northern 22
Utah & Northern 51
Utah & Northern-Union Pacific 62
Gilmore & Pittsburgh . . . 168-171

The Anaconda and St. Lawrence Mines at Butte, Montana, around the turn of the century. (Museum Collection)

Brigham City can be seen faintly etched along the base of the mountains in the distance, looking across the Salt Lake Valley from Corinne in this A. J. Russell view of 1869. (Union Pacific Railroad Collection)

Utah & Northern

the Narrow Gauge That Opened a Frontier

by Mallory Hope Ferrell

with Gordon Chappell and Cornelius W. Hauck

Picture, if you will, a three foot gauge railroad almost 500 miles long built across three frontier territories to a small Montana town that could count only 200 souls. Envision a narrow gauge line that was projected north from the Great Salt Lake by the Mormon Church, begun by farmers and settlers and completed by the mighty Union Pacific Railroad. Further envision a railroad that made possible a 1350-mile narrow gauge rail journey from Santa Fe, New Mexico to Garrison, Montana, and was powered by small Mason Bogies and a stable of other locomotives from the works of Grant, Brooks, Rhode Island and Baldwin. All this and more comprise the story of the Utah & Northern Railroad, a narrow gauge built daringly into a vast northern frontier.

Though its later history was in many ways typical of that of other narrow gauge railroads in the West, its early history was not, for it was spawned in the reactions of the Mormon Church heirarchy to economic conditions of the time. Persecuted because of their religious beliefs, the Mormons had fled and fled again, the last time emigrating across the "Mormon Trail" in 1847 from Nauvoo, Illinois to the valley of the Great Salt Lake. There Brigham Young and his followers in 1849 established what was intended to be an independent nation called "Deseret." But even before they had begun their hegira into what had been "terra incognita" of nominal Mexican sovereignty, the course of international events overtook their march, so that the land into which they had fled became part of the spoils of war fought in 1846 and 1847. The Treaty of Guadalupe Hidalgo of 1848 brought into United States possession the new "State of Deseret" even before its founding, so that instead of being head of an independent nation, Mormon leader Brigham Young found himself merely governor of just another American frontier territory — the Territory of Utah.

Nevertheless Young and Mormon Church leadership ran Utah almost as if it was a theocracy, and having been victims of persecution because of their religious beliefs elsewhere, some Mormons became persecutors of non-Mormons, or "gentiles" as they were called in Utah, who passed through or attempted to settle there. This combined with friction between Mormon leaders and "gentile" territorial officials appointed from Washington led to the so-called "Mormon War" of 1857-1858, which despite some armed clashes, was on the whole peaceably settled. When the Civil War broke out in 1861, Lincoln's government was still sufficiently uncertain of Mormon loyalty that a strong force of Union volunteer troops from California under

Colonel Patrick Edward Connor marched eastward to Salt Lake City, and established a new army garrison called Camp Douglas east of the city on the western slope of the Wasatch Range.

While the Civil War was still in progress a number of rich mining districts were opened up in Montana Territory, five hundred miles to the north. Virginia City, Helena, Butte and other such "boom towns" soon needed supplies, food, clothing and mining machinery.

About 1865 a settler named William H. Murphy, in what would later become McCammon, secured a franchise to operate a toll road between Ogden and Beaver Canyon on the Idaho-Montana territorial boundary. Murphy's route, after passing through the Malad Valley, went through the March and Portneuf Valleys. Known as the "Montana Trail," it traversed a huge area that was sparsely populated but rich in agricultural potential.

During the 1860's the freighting business between Utah and the gold fields grew steadily in importance. Large quantities of flour, bacon, sugar, clothing and other supplies were hauled into the mining regions each year. It was a slow trip, but more dependable than the equally tedious steamboat journey along the Missouri River route. A freight outfit consisted normally of three wagons hooked together in a "train" and hauled by horses, mules or oxen. The average pace over the "Montana Trail" was between 12 and 15 miles per day. The 500-mile haul was expensive; flour freighted across eastern Idaho to the mining towns sold for two dollars a pound. Furthermore, mining machinery and any goods not raised or manufactured in Utah had to come by wagon clear across the Overland Trail to Salt Lake or Ogden from the east, so that they traveled the base and the left side of a vast rectangle, the other two sides constituting the long route via the Missouri and by wagon from the head of navigation at Fort Benton to the mining camps. While better than the river route for agricultural crops and merchandise that could be produced in Utah, and in some respects better for shipment of goods from the east, the wagons could generally use the Montana Trail only between April and November — like the riverboats blocked during the winter, not merely by ice but by snow and mud.

An effort was made in 1866 and 1867 to open a new and more direct wagon road to Montana, stretching diagonally across central Wyoming from a point on the North Platte River a few days march west of Fort Laramie. Unfortunately this Bozeman Trail crossed the heart of Sioux and Northern Cheyenne lands and its use precipitated a disastrous two-year Indian war, culminated in 1868 with complete accession to Sioux demands and the abandonment of the trail.

Thus transportation to the Montana mining camps was at best poor, time-consuming and costly; at worst, during the winter, it was non-existent. The *Helena Herald* reported in the spring of 1869 that "more than thirty steamboats have left St. Louis for Fort Benton and the mines of Montana." How many of these shallow-draft boats made the entire trip to the headwaters of the Missouri was unreported, but treacherous currents and sandbars, rapids and snags took their toll each summer, and during the winter months the mighty river was blocked by ice. Steamboating on the upper Missouri was a dangerous occupation and accidents were frequent on the river. Furthermore, there was still a wagon haul to the mines from the head of navigation.

Another factor entering the equation (in which eventually the Utah & Northern would be a factor) was construction of the first transcontinental railroad, which would not only cross Utah Territory but whose two components, the rival Union Pacific and Central Pacific railroads, would meet in Utah at Promontory Summit northwest of Ogden. The railroad represented gentile economic penetration of the "Kingdom of the Saints," as this Great Basin political and economic domain of the Church of Jesus Christ of the Latter Day Saints — or Mormon Church — frequently was called. Nevertheless the Mormons welcomed it as an economic benefit to Utah which they, themselves, would not have been able to finance or build. Still, Brigham Young and Church leadership were unhappy that their efforts to have this transcontinental main line railroad pass through the territorial and ecclesiastical capital of Salt Lake City were unavailing; to do so, argued the Union Pacific engineers, would be to deviate many miles from the most suitable and inexpensive route, and neither the Central Pacific nor the Union Pacific could afford to do so.

Unhappy though they might be with the route chosen, via Ogden and around the north rather than via Salt Lake City and around the southern end of the Great Salt Lake, once the decision was made the Mormons nevertheless assisted the Union Pacific to completion. Subsequently the Mormons would incorporate their own short line, the Utah Central, to connect Ogden with Salt Lake City in 1870, and serve as a precedent for other "Mormon railroads," among them the Utah Northern.

The transcontinental railroad completed at Promontory Summit on May 10, 1869, changed the whole transportation equation as far as Montana was concerned, making the rail-wagon route far superior to the riverboat-wagon route via the Missouri. Furthermore, "gentile" business interests began to center at the new town of Corinne, Utah, 25 miles west of Ogden on the Union Pacific — actually on a portion of track between Ogden and Promontory Summit which in 1874 would be transferred to the Central Pacific. As a result of the efforts of gentile freighting firms, Corinne soon became the principal rail shipping point for traffic to the Montana mines. Montana merchants suffered such heavy losses shipping via the Missouri that they were eager to avail themselves of improved service by this route. When the large wagon freighting firm of Graham, Maurice & Company indicated that it was considering fast freight service between Montana and the East via Corinne and the railroad, a number of the businessmen of Helena wrote the firm on September 17, 1869:

> Gentlemen:
>
> Learning that you intend establishing a fast freight line from New York and other cities to this and other points in the Territory, via railroad to Corinne, thence by wagon train, we desire to tender you our support, with a view to the success of the enterprise. Navigation on the Missouri River is so precarious that we are anxious to avail ourselves of a route which offers a guarantee for the prompt delivery of our consignments. This we feel you can give by the means of transportation which you propose to employ.

Previous to completion of the Union Pacific, Ogden had been shipping point to the Montana mines, but Corinne, being closer and eliminating 25 miles of the wagon haul from Ogden to Montana, soon eclipsed the Mormon town to the east. A settlement had been platted there in February 1869 by Union Pacific chief engineer J. E. House. It was surveyed into hundreds of small lots and several large ones. An entire block was set aside for the Catholic Church. Within several weeks of its survey, about 500 wood frame buildings and tents were in evidence, and in typical "boom town" fashion lots were selling for from $100 to $1,000 each on land that a mere two months earlier had been a broad, arid salt flat at the mouth of the Bear River. The town was served not only by the new railroad but by the *City of Corinne*, a large, $45,000 Mississippi River-style steamboat that plied the waters of the Bear and the Great Salt Lake into which it emptied.

Often referred to as the "Burg on the Bear," Corinne prided itself in being Utah's principal non-Mormon community. Its newspapers were notoriously anti-Mormon, and of course Salt Lake City and Ogden newspapers responded by being equally anti-Corinne. It is said that Brigham Young had cursed Corinne and predicted that "grass will grow in the streets and the buildings will be torn down or moved to surrounding communities for barns and out houses," and beyond predicting the town's demise, would soon take steps to accomplish that goal. Nevertheless, for the time being Corinne prospered and was an irritating thorn in the side of Church leadership and the still-Church-dominated territorial government. There must be some way to wrest from Corinne control and some of the profits of this rich Montana trade!

Meanwhile Corinne continued its role as "supplier to the northern mines." In the spring of 1871, as it began its second season of shipping to the Montana mining districts, the city claimed warehouses for four freight lines: Kirkendall's Fast Freight & Express Company, Creighton & Munro's Freight & Express Line, the huge Diamond R. Freight & Express Lines, and Wells Fargo & Company Express. Other large east and west coast firms established branches in Corinne. These included the Oriental Powder Company of Boston, the Kimball Wagon & Carriage Manufacturing Company of San Francisco (soon to become a manufacturer also of railroad cars), Chicago's Schutler Wagon Factory and San Francisco's California Powder Works. Wells Fargo and the stage and mail line operated by Gilmer & Salisbury scheduled daily stages to Virginia City, Helena, Deer Lodge, Bozeman and other Montana Territory camps. The Idaho & Oregon Company stages departed for Boise City, Walla Walla, Umatilla and Portland each day.

The trip to the gold camps was no easier for the stage passenger than it was for the freight, despite the leather strap "springs" of the fancy Concord coaches. The drivers loved to pull into the next station in a cloud of dust, and liked to enter town with the horses at full gallop, much to the displeasure of the unsuspecting passenger. On one occasion, as the stage pulled into Eagle Rock, Idaho Territory, the driver saw his lone passenger leap from the stage, run across the yard to the outside wall of the station, and stand on his head with his feet propped against the wall. "Why in Hell are 'yer stand'in on yer head?" inquired the amazed driver. The passenger lowered his feet and replied, "Well, standing on my head is the only position I haven't been in during my ride in that thing you call a stage coach. I just thought I'd try it to make the cycle complete."

Freight shipments from Corinne resumed each spring as soon as the snows had melted. They continued until the snow was again so deep that the roads were closed. Springtime saw the greatest activity, when from half a million to a full million pounds of freight filled the warehouses and adjoining loading docks. In good weather, it took freight about thirty days to reach the camps from the time it left Chicago or St. Louis. The trip from San Francisco was somewhat shorter.

Corinne kept its place of prominence in the

Montana trade almost unopposed through 1872. Both Ogden and Logan challenged the "Burg on the Bear" for mail contracts, passenger and freight business, but unsuccessfully. Ogden was more than twenty miles farther from the gold camps than Corinne, and Logan was isolated and without a rail connection, although the Cache Valley around it did supply a small amount of local farm products during the spring and summer for shipment to Montana.

That this situation disturbed Mormon church leaders is an understatement. They soon took steps to remedy it, and Corinne lost the first battle. The two components of the transcontinental railroad had met at Promontory Summit, a desert junction far from any town or source of freight. This was eminently satisfactory to the Union Pacific which thus retained a monopoly on traffic not only eastbound but also west out of Ogden and the Great Salt Lake basin. It also left the Mormon communities vulnerable to monopolistic Union Pacific rates. But to the Central Pacific, as well as to the Mormons, this was most unsatisfactory, as one end of its lengthy railroad was blocked just short of access to at least Mormon traffic from Ogden west; the Union Pacific reaped all of the extra profits of all of that traffic originating on its line. The Central Pacific and the Mormon leaders were not without political influence; furthermore, working together they could extend a competitive Central Pacific line eastward from Promontory Summit, paralleling the Union Pacific not only as far as Ogden but beyond. It was to the interest of the Union Pacific to reach some amicable agreement allowing the Central Pacific access to the population centers of the Great Salt Lake Valley in exchange for no further penetration of Union Pacific territory. Corinne hoped to become the junction point, with attendant union depot and railroad roundhouse and shop facilities of both railroads and consequent increase in employment and population, but with Mormon influence thrown into the struggle, it was Ogden that won. Nevertheless, Corinne continued as transfer point for the Montana trade, and the Central Pacific Railroad, which took over the trackage between Promontory and Ogden in a transfer not finalized until 1874, erected a huge freight transfer warehouse there.

The next step facing the Mormon leadership was control of the freight traffic itself, and the way to do it was to replace the wagon freight route out of Corinne — or at least enough miles of it to achieve control of it — with a railroad, a railroad whose southern terminus would be Ogden rather than Corinne.

This was not, of course, the first railroad involvement of Mormons or the Mormon leadership. John W. Young, one of Brigham Young's eldest sons, had personally taken on a contract to build portions of the Union Pacific and Central Pacific main lines in the spring of 1868, netting between $45,000 and $50,000. With his brother Joseph A. Young (and other Mormons) he had been involved in construction of the standard gauge Utah Central, begun in 1869 to connect Ogden with Salt Lake City and completed on January 10, 1870. Subsequently he had been involved in the Utah Southern Railroad projected southward from Salt Lake City in 1871. Thus John Young and others had gained enough knowledge of railroad finance, construction and operation to contemplate the even larger enterprise of linking Mormon cities of Utah with the mining camps of Montana, bypassing Corinne and thus bringing Brigham's prophecy regarding that town to fulfillment. Most important, John Young had met and become closely associated with the rich and powerful men behind the Union Pacific and Central Pacific railroads.

Another Mormon Church leader, one who had been a subcontractor for Brigham Young on portions of the Union Pacific contracts, became interested in a railroad to Montana. During the summer of 1871 Bishop William B. Preston of Logan wrote Brigham Young that the Mormons in the Cache Valley were willing to do all that was necessary to see a railroad built into their territory. Young responded with encouragement to Preston and other church leaders of northern Utah, and asked his son, John, to assume personal responsibility for undertaking and successfully completing this "great work."

John W. Young was told by his father that the new project was to be a "people's road," that is, owned by the people who built it, and as with the other Mormon railroads, the farmers and Mormon citizens living along the projected route would be called upon to provide labor and teams in exchange for shares in the railroad. Nevertheless, John Young realized that the cost of the hardware — rails, spikes, locomotives, cars, iron bridges — would be greater than citizens of Utah and Idaho could afford. Consequently he traveled to New York where he met with Benjamin and Joseph Richardson, of Bridgeport, Connecticut, with whom he negotiated for funds to aid construction from Ogden 125 miles to Soda Springs. Joseph Richardson subsequently visited Salt Lake City where he met Brigham Young, who endorsed his son's project, and Richardson then agreed to supply the rail and rolling stock for the road.

In August 1871 John Young met with prominent Cache Valley Mormons in Logan, Utah. Although he had already expressed interest in just such a railroad, Presiding Bishop Preston was disturbed by the financial arrangement

John W. Young, right, assumed leadership of the Mormon effort to thwart Corinne and capture the Montana trade by building the Utah Northern narrow gauge. (Utah State Historical Society) The Church called upon the faithful to contribute their labor to the cause by building the railroad's grade, and the families (two?) shown below are working on the grade in the Cache Valley in 1872. (Harold B. Lee Library, Brigham Young University)

Young had made with the Richardsons, and on August 15 inquired of Brigham Young by telegram to Salt Lake City:

> Will it be wisdom for us in Cache County to grade and tie a railroad from Ogden to Soda Springs, with a view to Eastern capitalists ironing and stocking it [with locomotives, cars, and other hardware], thereby giving them control of the road? The people feel considerably spirited in taking stock to grade and tie, expecting to have a prominent voice in the control of it; but to let foreign capitalists iron and stock it will, if my judgment is correct, give them control.

To calm Preston's fears, Brigham Young replied that same day:

> The foreign capitalists in this enterprise do not seek the control; this is all understood. What they want, and what we want, is to push this road with all possible speed, if you decide to have one, so that it shall run through and benefit your settlements and reach Soda Springs as soon as possible.

Brigham Young's response satisfied Preston and he agreed to give his full support to construction of the new railroad — though in fact what Eastern capitalists were interested in was not merely to "push this road with all possible speed" or to "benefit your settlements" but to obtain a profitable return on their investment.

Bishop Preston and John W. Young arranged almost immediately to meet with the various ward bishops and other prominent Mormons of northern Utah to charter and organize the proposed road. At a meeting held in Logan on August 23, 1871, they incorporated the Utah Northern Railroad Company, capitalized at $2,000,000 divided into 20,000 shares, par value of $100 each. The road was specified to run from a junction with the Union Pacific, Central Pacific and Utah Central railroads at Ogden through Brigham City and Logan to Soda Springs, Idaho, a total of roughly 125 miles, at a cost of construction estimated at $1,500,000. It was implicitly understood that this was to be but the first phase of construction all the way to Montana. The Articles of Incorporation provided for thirteen directors; they were: Joseph Richardson and LeGrand Lockwood of New York City; John W. Young of Salt Lake City; Bishop William B. Preston and Hezekiah Thatcher of Logan, Utah; O. N. Liljenquist of Hyrum, Utah; William Maughan of Wellsville, Utah; Franklin D. Richards of Ogden, Utah; M. W. Merrill of Richmond, Utah; Samuel Roskelly of Smithfield, Utah; William Hyde of Hyde Park, Utah; and L. H. Hatch of Franklin, Idaho.

The seemingly large and potentially unmanageable Board of Directors was in fact a shrewd move on the part of organizer John Young, who thus was able to place on the Board a prominent citizen from each of the Mormon communities from which he needed to secure labor. Initial stockholders included, in addition to the 13 directors, a number of other citizens of northern Utah who had subscribed to stock, a total of $140,000 being sold at the beginning. Bishop Preston was the largest subscriber with 169 shares; John Young, using some of his profits from Union Pacific construction work in 1868 and 1869, purchased 95 shares; Joseph Richardson took 50 shares; others held blocks varying from 5 to 150 shares. Brigham Young was not among the initial stockholders. The Board elected John Young president and General Superintendent, Bishop Preston vice president, and Moses Thatcher secretary and treasurer.

The Ogden newspaper editorialized that same day:

> The Cache Valley people have contracted for the grading and ties for the road through that valley, and subscribed to stock to the amount of over $200,000. . . . This will be a splendid thing for the people of Cache Valley, as well as a benefit to Ogden, and will materially aid in the development of the Soda Springs country. Years ago we dreamed of the locomotive with a train of cars thundering across Cache Valley to Logan, and as we believe in a dream, . . . we expect to behold the reality. Cache Valley . . . will be the great grainery of Utah, and the new railroad will carry the vast products of that magnificent valley to the markets that mineral developments will make for them. Thousands of acres, now unoccupied, will yield rich treasures to the laborer, and thriving towns will spring up near the railroad track . . .

The newspaper naturally went on to note that:

> Ogden cannot fail to be benefitted greatly by the construction of this road. Here will be the great receiving and shipping point for the products of northern Utah and Idaho. Times will be lively, real estate will advance in value, and the city will spread out and improve in every direction. Success to the promoters of the new road, and fortune to all who help put it through.

The newspaper's optimism regarding the proposed railroad was typical of journalistic response to such projects throughout the West during that decade.

It was understood that this was the first section of a railroad to Montana. Once track had been laid as far as the northern Utah border, the distance from that point to Montana by wagon road would be much shorter than from Corinne and the much sought-after wagon trade could be expected to shift to the Utah Northern railhead. Cost of construction to Soda Springs was estimated at $1,500,000, exclusive of rail and equipment.

The directors decided to hire Colonel J. H. Martineau as Chief Surveyor of the new railroad. His work was familiar to John Young as he had surveyed the Utah Central, and before that had worked on Union Pacific construction. It was apparently also at one of the meetings in Logan that John Young, Moses Thatcher and Joseph Richardson decided to construct the Utah Northern as a narrow gauge — that is, with rails three feet apart rather than the standard gauge of 4 feet, 8½ inches, to which the transcontinental railroads and the Utah Central had been built. As early as August 25 the Salt Lake *Herald* reported the proposed gauge, noting the successful use of it in the Colorado Rockies. The Utah Northern was projected through country as mountainous as that facing Colorado's Denver & Rio Grande Railway, America's first major narrow gauge. Thus the Utah Northern would be the second major narrow gauge railroad begun in the United States.

The initial northern terminus at Soda Springs was selected at the request of Brigham Young, who with William Hooper and Horace Eldredge had purchased property there in 1869 and planned to establish a health resort at the mineral springs, but the area was also potentially rich farming country.

Meanwhile, John Young began the task of enlisting the aid of settlers in Box Elder and Weber counties, calling a meeting at Brigham City (23 miles north of Ogden) on August 26, 1871. The event was reported to the press the following day, appearing in the Ogden *Junction* of August 30:

> Brigham City, Aug. 27, 1871.
>
> Editor Ogden Junction:
>
> Dear Sir: — A preliminary subscription of nearly $12,000 was effected here yesterday, at our regular meeting, after Elder John W. Young had laid before the citizens the project of the building of a railroad from Ogden to Soda Springs.
>
> About sunset the city bell was ringing and the cannon roaring furiously. The rallying point was about a half mile due west of the Court House; there a place had been designated for the future railroad station of Brigham City, where the regular line will run.
>
> After some stakes had been put down by Mr. S. Wright, county surveyor, a dedicatory prayer was offered by Prest. L. Snow, who then handed a spade to John W. Young, Esq., requesting him to move the first dirt on the division of the contemplated line, which he did reluctantly, stating that he would rather have seen Prest. Snow do it. President Snow handled the spade next, followed by Hons. J. C. Wright, Judge S. Smith, Bishop A. Nichols, Major Loveland and Major H. P. Jensen. After which, a plow was put to work on the line, and several the citizens made a finished square of grade, around which we all formed a circle and listened to brief but spirited and deeply impressive speeches from John W. Young, L. Snow, J. C. Wright, S. Smith and A. Nichols. As it was quite dark, the young boys made a splendid illumination around the spot by firing the sage bush, while Captain J. Christensen's brass band played a number of enlivening national airs. The occasion will long be remembered by all present by reason of the spirit of pleasure and delight which animated the scene. The R.R. will be built.
>
> Respectfully, A.C.

Ogden, too, responded to the call from the Church. In September, Franklin D. Richards called a general meeting in Ogden similar to the August meeting in Brigham City. The Ogden *Junction* of September 20 quoted John Young as saying that the railroad would transport grain, butter, milk, chickens, and other products, and the coal fields in the Soda Springs vicinity would furnish traffic which alone would pay the cost of the railroad. He said construction of a narrow gauge would save 40 per cent of the cost of a standard gauge. Ogden, like the other Mormon communities, gave the project its hearty support. Franklin D. Richards asked the citizens to do the grading, furnish the ties and provide labor needed for the construction of the road paralleling the Central Pacific between Ogden and Willard. He received promises of labor and even a small amount of cash.

Typically, there were a few murmurs of dissent, particularly stemming from the decision of the management to start building the line from Willard, a point a few miles south of Brigham City where the narrow gauge would pass close to the Central Pacific line, rather than from Ogden. The newspaper dealt with this concern in an editorial in the same edition:

> The Starting Point of the U. N. R. R.
>
> Mr. Young, in his speech at the Mass Meeting on Saturday last, stated that, for the present, the Utah Northern would connect with the Central Pacific at Willard. Some persons present conceived the idea that this arrangement was designed to be permanent instead of temporary. It is singular that persons sitting side by side should differ so much in their understanding of a speaker's words. Mr. Young said distinctly that the road would undoubtedly connect with the Utah Central; stated that an effort was being made to obtain the unused C. P. grade reaching to Ogden, and that if that was unsuccess-

ful a new track would be built, but that to get the road into running order quickly, so as to make it pay at once, it was desirable to complete it as soon as possible to Logan, and connect with the C. P. at Willard as a saving of time.

Let no one hold back from working on this line, under the impression that the road is not coming to Ogden. Wherever the Utah Central terminates, there the Utah Northern will begin; there is no mistake about that. The Junction will be at Ogden. The two great roads still talk about moving to Harrisville, but they are not so crazy as to move from the natural spot, with all its advantages to a place totally unfit for their purpose, which would cost them ten times as much as the present locality to make it at all suitable, and then would not compare with what they have and can get without difficulty in Ogden.

Meanwhile, Joseph Richardson had returned to New York, where he placed orders for rail, spikes, splice bars, switch parts, locomotives and cars for the new railroad. The locomotives were ordered from the Grant Locomotive Works at Paterson, New Jersey, "the first to be delivered before the summer of 1872". Orders for cars were placed with Billmeyer & Small of York, Pennsylvania, and Jackson & Sharp of Wilmington, Delaware.

Colonel Martineau was at work during the rest of August on his surveys toward Soda Springs. First he ran a line north from Brigham City and then along the western base of the Wasatch Mountains for roughly 25 miles. From that point northward he had to choose between penetrating the Bear River Narrows (also known as Bear River Canyon), or crossing into the Cache Valley over Mendon Divide, known locally as Cache Hill. Both posed rough and difficult construction, the toughest the railroad faced, but the Narrows seemed to Martineau the better solution, eliminating heavy grades. When he reported back to the Board of Directors, however, they overruled him (Bishop Preston in particular) and selected the Mendon Divide route, because using it the railroad would pass through Logan whereas following the Bear River the line would bypass Logan.

Construction of grade begun so auspiciously at Brigham City on August 26 continued, with emphasis given at first to the line between Logan and Willard, the latter a point south of Brigham City on the Central Pacific. Thus the Central Pacific would temporarily provide rail service between Willard and Ogden until the Utah Northern could itself build into Ogden. It was in this initial construction that the unusual aspects of this railroad project became apparent. As with other so-called "Mormon railroads" such as the Utah Central and the Utah Southern, the Mormon Church placed its religious influence behind the project. Mormon farmers and businessmen along the line were encouraged to provide labor, teams and equipment for grading and bridge construction, being repaid in stock in the company equivalent to their effort. Local Mormon church leaders helped to recruit and organize these efforts. Groups of workers were organized by their wards or parishes, or their location along the right-of-way. Superintendents were assigned in each of the major areas of construction, probably covering segments of about twenty-five miles each. Construction progressed rapidly all along the line between Willard and Logan during the first week of September, and a contract was signed for 50,000 hand-hewn ties. By September 27, 1871, eight miles of grade had been completed in Box Elder County, and Cache Valley residents were hard at work on the difficult section over Cache Hill in the mountains separating the Box Elder and Cache Valleys. On October 7, 1871, the Ogden *Junction* quoted W. F. Fisher as saying that he and "joudy Hougen" were engaged in grading on the divide near Mendon and that the people throughout northern Utah had caught the spirit of railroading. Goudy Hogan himself recorded in his diary:

In the latter part of the summer there was a requirement made from [Mormon Church] headquarters to build a narrow gauge railroad from Ogden to Soda Springs and wished the people of Ogden, Boxelder and Cache Valleys to build road and own a good share of interest in it, for the people to do a certain portion of labor to each man. I rigged up my teams and started out in company with William Fisher and we worked out our portion of work. We were the first that started work in Cache Valley on the divide between Cache Valley and Salt Lake Valley. I had fitted out three teams, took my wife Christiana, and Harriet, my daughter, to cook, Ira and Nels, my sons, and one hired man. Fisher had four teams. We bought 70 yards of tent cloth and made a new tent. . . . We did the work that was alloted to us in three weeks and were going to start south to work, but John W. Young who had charge of the road wished us to stay and work on the Utah Northern. There were few could work on the road without some ready means having lost their crops for so many years, but Bro[ther]. Young promised to pay us a portion of ready pay . . . and take stock in the road for the balance. I worked three months . . . My estimate for eleven weeks amounted to $2600. Besides Fisher['s] work I had two hired men besides my own folks to pay in wheat and part in vouchers. These were railroad vouchers that circulated as money and paid off some of my debts.

Original equipment of the Utah Northern included little 4-wheel coal cars like that below (misletered "U&N"), as well as double-truck baggage car no. 1 (bottom). (Author's Collection) Amazingly, a journal-box lid from one of the original cars ("U.N.R.R.N.G.") has survived for over a century (above, Author's Photo).

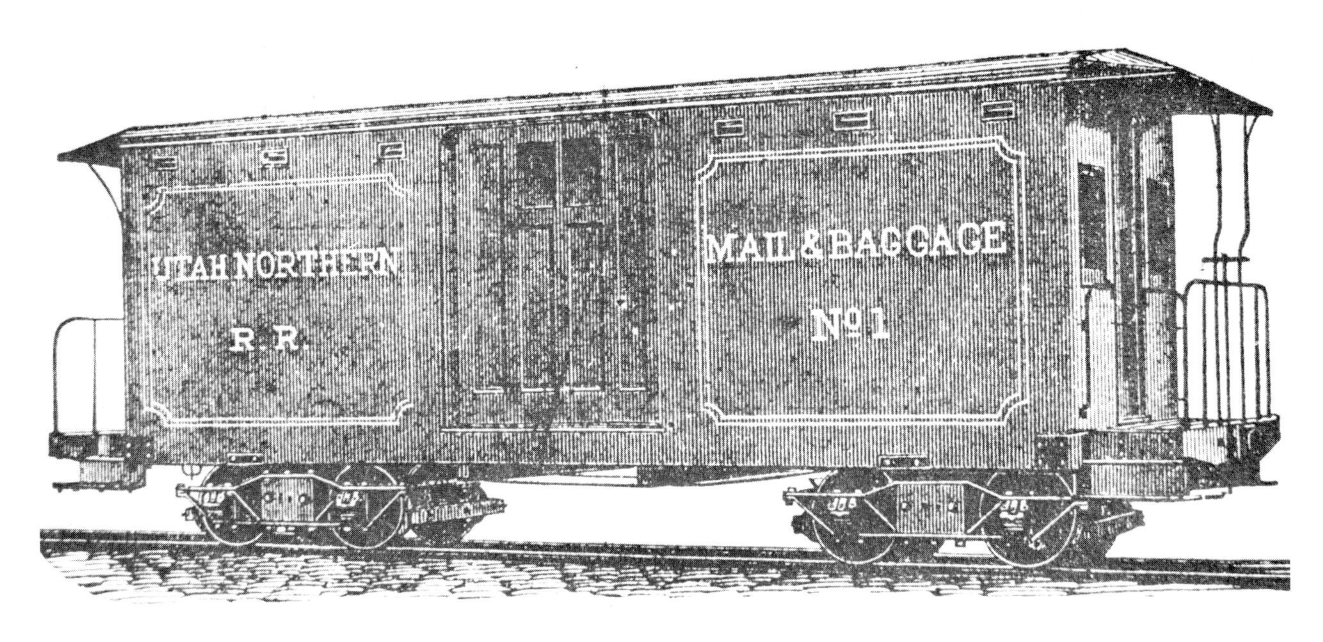

Shown in builder's photo above, the Franklin *was the first of three Grant tenwheelers to be received by the UN in 1872. The fancy natural wood, varnished cab appears too big for the locomotive, but the ornate striping and trim transforms the little engine into a veritable work of art. (Museum Collection) Below, this view of Arimo (or Oneida) station, in southern Idaho, in October 1878 shows — in addition to the busy freight platforms and one of the new Baldwin moguls at left — the only known view of the Utah Northern's first locomotive, an 1871 Grant 4-4-0 named* John W. Young. *(C. H. Peake Collection)*

Others such as Hogan pushed the work, with frequent interruptions when one or another left to harvest their crops. On November 29, 1871, the *Deseret News* in Salt Lake City reported:

> The construction of the Utah Northern Railroad is going on vigorously. For energy and enterprise, the people of Cache Valley are probably not excelled by any other body of people of the same numbers on this broad continent. They have given many evidences in favor of this among which is the great canyon road between Cache and Bear Lake Valleys, and now they are at work determindly and energetically making a railroad over the mountains and valleys northward.
>
> The portion of the road which the people of this country have undertaken to build commences at a point on the Brigham City road, four miles south of Pack's Springs. From that place to a point one mile beyond the summit of the mountain on the Cache Valley side of the divide, the entire contracts have been let, and most of the road over that distance is already graded and ready for ties. The greater portion of the work on the divide is very heavy, some of the cuts being through solid stone and gravel cement. There are three particularly heavy fills, the largest of which is that at Cottonwood hollow. It will take 50,000 cubic yards of earth to fill it, and the work has been contracted for by Marion Stevenson & Company, of Richmond [Utah]. Another, at Birch Creek will take 40,000 yards of filling, and the job has been taken by Colonel Thomas E. Ricks of Logan. The other, near Pack's Springs, will require 2,500 yards and Casper Whittle of Richmond, and his company are busy at work on it. Contracts for several thousand ties have been let, and a number of Cache Valley brethren are in the canyons getting them out. Should the weather continue open, it is thought that the grading will be completed in about eight weeks from now. It is apprehended, however, that the lower bottoms between Mendon and here will freeze up and stop the work. The work has been conducted under the supervision of Bishop Marriner W. Merrill of Richmond and Mr. George L. Farrell of this city.

The "apprehension" of writer J. Nicholson that the weather would soon bring the work to a halt was merited, the winter suspension leaving the roadbed from Willard to Mendon nearly ready for rails and the difficult grading over Cache Hill well along.

Meanwhile, equipment for the road began to arrive. In its Saturday, November 4 edition the Ogden *Junction* reported that "a handsome little narrow gauge locomotive, the 'John W. Young,' arrived at Ogden the beginning of the present week, and a telegram from Chicago announces that a complete construction train is on the way for the new line." Descriptions of the new locomotive are fragmentary and superficial; we are told that the underframe was finished in bright red enamel while the "engine" was painted black with gold leaf lettering. The boiler was "brass trimmed" and carried 120 pounds pressure; the firebox was of copper; water was supplied to the boiler with a cross-head pump (adequate running on the road, but in the yard the engineer would have to run her back and forth to maintain a sufficient water level); the tender had handbrakes, but the locomotive could only be stopped by reversing her with the Johnson bar. Subsequent research reveals the "Young" to have been a small 4-4-0, under 30 feet in length, about 14 tons weight, 44″ drivers and 10x16″ cylinders. The "construction train" mentioned in the wire apparently included the second locomotive, a 2-6-0 Mogul intended as the freight engine (the "Young" being the passenger engine) of very similar dimensions (Union Pacific records show 44″ drivers, 10x16″ cylinders, 28,750 pounds total weight), and named "Logan."

The first freight cars of the Utah Northern were small four wheel Billmeyer & Small products, very similar to those built for the Denver & Rio Grande in early 1871. The lone passenger car was also a product of the York Car Works and was supplied with eight wheels on a pair of extended archbar trucks.

Unfortunately, there was no track built to run the equipment on, or even put it on; it had to remain stored until the following spring. For by the time the locomotives and cars had arrived, so had winter, and with the onslaught of wind and snow and numbing cold grading ground to a halt.

With the spring thaw in 1872, construction of grade resumed, although not with the enthusiasm of the previous fall, as noted in his diary by the faithful Goudy Hogan:

> This spring there was a loud call for help to work on the Utah Northern Railroad. The men were rather slow to turn out to work because of no ready funds. The Bishop called on me and Fisher publicly to go as missionaries and work on the R.R. I again took my whole force and began work. Bro. Fisher and I finished the large Casper Whittle Fill and worked on the Hamtons Y at the station. I went home to arrange for someone to do my farm work but couldn't hire anyone as they were all engaged on the railroad.

Meanwhile, 30 pound rail and other track materials had been shipped from the East, and had arrived at Brigham City. On March 25, 1872,

John Young wired his father from Utah Northern R. R. Junction (Willard): "We drove the first spike on the Utah Northern R.R. at 11 a.m. today. Will lay about half a mile of track this afternoon."

Once again, the Utah Northern project was moving ahead. A March 29 report to the *Deseret News* indicated that "little progress has yet been made in tracklaying . . . the tracklayers being engaged most of the time unloading the iron which is now pouring in from the East. We are informed that forty additional carloads of rails are now at Ogden." About a mile of track had been quickly put down, and 25 miles of grade were said to be finished and ready for the iron. By mid-April, five miles of track were reported completed, and track was being put down a little better than a mile a week — not a break-neck pace! Work was slowed temporarily early in May, when the forces had to be diverted to repairing a section of the grade about two miles north of Brigham City that had been "washed away" in a spring storm.

The road was sufficiently operative by May 1 so that President Young devoted that day to having one of the road's little locomotives, with seven cars (probably mostly flats fitted with board seats), operate excursions between Willard (Utah Northern Junction) and Brigham City. The festive events were duly reported in the *Deseret News* on May 8:

> EXCURSION PARTY — The following came per the Deseret Telegraph line —
>
> Utah Northern Junction, May 1, 10 a.m. — President Young's party, about one hundred and fifty, parted with the missionaries at Ogden, who took their departure east. The party arrived here at eight a.m., and found seven cars of the Utah Northern, which we occupied to Brigham, making the trip (four miles) in ten minutes. We were met by Prest. L. Snow and 500 school children, with banners and music. The children and citizens all joined in three hearty cheers to President Young and party, also three more to the Utah Northern and its worthy president. We are now back at this place, where we will stay until 2 p.m., expecting to be in the city at 7:30 p.m. They have a beautiful May pole erected at this place and I notice about sixty teams laden with citizens and school children from Willard, with banners and music. The train now goes back for school children to Brigham. The day is beautiful, the scenery lovely and the music and cheerful countenances and happy hearts indicate a day of rare enjoyment.

By mid-May the track was reported as advancing at the rate of a half mile a day, and grading was being pushed towards Logan. The newspaper optimistically observed that "if the work of grading goes on as fast as anticipated . . . the cars will be in Logan . . . by the end of July," but this ignored the fact that the hard-pressed Mormon settlers would soon have to abandon railroad work for their farms if they were to avoid starving to death.

The June 7, 1872, edition of the daily *Deseret News* reported that the Utah Northern was said to "contemplate commencing to run trains to convey passengers and freight" from the Junction at Willard to Hampton's, about 25 miles, and this service was begun on June 13. Passengers could leave Salt Lake City at 5:00 AM and be in Hampton's by 10:00 AM, or leave at 2:45 PM and arrive at 9:00 PM. Returning, a train left Hampton's at 4:00 AM putting the traveller in Salt Lake City at 10:00 AM, or the afternoon schedule called for a 12:45 PM departure and a 7:30 PM arrival. It would appear that the morning train was a fast passenger schedule and the afternoon a mixed, if elapsed time is any indication.

A June 15 newspaper story dealt with the assembling and placing in operation at Brigham City of the Utah Northern's "first" locomotive, which was apparently a somewhat inaccurate report of the arrival of the first of the railroad's second batch of locomotives from the Grant works. This new engine, named the "Franklin," was a 4-6-0 and considerably heavier than the first two — nearly 19 tons, compared to 14-14½ tons. A July 1 report stated that two more locomotives (also 4-6-0's, the "Utah" and "Idaho") and "a number of passenger cars" were en route from the east and would arrive "shortly." The locomotives and equipment were by now badly needed, and the three Grant Tenwheelers, plus the two original smaller locomotives, would be all that the railroad would have until Union Pacific ownership provided a new infusion of equipment later in the decade.

Further track-laying progress was said to be impeded by slow work on a large fill at Cottonwood Hollow, and after its completion "there will be nothing to prevent the cars running to Mendon" on the edge of the Cache Valley.

Meanwhile the railroad attempted to build up a bit of traffic to Hampton's. Fare was set at $1.50 each way between Brigham City and Hampton's, and stage connections from that point to Montana were anticipated early in July. That did not prevent the Corinne *Daily Reporter* from deriding the whole undertaking in the July 8 issue:

> The traveler who takes a train on the Utah Northern narrow gauge at Brigham Station, may reach Hampton's in an hour or two, but arriving at the point of the mountain he'll find no coach or wagon awaiting to bear him onward, for long

> before that place is reached, the stage has passed on its more direct line several miles westward . . . We would like to see the officers of the Utah Northern throw out a hint to the green tourist that there is no stage line in any way connected with the road . . . only from the Central Pacific Railroad at Corinne do the stages and freighting for Montana depart every day.

What the Corinne paper claimed was true! Despite its more than 25 miles of track in operation and a stable of five locomotives, the Utah Northern had thus far made no dent in Corinne's monopoly of the Montana trade, for the freighting firms were not especially eager to lose part of their wagon haul to the railroad, and the railroad had not yet penetrated far enough north to command a part of the trade.

Corinne nevertheless trembled at the implications of every proposed railroad which had any potential of infringing on its strategic position as transfer point for the Montana trade, and even more when one of the proposals materialized into grade, then track, and finally trains. Meetings were held to discuss the situation, and leading citizens of Corinne inevitably gravitated towards the only answer; If a railroad threatened to destroy Corinne by taking away the Montana wagon traffic and bypassing Corinne, Corinne could respond only by replacing its profitable wagon traffic with a railroad of its own to the Montana mines. As early as March 1872, when the Utah Northern began to lay iron, Corinne's leading citizens commenced a campaign to obtain sufficient support to incorporate a railroad in the territory. The result was the Utah, Idaho & Montana Railroad, incorporated April 13, 1872 and projected from Corinne via the Bear River and Malad Valleys to the northern boundary of Utah Territory, some thirty miles, estimated to cost $1,000,000. President of the new company was General Patrick Edward Connor, former commander of the Camp Douglas garrison during the Civil War, now a non-Mormon Salt Lake City businessman. His company applied to Congress and obtained on June 1, 1872 a grant of right-of-way across all public land which lay on the route not only across Utah but all the way to a point on the projected line of the Northern Pacific Railroad in Montana Territory. The Utah, Idaho & Montana subsequently amended its charter to extend the road into Montana and to increase its capital stock to $12,000,000. A rip-roaring ground-breaking ceremony for the Utah Northern's competitor took place in Corinne on June 17, 1872, with the town's streets filled with both inhabitants and visitors and with beer flowing freely. Connor turned the first spade of earth and a number of speakers harangued the populace. Survey work followed, as well as construction of a few miles of grade north of Corinne, whereafter the Utah, Idaho & Montana Railroad subsided into a paper enterprise of no economic significance. No engine bearing its lettering ever turned a wheel.

Construction of the Utah Northern, meanwhile, progressed slowly. The most difficult part of its initial route lay over Cache Hill between the Box Elder and Cache Valleys. A large number of men and teams were at work on cuts and fills over the hill most of the summer, and the longest and deepest fill at Cottonwood Hollow, some 400 feet long and up to 100 feet deep, crossed a three-by-six foot stone culvert designed to carry heavy spring runoff. It took fifty men and teams much of the summer to finish this fill alone, and it was not until the end of September that all of the grading over Cache Hill was completed. Then tracklaying resumed, hampered by fall and winter snows. On December 22, 1872, Engineer Charley Paul ran Engine No. 1 and four cars over Cache Hill, while people who lived in the vicinity gathered to watch, some doubting the capacity of the diminutive engine to make the grade. At the summit, Engineer Paul stopped the train and from there gave a number of children a free ride to Mendon station.

On January 31, 1873 at 5 PM Engineer Evan Jones brought the first train into Logan. Already under construction at that town were a substantial roundhouse and machine shop, water tank and fuel bins, and 10,540 feet of sidings. Nearby, workmen were finishing the passenger depot and freight shed. The first train was met at the unfinished depot by a large crowd and honored by speeches and a banquet.

On February 3 the weather closed in and snow shut down operation over the hill until February 12. Within a week of the line's completion to Logan, Chief Surveyor Martineau's objections to the hill route were dramatically confirmed, and prophetic of things to come. Each winter the Cache Hill crossing would prove an Achilles' heel to the Utah Northern.

The weather slowed further work on the Utah Northern — when the line was blocked again over Cache Hill early in March, citizens of Logan and surrounding towns turned out *en masse* to dig out the line. Worsening economic conditions intervened, too. The Ogden *Junction's* editor observed that "this is a dull time, money is scarce, or else it is lying in secret." He went on to complain that "cash, to be of any use, must be circulated." The Utah Northern still had a bit of cash to circulate, and was pushing its line north of Logan. An April 15 dispatch from Franklin, 20 miles north of Logan, claimed that grading was nearing completion and ties cut for another 30 miles of line, and by June

The old map at right shows both the original UN line from Ogden through Brigham, Hamptons, Logan and Franklin and the later relocation through Cache Junction and along the Bear River. (Museum Collection) Below, the "Burg on the Bear," Corinne, in 1869. (Union Pacific Railroad Collection)

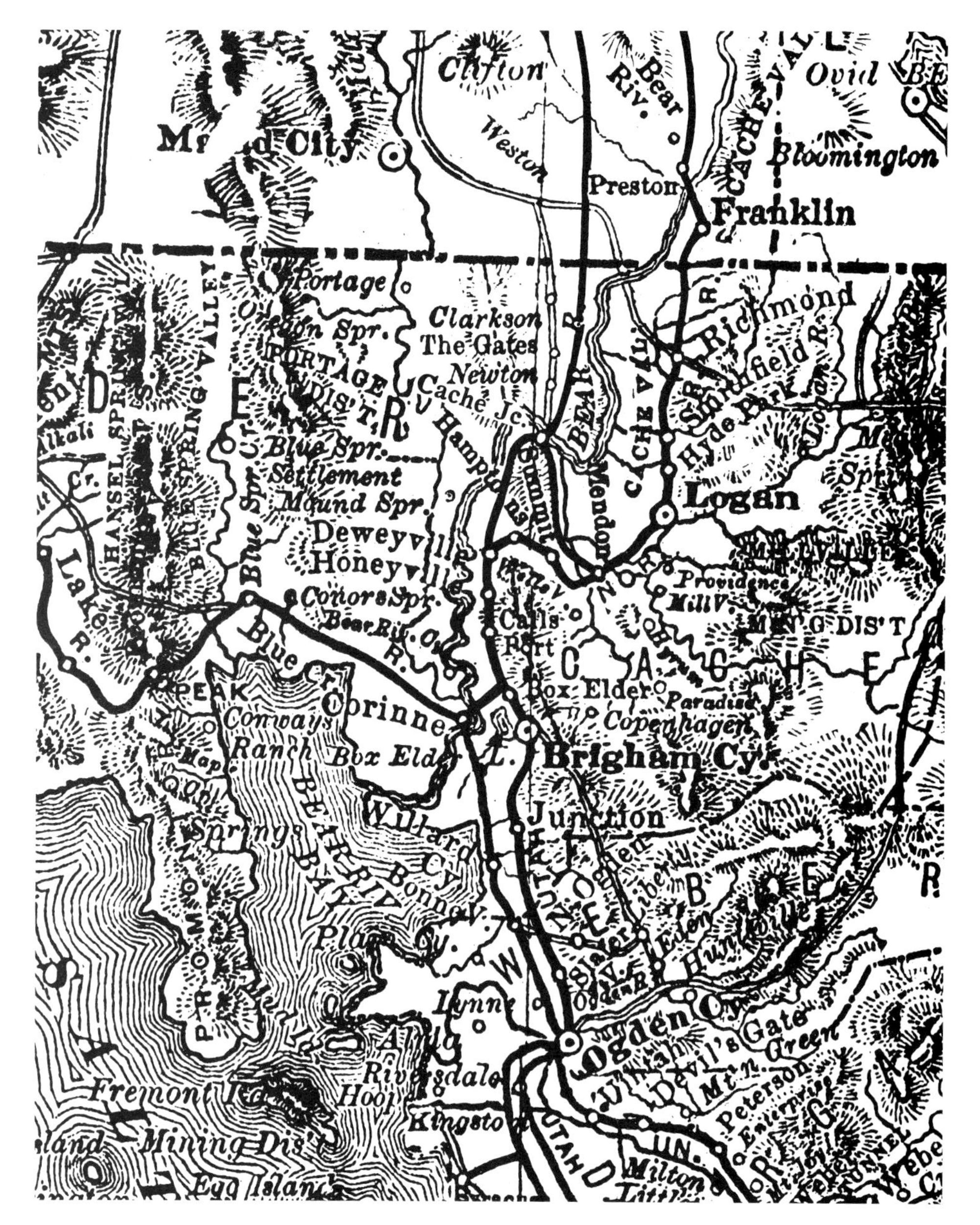

track was said to be nearing the Bear River bridge.

Utah Northern management also moved to nullify the threat from Corinne's planned Utah, Idaho & Montana Railroad by building a short branch into that town. The 4.11 mile line was completed and put into operation on June 9, 1873; the most difficult part of the project (and one which delayed its completion) was the construction of a substantial bridge over the Bear River at the edge of town. A large freight house that had belonged to the Diamond R Freight Line was purchased and converted into a combination freight and passenger depot. A flag-decorated UN locomotive and short train steamed into Corinne over the new line on June 11 — not generating much excitement or fanfare — and regular mixed train service began the next day.

On June 19 a large contingent of Logan citizens decided that the completion of the Corinne branch might afford an opportunity for a fine railroad excursion, and so they set forth — 403 of them — on the UN at 8:30 in the morning to visit the "Burg on the Bear." The account of the trip filed with the Ogden *Junction* by one of the tourists affords a particularly clear picture of the railroad and the towns:

> Dear Sir — At half-past eight this a.m. four hundred and three passengers, including the Logan Brass Band, about seventy-five adults, Sabbath school teachers, and the balance of the company children, from the ages of four to sixteen, started on a trip per Utah Northern Railroad to Corinne and Brigham cities. We were provided with two passenger and five flat cars, the latter nicely and comfortably arranged with seats, awnings, etc., and all were crowded to the guards. The ride across the Logan and Mendon bottoms was very pleasant, a gentle breeze from the north blew off the smoke and cinders, as the train was going west, and kept us all nice and cool.
>
> Passing the flourishing little town of Mendon, on the left some ten miles from Logan, we began to ascend the divide between Cache and Malad counties. This is a gradual rise of rolling hills covered with splendid bunch grass, making excellent pasturage for the animals that belong to the many ranchers and dairymen whose houses dot the hills at almost every curve of the road.
>
> We made the ascent easily and comfortably, although the grade at some points is ninety feet or over to the mile. From this summit we have a beautiful view of Cache Valley. Eight towns can be seen in the distance, toward the south, east and north, with their fertile fields. Stopping at Hampton's a few minutes, we sped on through fields of grain, which are rather in advance of those of Cache county, and reached Corinne about noon. A large C. P. freight train was just passing out as we entered, making a very pleasant sight for our little folks.
>
> This being our first ride over this portion of the road, we could not help noticing the amount of work that had been done in bridging these bottoms, covered with rushing water from one to ten feet deep besides the cost of spanning Bear River. Pulling alongside the depot, the folks, little and big, poured out of the cars, all anxious to see Corinne. No sooner had we landed than we were kindly invited to the Opera House, the Band leading the way and playing. The company followed with their pic-nic to the above-name place, where we found comfortable seats and a kind reception. Nor was this all, for in a very short space of time, gentlemen were busy serving the company with lemonade, which we all enjoyed hugely, and I rather think they thought so from the amount that was imbibed. The ladies and gentlemen were very kind to us and regretted that we had not informed them of our intention to visit them, that they might have been prepared with ample provision and better accommodations. We sincerely believed them, and were quite willing to accept the will for the deed with hearty thanks.

The inhabitants of Corinne who had this swarm of 403 Mormons descend upon them unannounced reacted a little differently, as was recorded in the following report in a subsequent issue of the *Junction*:

> Excursion from Logan — Without a moment's warning, yesterday morning, a party of about four hundred excursionists arrived here at half-past eleven o'clock. No one was over at the depot to bid them welcome, or to escort them around the city, but it was because no one knew anything at all about their coming. As soon as the train came to a stand-still, however, the little fellows alighted, and immediately began reconnoitering the city, rushing from one street to another, stopping at every candy shop and soda fountain, and gazing with wonder at all the fine sights, which can be seen in cities of this size only. A fine brass band was along, and at noon the excursionists fell into line behind the music and paraded the streets, being conducted by a couple of our citizens. The procession drew up at the Opera House, where the children belonging to party were drawn up in a line, and, led by their teacher, they sang several very beautiful songs. No refreshments were tendered them except something in the way of cool beverages, which were swallowed by them with the greatest avidity after tromping through the hot

and dusty streets. After an address by our worthy Mayor welcoming this, the first, excursion that ever visited this city from the Mormon settlements, and extending to them a cordial invitation to return often, the delighted audience filed out of the building, and to the tune of "Tramp, Tramp" marched slowly back to the cars, which were in readiness for them, and were seen flying over the rails to Brigham City. We are told, by the way, that their coming was as little known there as here, and that no preparations had been made to receive them.

The Corinne branch enjoyed brisk business until the line was completed from Willard (Junction) into Ogden, on February 5, 1874. The UN then extended from Ogden (and a direct connection with the Central Pacific, Union Pacific and Utah Central railroads) to Franklin, 78 miles. Another 14 miles of grade beyond Franklin were said to be ready for iron, but no additional track would be laid. The country was suffering from the effects of the Panic of 1873, and no money was available for new railroad construction — or would be for several years. When construction would finally be resumed, under the aegis of the great Union Pacific System, the planned route to Soda Springs would be dropped for a more favorable route through the Marsh and Portneuf Valleys to the Snake River plain.

299 UTAH NORTHERN RAILROAD.

JOHN W. YOUNG, President.
WM. B. PRESTON, Vice-President.
MOSES THATCHER, Secretary and Gen. Superintendent.

CHAS. NIBLEY, Gen. Freight and Ticket Agent.
General Offices—Logan, Utah.

	Pass'ger.	Mls	STATIONS.	Mls	Pass'ger.
Salt Lake time.	7 00 P.M.	0	lve....Brigham...arr.	61	12 30 NO'N
	7 20 "	4	.......Box Elder.......	57	12 10 NO'N
	7 45 "	11	.......Call's Fort........	50	11 45 A.M.
	7 55 "	14	.......Honeyville......	47	11 35 "
	8 15 "	18	......Deweyville.......	43	11 15 "
	8 50 "	24	........Hampton's	37	10 40 "
	9 15 "	28	.........Summit........	33	10 25 "
	9 50 "	34	.........Mendon........	27	9 40 "
	10 30 P.M.	41	arr......Logan....lve	20	9 00 A.M.
		45	......Hyde Park......	16	
		49	........Smithfield.......	12	
		55	........Richmond......	6	
		61	arr....Franklin...lve.	0	

This schedule would indicate that, when the UN RR was first extended to Franklin, there was not sufficient traffic in prospect to warrant extending the daily passenger train beyond Logan. (Museum Coll.) When through Ogden-Franklin service was put into effect, the northbound train left Ogden at 9:30 AM and arrived at Franklin at 4:45 PM; southbound times were 9:00 AM and 4:30 PM.

Although the Utah Northern was at last a railroad that actually *went* somewhere, financial success seemed to elude it. Local traffic was not sufficient to repay construction costs and generate profits, and the Montana trade did not develop in the volume that had been expected — much of the rush to supply the new bonanza mining districts had subsided, some of the districts themselves were already showing signs of playing out, and the impact of the Panic of 1873 was being keenly felt in the mining industry. Further, the 78 miles of UN track reaching north from Ogden was not sufficient to give the UN indisputable claim to what Montana traffic there was; other routes still competed, and the teamsters were loathe to "short-haul" themselves by turning their loads over to the UN at Franklin or Logan. The railroad company was unable to redeem the vouchers given local citizens in exchange for their work and supplies used in the building of the line. Accordingly, the Church arranged to redeem the vouchers in public hands, taking stock in the railroad in exchange — in that way becoming a major stockholder in the company. Dividends were non-existent, and the railroad's bonds, issued at 70% of par, sank further in value.

Passengers neither flocked to the road's trains nor found them terribly impressive, if one Army officer's comments about a ride over the Utah Northern can be taken as representative. Second Lieutenant John Gregory Bourke, Third United States Cavalry, was traveling on military business from Ogden to Fort Hall, Idaho (near present-day Pocatello), and the struggling little narrow gauge offered him rail transportation for part of the trip. Bourke, a Civil War veteran and West Point graduate, was then serving as aide to Brigadier General George Crook. Much more the intellectual than the average cavalry officer, Bourke was an indefatigable diarist who in twenty years would fill more than a hundred and twenty diaries, as well as carrying out an extensive personal and professional correspondence and writing a number of books. Bourke's initial impressions of the Utah Northern, during the trip to Fort Hall, were recorded in one of his diaries. And, his first impression as recorded in his diary was something less than flattering:

> The *"Utah Northern"* is a very funny looking specimen of a Railway; of narrow gauge, 3 feet, it is poorly built and not up to mediocrity in the condition of its rolling stock; the locomotive is of about ten teakettle power. Each train consists of locomotive, tender, two freight and one passenger cars. While the aim of this little tramway is ambitious in seeking to make *Helena, Montana,* its final terminus, it is hard to predict an early attainment of its hopes, judging from the amount of patronage favoring the section already in operation; our car is capable of seating forty-eight (48) passengers, but at no time did it have ten occupants. The inclement weather may have had much to do with this small percentage of travel. To work this road cannot cost very much; the conductor

> acts as brakeman when necessary; checks baggage, or rather don't check it but puts it away in baggage car, (they don't use checks on this line,) and deals out the mails at the stations as we come along.

Bourke couldn't resist comparing the little line with the Central Pacific and Union Pacific, completed through Utah a mere six years earlier:

> The accommodations for passengers approximate to those on the emigrant cars of the Pacific roads. The speed attained is on an average about 10 miles an hour; nearing *Corinne*, our engineer nearly took our breath away by making a brief spurt at the soul-destroying velocity of 13 miles [an hour]. I would not write this did I not have corroborative evidence from the other passengers.

Having enjoyed a bit of sarcasm at the expense of the Utah Northern, the perspicacious officer could not help recording a more positive word or two about the line:

> People who know of the comfort and elegance guaranteed on the Eastern roads would turn up their noses at this little narrow gauge line running from *Utah* to *Idaho*. Everything, however, must have a beginning; this kind of travelling is as good as the best thirty years ago; it is better than walking even now; or for that matter than stage-riding. In new communities where money is always scarce, the "narrow gauge" is the salvation of the people; it can be built, equipped and operated for not more than half to two-thirds the cost of laying the track alone of the *"Broad-Gauge."*

Bourke must have done more than merely observe. When opportunity offered, the lieutenant must have talked with members of the crew, and after watching his little train buck some snow, noted:

> One disadvantage in a wintry climate is the inability of the weak little [narrow gauge] engine to break a path through the snow-drifts; but in climbing heavy grades, narrow gauge locomotives can accomplish more than the heavy engines.

"This *'Utah Northern' R.R.* consumes nearly a whole day in going 75 miles from Ogden to Franklin, a small town some few hundred yards north of the southern boundary of Idaho," Bourke complained at the end of his rail trip, though he was soon to find it preferable to what was yet to come. His account of the stage trip offered a contrast to the comparative speed and comfort of travel by rail even on a primitive little back-country narrow gauge. It began with a stop at the principal hostelry in Franklin:

> The *"Keeney House"* offers rest and refreshment to the traveller passing over this road; most of the business of the place seems to be done with people from *Helena, Virginia City* and *Bozeman, Montana*. Of the hotel, it might perhaps be unjust to speak too critically; it is the noisiest hostelry I ever put up at, the hum of voices lasting well through the night.

And while it might be preferable to a hard cavalry campaign, a stagecoach in winter had its unpleasant aspects:

> The stage line to *Helena* is a poor enough apology for rapid transit; recollections of my recent experience in Utah made it seem a luxurious mode of travel. The only passenger besides myself was an old lady traveling from New Hampshire to join her boy in Montana; her case was another illustration of the folly of wisdom where ignorance is bliss; her ideas of the perils and discomforts to be encountered were blissfully vague and indefinite, and I thought it a duty to keep her in ignorance. Snow and mud clogged up the road to such an extent that we made only 58 miles in 24 hours; several times on the way, the old lady nearly fainted from cold, hunger and exhaustion; luckily, some whiskey was handy and a liberal dosing with it restored her.

Bourke's reservations notwithstanding, it was clear to some — and to Joseph Richardson in particular — that the Utah Northern would never be a "paying proposition" unless it was extended to Montana, where the only existing sources of substantial traffic could be identified. Richardson was understandably reluctant to invest further in this so-far losing venture, at least without a great deal of support from some other sources. The Mormon Church was in no position to help appreciably; the Church had little wealth to devote to the project, and no settlers north of Franklin to call out for free labor. Richardson continued efforts in 1875 to gain financial aid from the Idaho and Montana territories, but Idaho's politicians made it clear they were not interested, and Montana's railroad boosters were split into factions — the towns along the proposed UN route were disposed to aid the narrow gauge, but other towns not so favored were inclined to direct public aid toward the projected Northern Pacific.

Not surprisingly, Richardson talked at length with the Union Pacific — which was then desperately casting about for viable feeder lines with which to build up traffic on its Omaha-Ogden main line — and Sidney Dillon expressed tentative interest. But there were many impediments to cooperative action, one being the waning interest of the Mormon Church in any extension beyond Soda Springs. This dichotomy was resolved in October 1875 when John W. Young resigned as president of the UN, to be succeeded by Royal M. Bassett of Connecticut, a businessman and investor.

Richardson and Sidney Dillon of the Union

Pacific now looked to the question of how they could finance the critical Montana extension. Not unexpectedly, they turned first to gaining a suitable subsidy from the Territory of Montana. A proposal was put before the Montana Legislature with the help and backing of such influential supporters as Samuel T. Hauser of Helena and others, and as a result the Legislature did pass a subsidy bill in February 1876 — but not with the terms proposed by Richardson and the Union Pacific, as is made clear in the following story from the Salt Lake *Herald*:

> The subsidy bill passed by the Montana Legislature provides for the issue to the company of 7 per cent, 20 year coupon bonds to the amount of $4,500 per mile, for every mile of road completed and stocked, from Franklin, Idaho, to the mouth of the Big Hole River, Montana. The road is to be finished within two years from the signing of the contract. After the completion of the first 50 miles of the road the company is to receive 60 per cent of the bonds due, and the remaining 40 per cent when the road shall be finished; the second 50 miles, 70 per cent on completion of the section and 30 per cent when the road shall be finished; for the third 50-mile section, 80 per cent on its completion, and the remainder when the road reaches the terminus; for the fourth 50-mile section, 90 per cent on its completion, and the balance when the road is finished; for the remainder of the road to the Big Hole the full amount of bonds shall be paid upon the completion of each 50-mile section. The bill provides for taxing the road the same as other property is taxed in the territory, and limits the rates of fares and freight charges as follows: Through first-class passenger fare, 6 cents per mile; local passenger fare, 7 cents per mile; through freights, 2½ cents per ton per mile; local freights, 3 cents per ton per mile. The act is to be submitted to a vote of the people for adoption or rejection, and if it is ratified then a special tax is to be levied in each county for the purpose of paying interest on the bonds. The proposition of Mr. Joseph Richardson and the Utah Northern Company was to build the road for bonds at the rate of $6,000 per mile, the complement due to be paid on the completion of each 20 miles. Mr. Sidney Dillon, on behalf of the Union Pacific, agreed to aid in carrying out the proposition if accepted by Montana.
>
> It is thought that the people of the territory will ratify the act, and that the Utah Northern will accept the subsidy and build the road.

Contrary to the *Herald's* "thoughts," Richardson and the Union Pacific found the proffered subsidy unsatisfactory and rejected it out-of-hand. It was pointed out that the UN would have to build 200 miles of road to gain any subsidy, and that the subsidy would then only come in installments that would be inadequate. There was uncertainty about the Territory's authority to grant such aid, and the UN pointed out that if it should "transpire that the Territory could not grant the aid without the consent of Congress, the Utah Northern would be considerably out of pocket." Further, comparable aid was to be extended to the Northern Pacific, and the UN noted that if accepted the Territorial indebtedness would then amount to $4,000,000, "which would bankrupt Montana and make its securities valueless." In fact, Richardson expressed the opinion that in his view the Montana bonds, if issued, would be so suspect in value that they would be unsaleable in the bond markets for any reasonable price, thus rendering the whole exercise futile.

The Salt Lake *Herald* of March 25 quoted UN President Bassett as saying that "the road will be built to Fort Hall anyway, when the terminus will be only 250 miles from the heart of Montana. If the people then feel like voting a decent subsidy, with less objectionable restrictions . . . (we) will build the road" on to Butte and Helena. Brave talk — and UN management backed it up with a superficial flurry of activity beyond Franklin. In May the Salt Lake *Herald* enthusiastically reported that

> work of grading on the extension of the Utah Northern in the direction of Montana is progressing rapidly. Fifteen miles of the new grade is ready for the iron. Another section of 10 miles will be completed by June 1, and the management intend to have cars running to Cottonwood, 30 miles beyond Franklin, in September. This will cut down freighting and staging to Montana about 100 miles.

Little came of this, largely because the financial problems still were unresolved — and remained unresolved all throught 1876. Some of the UN's supporters, like Hauser, continued to search for support; but others (in Utah and Montana alike) began to ridicule "the wheelbarrow line" as a useless streak of rust.

Finally, a new "syndicate" was organized to build the line north of Franklin, based on the hope of a new $1,700,000 Montana subsidy. A new corporation, called the Utah & Northern Railroad Company, was drawn up on January 31, 1877. The company was chartered under Utah Territory law with the purpose of "owning a railroad along the route of the Utah Northern of 1871 to the northern border of the Territory and under Idaho or Montana law to Butte, Montana Territory." Stockholders included Jay Gould (265 shares), Sidney Dillon (264 shares), Joseph Richardson (264 shares), and one share

Photographs of the Utah Northern in early years are rare, but these two views do show the overall railroad facilities at Ogden during the period. Above, looking south at the yards, the ramshackle string of buildings at left represents the combined depot facilities (UN at far left). (Utah State Historical Society) Below, looking east at Ogden, with the same "Union Depot" visible at extreme right. At left, beyond CP standard gauge tracks, can be seen a string of narrow gauge U&N cars standing in front of what appears to be an old one stall narrow gauge engine house. (Union Pacific Railroad Collection)

The Utah-Idaho Central interurban above is traversing the old grade of the UN over Cache Hill between Dewey and Mendon, in this 1947 view; the cars are just out of Dewey northbound. (Henry R. Griffiths Collection) By taking this route the UN avoided the heavy construction in Bear River Canyon (below) that was later undertaken by the Union Pacific. Here, UP 2-10-2 no. 5306 is headed northbound in the canyon on August 28, 1948, just approaching Cache Junction. (Emil Albrecht Photo)

In this May 1940 view UP extra 2524 smokes through Cache Junction with a very mixed consist. The "beanery" or lunch room at left is still in use, but the trappings of the steam era in the background have long since disappeared. Below, UP 4-6-6-4 no. 3703 streaks across the broad valley north of Cache Junction with a seemingly endless string of high cars; the date is March 4, 1956, and steam operation was about to end. (Both, Emil Albrecht Photos)

The original Utah Northern line (later abandoned by the UP) crossed the Bear River at right center above, where the old UN bridge piers can still be seen, and the outline of the right of way is still visible stretching across the fields. A division point town and yards were established here and called Battle Creek, after an Indian massacre of 1863. Beyond the houses and trees in the distance to the north the line turned left and climbed up a gulch between the hills at far left. Below, the old grade of the line dropping down into the valley from the south is still clearly visible in this 1975 photo. (Both photos, Henry R. Griffiths)

for a Utah stockholder. Bassett and the Utah Mormons would no longer be involved in the extension. However, when the subsidy legislation was enacted, it proved unacceptable to the railroad group, just as the previous proposal had been. And the UN (or U&N) was still stalled at Franklin. Talk resumed about laying rail on the grade north into Idaho, and in July the *Railroad Gazette* carried the following brief item:

> Utah Northern.
>
> This company is trying to secure some local subsidy for an extension of its road from the present terminus at Franklin, Idaho, to Cottonwood, about 25 miles. It is promised that if the extension is made the bulk of the Idaho and Montana freight coming over the Union Pacific will be sent to Cottonwood, for transfer to teams at that point.

A report of somewhat more substance appeared in the Salt Lake *Herald* on October 6:

> The Union Pacific magnates, Sidney Dillon, Jay Gould and S. H. H. Clark, were in Salt Lake City Thursday, having come down from Ogden on a business visit in connection with the Utah Northern Railroad. On the occasion of the visit of these gentlemen last Summer negotiations began, looking to the Union Pacific assuming control of the Northern, and extending it toward Montana so as to control the carrying trade. The negotiations were concluded Thursday, the necessary papers receiving the signatures of the Union Pacific officials. The Utah Northern is to be extended northward for some distance, the intention being to have the winter terminus somewhere in the vicinity of Fort Hall. Contracts will be let and work commenced immediately, and by the time the grade is ready the rails will be on the ground. There is a quantity of rails already at hand, besides a vast number of ties. Probably within a few weeks the engine will be running beyond Franklin, and by the time snow falls and winter sets in 25 or 30 miles of additional road will be in use.

Clearly, the Utah Northern was becoming an appendage of the Union Pacific — if the process was a slow one. Gould and the UP management were more convinced than ever that western Montana offered an attractive source of traffic, but from the beginning the Union Pacific's officers held to the belief that their road could not absorb the capitalization of the original Utah Northern *and* finance the extension to Montana on a profitable basis. The task now became one of acquiring the physical assets and franchise of the old Utah Northern at minimal cost — by washing out the original investors for a few cents on the dollar. Royal Bassett and Joseph Richardson and many smaller stockholders, weary of the whole business, complied. John Young traded Mormon stock for some railroad equipment. Only the final liquidation of the Utah Northern remained to be accomplished, and this was done on April 3, 1878, when it was sold at foreclosure in Salt Lake City to satisfy action brought by the Union Trust Company as trustee for the bondholders. S. H. H. Clark, a Union Pacific official, bid in the road at $100,139 ($89,600 in old UN bonds and $10,539 in cash). The road was then conveyed to a new corporation incorporated in Utah on April 30, 1878 — the Utah & Northern *Railway* Company. (The Utah & Northern *Railroad* Company incorporation of 1877 was apparently never implemented and was voided at the end of that year.) To acquire the line for $100,139, however, Gould had paid Richardson $400,000 for his interest (or about 40% of his cost), and had acquired some $800,000-worth of stock held in Utah hands for a mere $80,000.

Gould and the Union Pacific now resumed efforts to gain some acceptable subsidies from Montana — either cash or tax exemptions — but by now many Montanans accepted the thesis that the railroad would come anyway, so why offer subsidies? And that is what happened.

Gould was anxious to get to Montana as quickly as possible, and had not waited for negotiations to be concluded. In October 1877 he elected to start building the line on his own account, and wired the Union Pacific's Chief Engineer accordingly:

> New York, October 24, 1877
>
> Washington Dunn, Engineer:
>
> Let a contract in my name for 10 or 20 miles, by the Marsh Valley route at once.
>
> J. Gould

Dunn, who was to be prominent in the Utah & Northern Railway's affairs all the way to Montana Territory, at once arranged with Moses Thatcher and other Mormons to grade twelve miles of road north from Franklin, Idaho. The route was a new one via the Marsh and Portneuf valleys to the Snake River Plain, and Jay Gould intended to get as far as Eagle Rock (now Idaho Falls) within the year. The old route to Soda Springs was abandoned, and the unused grade can still be seen beside the highway north of Franklin.

With the reorganization in process, the Union Pacific began pushing the extension with vigor. By April 12, 1878, the *Railroad Gazette* was able to report that track on the extension "is now laid from Franklin, Idaho, northward 10 miles. Work is being pushed actively; the bridges over Cub and Bear rivers are finished, all the trestle-

Two key figures in the expansion of the Utah & Northern under the Union Pacific were Sidney Dillon (left above) and Jay Gould (right above). (Both, Union Pacific Railroad Collection) The U&N construction into Idaho brought the line into the Marsh Valley, where a station was opened at Oneida, now Arimo. The event was commemorated in a monument erected by the Daughters of Utah Pioneers many years later. (Right, Arthur Petersen photo)

work in place, and a contract has been let for laying 36 miles of track, to be done as fast as the ties can be procured." By July the track had reached the Portneuf Canyon, 45 miles above Franklin, and it was reported that "iron is still going forward, and the company expects to reach Snake River before winter."

First Lieutenant John Bourke, who rode over the UN in 1875 and recorded his impressions then, as noted previously, once again travelled over the now resurgent U&N in the spring of 1878 and commented further. His northbound train stopped at Hampton's for dinner — "a good, honest, God-fearing meal, one that could look you squarely in the eyes and ask for 50 cents" — where his train met the down train, and Bourke sat beside a Montana miner who filled him with tales of the "recent wonderfully rich strikes in gold 'diggings' in that Territory." Reaching Franklin, he met Colonel John Gibbon en route from Montana to Washington, who regaled him with the story of a fabulously rich new mine. Bourke related that "this mine, or to speak more strictly, hole in the ground, is not over 70 feet deep and about 12 feet square at the surface. In the past 45 days, the owner has taken out *$50,000* . . . Every bit of the quartz showed free gold; a piece of the quartz shown me by General Gibbon was assuredly very remarkable, showing free gold to the naked eye, on every side. *Montana* is one of the most promising of our territories, whether as a mining, pastoral or agricultural country: the extension of the *Utah Northern Rail Road* will do wonders for its development."

Bourke noted the signs of activity along the way, including "great piles of ties and rails for the extension" stockpiled at Logan. Before retiring for the night at Franklin, Bourke walked around town "looking at the preparations for continuing the Rail Road to the north: the rails for the new portions of the road weigh more than those on the old line, and the ties are heavier, broader and longer, which circumstances will make the new part of the line much firmer and easier to travel on. A few miles north of Franklin, there is an extensive deposit of 'drift' gravel, that the company can use upon its road-bed."

The Union Pacific was apparently going to build a first class railroad, even if it *was* narrow gauge. Some work must already have been done on the Ogden-Franklin line since Bourke's trip in 1875; the editor of the Helena (Montana) *Herald* rode over the line early in 1878 and commented very favorably on the trip. He claimed that the train maintained a steady speed of 14 to 18 miles per hour, with one 14 mile stretch being covered in 28 minutes — a 30 mph average. With the Union Pacific funneling freight to the line, traffic picked up, too — in April the *Deseret News* reported 10 to 20 cars of freight going forward on the line daily, which must have been an appreciable increase.

Bourke had the interesting experience of riding north from Franklin on a construction train, regular service not having been begun. He was "shaken out of bed between 4 and 5 o'clock" and, after a breakfast of sorts, by six o'clock "we were off on the 'construction' train, for Bear River, Idaho, twelve (12) miles north of us. Train consisted of a dozen 'flat' cars, loaded with Rail Road iron. Mr. Jim Henderson, the Stage Agent, lent us three wooden chairs, upon which we sat comfortably during our ride. Wrapped in our buffalo robes and heavy over-coats, it was an exhilarating journey, even if the air blew a little keenly at first." The trip back was made several days later in similar style, except that empty spike kegs had to be pressed into service as seats, and was accomplished in just an hour — not bad for a construction train on new track, with a couple of stops. All this activity on the road must have been taxing the five little Grant locomotives, as Bourke also reported that a couple of engines from the Summit County Railroad, a little narrow gauge east of Ogden, were in use on the Utah & Northern at Ogden. These would be just the first of a stream of narrow gauge locomotives that the Union Pacific would bring in from its other narrow gauge subsidiaries (such as the South Park) when influxes of traffic would inundate the U&N in later years. However, to provide the new motive power that the extended line would require, the Union Pacific ordered sixteen new 2-6-0 Mogul type locomotives from Baldwin, which were received between September 1878 and June 1880. They were in turn followed by twenty-three larger Moguls from the Brooks works in 1881-1882. In addition, large numbers of freight and passenger cars were ordered from the eastern car-builders. A new day was dawning for the narrow gauge.

From Red Rock Pass, twenty-five miles northwest of Franklin, to the crossing of the Blackfoot River, a distance of seventy miles, the Utah & Northern route traversed the Fort Hall Indian Reservation. As originally established in 1869, the reservation comprised some 1,300,000 acres and had been set aside as a home for the Bannock and Shoshone Indians. As the Utah & Northern survey crews approached the reservation, trouble began. Guards had to be posted around the camps and when the survey line came closer to the reservation the Indians held a war dance to show their displeasure. Congress approved an act on June 20, 1878 that gave the railroad a right of way across the reservation and the redskins a large sum of money.

The right of way across the reservation was

The Utah Northern line passed from the Bear River valley into the Snake River valley through a low saddle called Red Rock Pass, formed when ancient Lake Bonneville (now Salt Lake) spilled over and drained into the Snake River. The old advertising cut at right shows a U&N narrow gauge train passing Red Rock and Swan Lake. (Museum Collection) Below, almost a century later a modern Union Pacific freight highballs northward over the same route. (Henry R. Griffiths photo)

The line from McCammon to Pocatello through Inkom (left) was relocated in 1881 with the coming of the standard gauge Oregon Short Line, and this work train may have been removing the narrow gauge line. The Baldwin mogul was probably one of those acquired from the Summit County. (Union Pacific Railroad Collection) The two Union Pacific 2-10-2's below (nos. 5037 and 5087) were wheeling an extra south of McCammon in 1948 when Emil Albrecht made this view.

not secured without some problems. Head of the Shoshoni was Chief Dono-Oso (meaning Buffalo Robe), whom the white man called "Pocatello." Chief Pocatello was a rather large, heavy Indian and was particularly fond of pork and tallow. It is said that the soldiers at Fort Hall called him "Pork 'n Tallow," the phrase being condensed to "Pocatello." The word is not of Indian origin and only the white men referred to the chief in that manner. In any event, the Chief stated that he would allow the steam trains to cross the reservation if he would be allowed to ride inside the cars (rather than on top of the cars) in a sleeping wagon (Pullman). The Chief told Assistant Attorney General Joseph K. McCammon that he wanted "the great white man (president) to put down his hand hard on the paper," to insure that the Chief could ride as he desired. Chief Pocatello got his wish and the Utah & Northern got its right of way, building the line through the reservation early in 1879. At that time, the town of Pocatello had only a box car set out beside the narrow gauge near Pocatello Creek, a short distance from the present city. The box car served both as station and as section house.

Railroad officials chose Eagle Rock as their division point. The spot, now called Idaho Falls, was where the narrow gauge would cross the Snake River, twenty seven miles north of the Fort Hall Reservation. One hundred acres of land were purchased, and during the winter of 1880-1881 the U&N built its main repair shops and a number of houses for railroad employees on the site. Eventually some two to three hundred men were employed at the facilities. The location was a logical one, as a small community had already grown up there around an important toll bridge on the freighting route from Utah to Montana.

The crossing-point had been an important one for fifteen years. On December 10, 1864 a franchise had been granted to Edward M. Morgan, James M. (Matt) Taylor and William F. Bartlett to operate a ferry across the Snake River, one and a half miles below Cedar Island at Eagle Rock, the present site of Idaho Falls. Matt Taylor selected a bridge site in 1864-65 at Black Canyon. An 83-foot long modified Queen's Truss wooden bridge was built across the Snake, anchored in solid rock at each end, in 1865. This bridge eased the problems for freighters along the "Montana Trail," as it avoided the dangerous ferry crossing of the Snake River, which was sometimes impossible to use due to flooding each spring. Taylor's bridge was washed out in the spring of 1867, but was promptly rebuilt.

With the completion of the line to Blackfoot, on the Snake River some ten miles above old Fort Hall, in 1878, regular service was quickly extended to that point. The line soon was attracting the attention of the western travel publicists and guidebook publishers (with some urging from the Union Pacific's own promotion people, of course), and a detailed description of the route and towns served appeared in *Crofutt's New Overland Tourist* in 1879. A few passages quoted from the account will provide a little added background on the route:

> Trains leave Ogden opposite the Union Depot to the eastward.
>
> Leaving the depot, the road skirts the western edge of the city, across rich, broad, and well-cultivated fields, orchards and gardens, with the Wasatch Mountains towering to the right.
>
> From the cars an occasional glimpse of Salt Lake can be obtained, with its numerous islands, lifting their peaks far far above the briny waters.
>
> With the rugged mountains on our right and the waters of the lake seen at times on our left, we find objects of interest continually rising around us. Far up the sides of the mountain, stretching along in one unbroken line, save where it is sundered by canyons, gulches, and ravines, is the old water-mark of the ancient lake, showing that at one time this lake was a mighty sea, washing the mountain sides several hundred feet above us.
>
> We are gradually rising up on to a high bench and will continue along near the base of the mountains for the next thirty miles. In places the view will be grand. The Great Lake at the southwest with its numerous islands in the distance, the well-cultivated fields in the foreground.
>
> WILLARD — This is a quiet Mormon town of 700 inhabitants, and contains some fine buildings, but the greater portion are built of logs and adobe, yet neat and cosy.
>
> BRIGHAM — This is the county seat of Box Elder county, situated near the mouth of Box Elder and Wellsville Canyon. Like Willard, it nestles close under the shadow of the Wasatch, and is embowered in fruit trees. Population, 1,800. The buildings are mostly of adobe. A thriving trade and rapidly increasing population attest the importance of the place. The public buildings include a court-house and tabernacle, two hotels, and no saloons.
>
> DEWEYVILLE . . . some good farms and a grist mill. Curving around the point of the mountain and heading for the north, up Bear Valley, the grade increases; sage is the rule, pines and cedars appear in the mountain gorges, and up we climb. To the west on the opposite side of Bear River, about five miles above the station, is located a village of Shoshone

Indians, about 100 in number. The tepees — lodges — can be plainly seen. These Indians took up this land in 1874, under the pre-emption laws of the United States, and abandoned their tribal relations. They own some large herds of cattle and bands of horses, and are very quiet and peaceably disposed.

Passing on up a heavy grade through deep cuts for five miles and we are at

COLLINSTON — formerly Hamptons, once an eating station. Now abandoned. Meals are served at Logan, sixteen miles east.

Just before reaching this station, the road cuts through a spur of the mountain that juts out to the westward into the valley, leaving a high, isolated peak. Let us climb this peak and take a look. To the north, six miles, the Bear River canyons through a low spur of the Wasatch which reaches away to the northwest. To the west of this spur lies the Malad Valley, the Malad River; the latter and the Bear come close together into the valley, immediately to the west of where we stand; then flow close together down the valley to the south parallel for ten miles before they unite, in some places not more than 20 feet apart. To the west of this valley rise the long range of the Malad Mountains, which, commencing near Corinne, runs nearly north to opposite this point, and then bears away to the northwest.

Only a small portion of the lands in the Bear or Malad valleys are cultivated; cattle and sheep are plenty. Leaving Collinston, our road is up to a 100 foot grade, curving around to raise the spur of the Wasatch above alluded to, through which Bear River canyons a few miles to the northward. Finally the

SUMMIT — is reached and passed four miles from Collinston and we curve to the east and then to the south, around the narrow spur alluded to, which separated Bear Valley from Cache Valley.

From the Summit we have been rapidly descending into Cache Valley, which is on our left, and is one of the most productive in Utah Territory. The valley heads in the Wasatch Mountains, northeast of Ogden, and is 40 miles long with an average width of six miles, to where it intersects Marsh Valley on the north, five miles distant. The Logan River runs through the lower portion of this valley, and is composed of the Little Bear, Blacksmith Fork, and Logan creeks, making a stream of ample volume to irrigate all the land in the valley, much of which is yet open for pre-emption.

In an ordinary season the shipments from this valley average 500 car-loads of wheat, 200 car-loads of oats, and 100 car-loads of potatoes, most of which go to California. Wheat often yields 50 bushels to the acre.

MENDON — is the first station from the Summit, 5.5 miles distant, on the west side of the valley, and contains about 700 population.

LOGAN — This city is the county seat of Cache county, situated on the east side of Cache Valley, just below the mouth of Logan Canyon. It is the largest place in the valley — containing a population of about 3,000, most of whom are engaged in agricultural and pastoral pursuits.

Leaving Logan, our road runs north, along the base of the Wasatch Mountains — having made a great horse-shoe curve from the summit.

FRANKLIN — This town is one mile north of the line, between Utah and Idaho, and, consequently, is in Idaho Territory; population about 400. It is situated in Cache Valley, Oneida county, Idaho, on Chubb Creek about one mile from the station to the northeast, at the base of the Wasatch Mountains.

From Franklin, we turn westward and cross Chubb and Worm Creeks, along which are some fine farming lands; pass through a number of deep cuts and find Bear River on our left, far below our road, with narrow bottom lands on each side. The road turns north and runs up on the east bank of the river a few miles where it crosses to the west and stops at a small side track called

BATTLE CREEK — twelve miles from Franklin. Soon after leaving the station the road turns west up CONNOR'S CANYON, where, in the winter of 1863-4, Gen. Connor had his celebrated fight with the Shoshone Indians. At the time of his fight there was two foot of snow on the ground, and the weather very cold. The Indians — some hundreds — were hid in the Canyon among the willows along the Creek, and in the cedars to the right along the bluffs. By a vigorous charge of the troops, the Indians were completely overcome, and with few exceptions, none were left alive to tell the tale. The bones of the dead are still to be seen near the station.

In ascending the Canyon the grade is heavy, deep cuts are numerous, sage brush abounds, and the country is very broken, only adapted to stock raising.

ONEIDA — a small town of perhaps fifty people. The famous Soda Springs of Idaho, are 30 miles east of this station, where are ample hotel accommodations for tourists.

Leaving Oneida, a low cut in the mountains about five miles distant to the northeast, marks the passage of Port Neuf River through Port Neuf Gap. The old stage road is on our right, along the base of the mountain. After crossing a number of small creeks, and about eight miles

> from Oneida we come to Port Neuf River, and follow it for the next thirty-six miles.
>
> Along this river are many peculiar rock formations. In places the rocks rise like a solid wall, from 20 to 100 feet from the ground in a line of uniform height for miles in extent, resembling huge fortifications. In several places along the road there are two and sometimes three of these walls running parallel with each other. Proceeding down the river we come to "Robbers' Roost" on the right, about four miles before reaching the next station. It is the point where the Montana stage robbery was committed in 1864.
>
> BLACKFOOT — named for the Blackfoot Indians, has a population of about 350 (March 1879). It has several hotels, stores of various kinds, a bank, express, telegraph, freight, and stage offices. It is situated on a broad sage-covered plain, with the Blackfoot River one mile to the south; the Snake, about one mile to the northwest, marked by a dense growth of cottonwood and willows.

Although tracklaying had stopped at Blackfoot about the first of December in 1878, advance work extended some distance beyond. One report stated that grading was nearly complete to the crossing of the Snake at Eagle Rock, and the Union Pacific had put Captain Edward L. Berthoud, architect of the Colorado Central narrow gauge, and a large survey crew in the field all summer, mapping out the route to Montana. Tracklaying did not resume until the end of March, and the railhead slowly advanced on Eagle Rock during April and May. The large bridge across the Snake at Eagle Rock — involving two spans of 130 and 160 feet each — had to be completed before the railroad could proceed beyond that point. By July 4, 1879, the *Railroad Gazette* could report that

> Trains now run regularly to Eagle Rock, Idaho, 207 miles from Ogden, Utah. A heavy business is reported, and the company has 16 engines and 300 cars in constant use. The grading is finished to Camas, 40 miles from Eagle Rock, and track is laid to a point 20 miles beyond Eagle Rock.

Ten of the sixteen locomotives mentioned were new Baldwin Moguls, received since the previous fall. They had been badly needed.

Camas was reached by mid-July, and "Devil's Dive," 40 miles further north, by late September. Some references cite further extension into Montana in the winter of 1879, but this was apparently confined to advance grading work. Railhead for the winter was established at Beaver Canyon, 30 miles north of Camas and a dozen miles short of the border at Monida.

Although Montana was the objective of the U&N, the mountainous regions of Idaho west of the new U&N line were attracting great interest for their rich placer gold deposits along streams such as the Snake, Salmon and Lemhi. In his 1879 guidebook, *To the Rockies and Beyond,* Robert E. Strahorn discussed at length the attractions of these areas, and the importance of the U&N and Eagle Rock as the preferred route for reaching them:

> This vast new region, already awakened by the rumble of the Utah & Northern locomotives, is as easily accessible as any railroad point in the west. Its discovery just at this time augurs brightly for the Montana branch of the Union Pacific. Eagle Rock, at which point the Utah & Northern Railroad crosses Snake River, is within a few moments' walk of some of the bars referred to above — indeed, the soil for miles thereabouts will, it is said, show good "prospects" of this fine gold. Miners' outfits are obtainable at Blackfoot or Eagle Rock, at reasonable prices.
>
> *Eagle Rock* — Northward from Blackfoot, 30 miles, or from Ogden, 206 miles, is old Eagle Rock Bridge across Snake River, and the present (April, 1879) temporary terminus of the Utah & Northern Railroad. It is one of the most interesting spots between the Union Pacific Railroad and the Montana line, although a misnomer, as Eagle Rock, a black lava crag in mid-river, is 10 miles further up the Snake. The majestic and navigable flood, the noblest of Idaho rivers, here dashes its entire volume through an ominous rock-walled fissure less than 50 feet wide. The staunch old wagon bridge resting at either end on the singular lava palisades, is 60 feet above low water mark. Soundings of the deep blue stream made from the bridge failed to discover bottom *at 240 feet.* It is near here that a striking resemblance of the formation to that of the Giant's Causeway in the old world, is noticeable. A few yards below the old bridge the splendid new iron structure of the Utah & Northern spans the stream. Snake River abounds in salmon trout of great size and voracious appetites. They are a welcome feature of bills of fare at eating stations along the road. The stream is over 1000 miles long, and waters a vast area of fine farming and grazing lands.
>
> Near here we obtain excellent views of those noted landmarks, the Three Tetons, 100 miles away to the northeast; the Salmon River range, about the same distance on the west, and Black Butte, 50 miles to the northward. Never have I seen such jagged, sharp-pinnacled, and apparently insurmountable landmarks as the glacier-crowned Tetons.
>
> The view from Eagle Rock to the northwest, as already indicated, takes in an almost boundless and an exquisitely beautiful vista of rugged, snow-capped

mountains. The central group of these is the great Salmon River range, 125 miles away, a region which is just now deservedly attracting much attention in western mining circles, but which is only recognized in the busy eastern world as a real *terra incognita*. The Salmon River, Yankee Fork and Loon Creek gulch mines have long been quietly sending southward fine lots of nuggets and dust. But it has remained for the railway era to open up the wonderfully rich quartz mines which have been systematically worked the past season. The principal quartz districts lie along Salmon River and its tributaries, covering an area of some 10,000 square miles. The entire region is abundantly watered with clear, swift mountain streams, and timbered with pine, spruce, cedar and other varieties of soft wood. The Salmon River range occupies almost the entire area, and renders it one of the roughest and most difficult of access in the whole Rocky Mountain country. The two or three arable valleys of any considerable extent, having an altitude of only from 3,800 to 5,000 feet above the sea, and being extremely fertile, are already being rapidly turned into productive farms and garden spots. Road-making has been necessarily slow, and the different camps, far from railways, often harassed by savages, and having, until the past season, only been linked by trails, have not done much to attract even the slightest notice from the outside world. Nearly all merchandise has been distributed from Salmon City to the various camps, from 25 to 100 miles distant, on pack-mules, while ores have been brought back the same way. However, the marvelous richness of the ores in different mines, the rapid extension of the Utah & Northern Railroad, and the great interest recently manifested by outside capitalists in the various districts, are bringing about the natural results. From now henceforward the construction of roads, bridges, mills and other needed improvements is assured, and the wealth of the Salmon River mines will be as familiar a theme as that of any of the bonanza districts of Colorado, Montana or Nevada.

The mines are in numerous instances well defined ledges of both gold and silver. In the Yankee Fork district, 90 miles southwest of Salmon City, are the noted "Chas. Dickens" and "Ramshorn" mines, carrying ores which yield from $300 to $1,000 in silver to the ton, and a considerable percentage of gold. A shipment of 100 tons of ore to Salt Lake City the past summer yielded an average of $550 per ton. The "Ramshorn" produced $40,000 last year.

The road now most extensively traveled by Salmon River freighters and miners turned directly westward from a station called Sand Hole, on the regular Montana stage route. Tri-weekly coaches of the Salisbury line run direct to Salmon City in from 50 to 60 hours. Fare from the temporary terminus of the Utah & Northern Railroad to Salmon City, $45. The road entering the Salmon River region at Challis turns off directly to the northwest from Blackfoot Station, crossing Snake River at Central Ferry and reaching Challis in 135 miles. Wood, water and grass are plentiful enough for campers on either route. Miners' or farmers' outfits can be purchased at reasonable rates at the terminus or, with the cost of freight added, at either Challis or Salmon City. Transient board at the latter points from $2 to $2.50 per day, or by the week from $10 to $14.

For the benefit of those going to Montana, Strahorn gives a complete resume of the various stage lines to the major Montana camps, with distances, fares and times:

> *For Montana.*—Gilmer, Salisbury & Co's line of daily Concord coaches, carrying the mails and Union Pacific Express, connects with Utah & Northern trains at the terminus for all cities, towns and mining camps in Montana and Eastern Idaho. The telegraph also continues northward into the Montana settlements. Graders and track-layers are busily engaged in pushing the Utah & Northern onward in the wake of the pioneering institutions to the Montana line, now only 100 miles away. Thus by early autumn the Territory will be reached, and that beautiful wonderland, Yellowstone Park, will be within less than 15 hours' staging distance from the Pullman and parlor coaches of this splendid narrow gauge. Distances by stage from Eagle Rock are about as follows: Lovell's, Montana, 163 miles; Bannack, 190; Salisbury, 200; Virginia City, 228; Glendale, 230; Butte, 253; Deer Lodge, 280; Helena, 290; Bozeman, 300; Missoula, 325. The stages consume from 36 to 72 hours in reaching these different points. On April 1, 1879, the following rates were in effect: From Omaha to the prominent Montana points, 1st class, $100; 2d class, $75; emigrant, $45. Holders of 2d class and emigrant tickets, via Gilmer, Salisbury & Co's line, will both be carried from the railway terminus to destination in covered mail wagons. One hundred pounds of baggage carried free by rail; forty pounds free by stage, on first-class; fifty pounds free by wagon on 2d class and emigrant; extra baggage on stage and wagon lines, fifteen cents per pound. Stages and wagons run daily.

Blackfoot (below) became a terminus for connecting stage and freighting outfits upon arrival of the Utah & Northern; piles of rails and ties are still apparent in this view. (C. H. Peake Coll.) The plat at right shows the alignment of the U&N at Eagle Rock; the railroad made a quarter-circle turn to the west to cross the river, with the depot being placed at the end of the sweeping curve. (Author's Coll.)

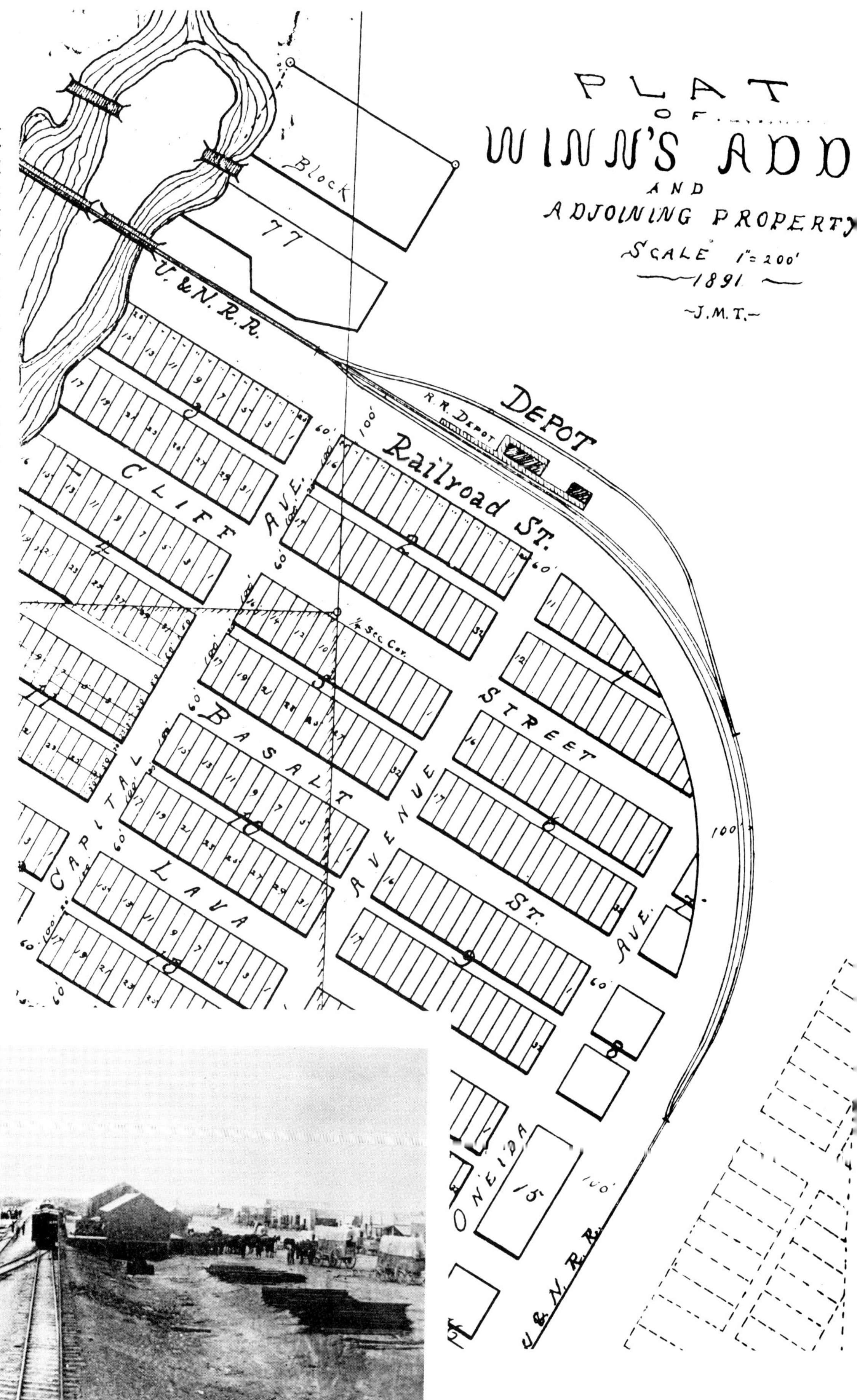

Two views of the bridges at Eagle Rock: the woodcut above is looking downstream at the wagon bridge in the foreground, while the 1879 photo below is looking upstream, with the railroad's "great iron truss" bridges prominent and the two wagon bridges visible beyond, left and right, beneath the railroad bridges. In the background, right, are the railroad shop buildings. (Above, J. D. Marker; below, C. H. Peake Collection)

This dramatic view shows one of the U&N's Brooks moguls, handsomely lettered and striped and displaying a towering Congdon stack, posed on one span of the railroad's impressive bridge. Immediately behind it is a span of the wagon bridge, while the vast shop buildings and roundhouse at Eagle Rock can be seen silhouetted in the distance. (Author's Collection) Right above, Utah & Northern no. 85 (originally no. 28), another Brooks mogul, pictured in front of the roundhouse in 1886 with huge wedge plow and extensive cab and tender curtains for snow fighting. In the period of several years, fancy striping and spit-and-polish have disappeared, as has the Congdon stack. (Arthur Petersen Collection) Right below, a broad view of the roundhouse and shop buildings in the 1880's. (Idaho Historical Society Collection)

85

285

The shop force at Eagle Rock turned out in 1885 for this group photo, while several contemporaries posed (right) by a freshly varnished U&N Pullman before the car shop. A three-wheel "Irish Mail" handcar is in center. Another popular photo locale was the great bridge at Eagle Rock; here (below) a crew poses with their freight train in 1886. (Author's Collection)

At the time the Utah & Northern was being operated from Ogden to Beaver Canyon, the superintendent of the road was G. W. Thatcher, who had been retained by the Union Pacific from the original Utah Northern. Thatcher was headquartered at Logan, Utah. All of the matters pertaining to new construction on the narrow gauge were handled by Colonel Washington Dunn, as superintendent of construction, under the direction of Union Pacific Chief Engineer Jacob Blickensderfer in Omaha, Nebraska. The general contract for all the grading was let to Bishop Mariner W. Merrill of Franklin, but there were a large number of sub-contractors. Bridges and buildings were constructed by the firm of Dakin & Pinkham.

Tracklaying was resumed as early as possible in 1880, and U&N rails reached the Montana Territorial line on March 9. A huge celebration was arranged, with an elaborate ceremony of driving the first spike in Montana being held that midday. A special train of three cars of participating dignitaries left Beaver Canyon at 10:00 AM, arriving at Monida before noon. The "first" spike was attached to a telegraph instrument, so that the blows of the sledge driving it home could be telegraphed to places such as Butte, where the citizenry gathered in a large hall to hear the event take place. The spike was driven at twenty minutes before one, after which speeches and celebrations lasted well into the afternoon. The Utah & Northern had at last accomplished the feat of being the first railroad to enter Montana.

The track was quickly pushed on to Red Rock, nearly a hundred miles from Eagle Rock and 304 miles from Ogden; there a new terminus was established while further surveys were run for lines towards Helena and Deer Lodge (maps of the 1879 period indicate that the final route still had not been decided upon). Train service was established on the following schedule:

6:30 PM	0	Ogden	8:55 AM
5:40 AM	158	Pocatello	10:25 PM
9:00 AM	207	Eagle Rock	7:05 PM
3:15 PM	304	Red Rock	12:45 PM

Quite an improvement over the stage trip of just a year or two previous!

The Deer Lodge route was chosen and tracklaying resumed during the summer, with the new town of Dillon (named, obviously, after Sidney Dillon of the Union Pacific) being reached by October. 46 miles beyond Red Rock and 350 miles from Ogden, Dillon became the new terminus for the winter of 1880-1881.

The growing equipment roster now numbered 21 locomotives, 177 box cars, 12 stock cars, 124 flat cars, 15 non-revenue cars and 5 cabooses. The passenger equipment was soon augmented by the addition of five new Pullman sleepers that arrived in 1881. The five cars came from the Jackson & Sharp Works of Wilmington, Delaware. Each of the five cars cost $5,000, and they carried these names:

"Rambler"
"Advance"
"Security"
"Ogden"
"Soda Springs"

The "Security" was misnamed, for she continually derailed and ended up "in the ditch" or off the track. One passenger said of the narrow gauge Pullmans: "You have to double yourself up like a jackknife in order to get a night's rest. And at that you had to hang on in your sleep to keep from being dashed out onto the floor of the coach as it rounded a curve."

Tracklaying resumed once again in the spring of 1881, although the pace did seem to be slowing down. Perhaps, now that the U&N was in the "pay dirt" of Montana and the only potential competition (the Northern Pacific) was still over the horizon, the Union Pacific felt haste was unnecessary. At any rate, Melrose, 30 miles north of Dillon, was reached in July and Silver Bow, just west of Butte, in October. The main line would be continued north through Deer Lodge to a point west of Helena, where it would intersect the Northern Pacific when that line was completed — a point subsequently named Garrison.

While the main line was being constructed, many branch line projects were discussed, rumored, even planned. One involved a branch from Beaver Canyon east to Yellowstone National Park; another to Helena via Three Forks; an extension to Fort Benton; and lines to Virginia City, Bozeman and Missoula. Most of this was pure speculation. One branch that was essential to the U&N's plans, however, was the short branch from Silver Bow into Butte. The road was prepared to build this line as quickly as it could after reaching Silver Bow— but a pesky problem arose. The route ran through some old placer mine claims, and the claim owners perceived an opportunity to reap some reward from their claims that they had not been able to extract by panning for gold — so they held out for unspecified but sumptuous amounts of money. Because the line was not part of the main line, the U&N could not condemn the properties under its charter. When negotiations bogged down into a confused impasse, the railroad decided to establish the terminus at Silver Bow for the interim. If Butte did not get its railroad, the U&N hoped, responsible elements in the town might help solve the problem; and to bring added pressure to bear, the railroad let it be known that it would turn all efforts towards extending the

As the railroad moved north through Idaho, the countryside took on a desolate, mountainous appearance — typified by the isolated station of High Bridge, shown below. The Eclipse windmill in the foreground and the steam pump-house were both needed to provide water for the big tank, which towers over the little frame station and box-car section house. (Henry R. Griffiths Collection) Further north, the "U&N Eating House" at Lima (originally Spring Hill) seen in the sunny view at left must have been a more welcome sight to U&N crews. (Arthur Petersen Collection)

line on to Deer Lodge (and, perhaps, the hated rival town of Helena beyond?). The strategy worked: Butte's civic leaders reacted in alarm, twisted some claim-owners' arms, and negotiated a price of $8,400 to settle the claims. Butte raised $3,400 of the amount through popular subscriptions, and the Union Pacific provided the other $5,000, and Butte greeted its first train on December 26.

During 1882 the U&N was extended to Deer Lodge, and on to Garrison the following November, 454 miles from Ogden. There the U&N would establish a junction with the Northern Pacific. The plan would be for the U&N to reach Helena over NP rails, and the Northern Pacific to reach Butte with another third rail over the Utah & Northern.

In mid-February 1883 a meeting was held in New York between the officials of the Northern Pacific Railway and the Union Pacific Railway. The February 23, 1883 issue of the *Railroad Gazette* stated that a satisfactory agreement had been made between the two roads whereas: "Upon the completion of the Northern Pacific Railroad to Little Blackfoot, Montana Territory, a point about 48 miles west of Helena, where it intersects the Utah & Northern and which point will be reached some time in July, the Northern Pacific Railroad will lay a third rail between Helena and Little Blackfoot. The Utah & Northern will also lay a third rail between Little Blackfoot and Butte City, thus giving to each line a through rail connection to the most important cities of Montana."

The actual meeting point was at Garrison, 12 miles north of Deer Lodge. As soon as the line to Garrison and the Northern Pacific was spiked down, Utah & Northern construction crews began work on two short branches to serve the mines and smelters of the Butte District. One line ran from Anaconda to Stuart, while the other served the St. Lawrence mine. Elsewhere the survey crews were busy running a line from Beaver Canyon, Idaho toward the western boundary of the Yellowstone National Park, a distance of some 75 miles.

On October 18, 1883 *Railway Age* commented: "It is reported that the work of putting a third rail to make a standard gauge on this road from Butte to the Northern Pacific junction has been suspended, on account of some disagreement between the company and the Northern Pacific; and that the latter company will build an independent line to Butte, Montana, while the narrow gauge extension will be constructed from Butte to Helena by the Utah & Northern." Alas, the U&N never did reach Helena.

At this time the Union Pacific was building a standard gauge railroad from its mainline at Granger, Wyoming, to the Pacific Northwest under the name of the Oregon Short Line Railway Company. This railroad was incorporated on April 11, 1881 and eventually built a railroad from Granger to Huntington, Oregon, a distance of 541 miles, with branches bringing the total length to 612 miles. The Oregon Short Line met the Utah & Northern's mainline at McCammon, Idaho and utilized a third rail on the U&N line from that point to Pocatello, Idaho Territory, a distance of 22.81 miles. An interesting sidelight in the construction of the Oregon Short Line was the construction (in 1882) of some 16 miles of narrow gauge trackage on standard gauge ties from Pocatello west toward American Falls, prior to the standard gauge mainline reaching a junction with the narrow gauge at McCammon. As soon as the Oregon Short Line link-up was made, the narrow gauge west of Pocatello was widened.

During June of 1882 the Oregon Short Line crews were pulled off the standard gauge to rebuild a section of the old Utah Northern through the Marsh Valley. This line had given trouble each spring due to flooding, so it was decided to relocate the line from Arimo for a distance of seven miles, joining the Oregon Short Line and then following that road the remaining 30 miles into Pocatello. The new narrow gauge route was slightly longer, but was free from constant spring flooding.

Traffic on the Butte and Garrison to Pocatello line was so heavy that a number of locomotives were transferred from the Union Pacific's Colorado lines. The Utah & Northern's own roster boasted some 45 locomotives and still more were needed. A number of Mason Bogie type 2-6-6T engines were brought over to the Utah & Northern, along with several Brooks 2-6-0s from the Denver, South Park & Pacific. The Denver, South Park & Pacific at that time extended from Denver to Gunnison, Colorado via the famed Alpine Tunnel route, with branches to Breckenridge, Morrison and Buena Vista.

The Utah Northern had its share of wrecks and similar unpleasantries, although many probably went undocumented. The first fatality noted in train service occurred early in 1873, when an Indian made the mistake of lying down on the track to take a nap and was dispatched to the happy hunting grounds by the southbound accommodation from Logan. A young construction worker, helping to erect the bridge at Corinne on that branch, fell into the river and was drowned in a whirlpool. Although no fatalities resulted, a more spectacular affair was the collision somewhere north of Salt Lake City in January 1885, when three engines were said to have been "wrecked". The nature of the country contributed to the road's problems; the untamed wilderness was still

Dillon was one of the more important towns to spring up as the U&N marched north through Montana, and quickly became an important freight forwarding point for the more remote mountain camps (below). At left, a small group of Indians waits stolidly on the Dillon depot platform for a train to carry them off to some unknown destination. (Both, Montana Historical Society) Right above, the new freight house at Dillon and a U&N narrow gauge engine are festooned with a group of citizens anxious to sit for their photo. (Beaverhead Co. Museum Coll.) Below, the water tank at Dillon also eventually acquired its Eclipse windmill. (Arthur Petersen Collection)

When the U&N finally reached Garrison, Montana, construction stopped to await a connection with the Northern Pacific for an entry into Helena, which never materialized. Above is the only known photo of a U&N narrow gauge train at Garrison, powered by a borrowed Denver, South Park & Pacific Mason Bogie no. 55. (Arthur Petersen Collection) Below, a small community quickly cropped up at railhead, centering around the saloon and Hotel Garrison shown here. (C. H. Peake Collection)

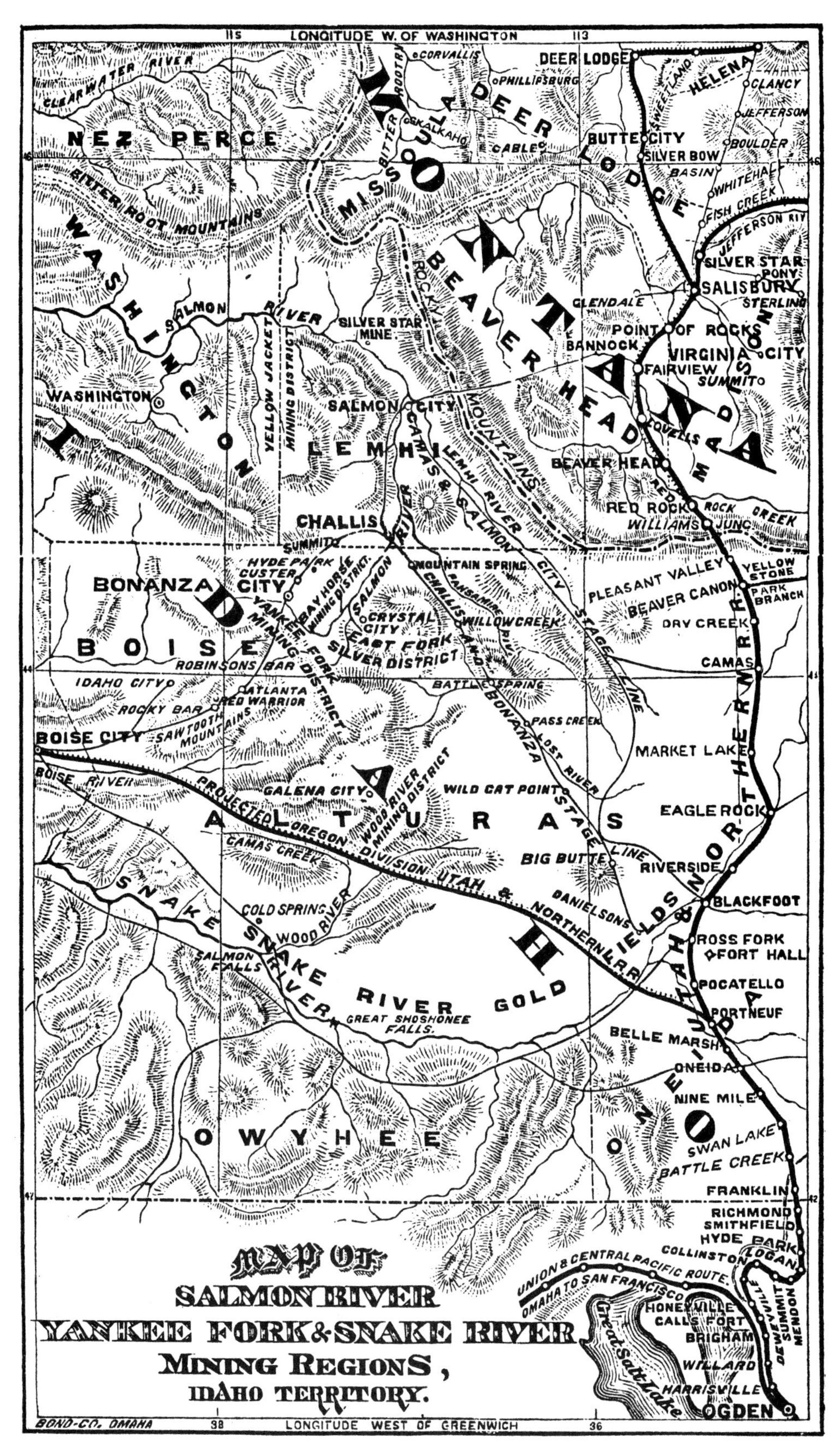

This 1880 map from Strahorn's To The Rockies and Beyond *shows the U&N as built at that time — as far as Red Rock, Montana — plus any number of ambitious extensions and branches. Particularly interesting is the projected "Oregon Division" from Portneuf west through Boise City over a route somewhat north of that taken soon after by the standard gauge Oregon Short Line. Mines around Challis and Bonanza City, in central Idaho, declined before the U&N could consider building into that area.*

One of the best views of early U&N trains is that above at Logan, Utah, in the early 1880's, capturing Baldwin No. 11 with a 5-car mixed. A sister Baldwin mogul appears at left with the assembled employees at Battle Creek about the same time. (Both, Arthur Petersen Collection) Below, Brooks mogul No. 100 poses with a piledriver somewhere near Logan in the mid-1880's. (Author's Collection)

apparent in July 1883 when the driver of a connecting Wells, Fargo stage was killed by "robbers". Another aspect of danger in the wilderness was spelled out in a January 29, 1885, story in *Railway Age*. Under the heading "Wholesale Slaughter of Deer by Railway Trains", the article revealed that "four deer were killed near McCammon, on the Utah & Northern, by the northbound passenger train . . . When the weather is exceedingly cold, the deer seem to fancy railroad tracks as a good place to obtain shelter from the wind." Apparently the deer would huddle in the deep cuts to escape the wind, and could not escape when the train bore down upon them.

One accident on the Utah & Northern in 1886 was so spectacular, however, that it received attention from the press all over the west. It occurred at Dry Creek, Idaho, in the upper end of Beaver Canyon, on May 12, 1886, and is covered in thorough detail in the following account from the Butte *Daily Miner* of Friday, May 14:

WRECK ON UTAH NORTHERN.
A Curious Accident Causes a Collision
Between Freights Near Dry
Creek, Idaho.

The Result, One Man Killed, and Two
Others are Not Expected to
Live.
Damage to the Company Property Not
Known, But it is Surely
Very Extensive.

Special to the MINER.

DRY CREEK, Idaho, May 13. — Last night near this point there occurred one of the most disastrous accidents that has ever occurred on the Utah & Northern road, involving in addition to a loss of life a very heavy loss of property. It appears that about 8 o'clock Conductor Quinn, in charge of freight train No. 618 from Spring Hill going south, was intercepted by orders to side track at Dry Creek in order to allow a very heavy triple header from Eagle Rock to pass. When the point was reached he proceeded to obey orders, and at once discovered that the side track was occupied with a lot of empty box cars and eleven cars laden with steel rails. He sent brakeman Taylor ahead to release the standing stock, and pulled in, as is usual, when the engine of 618 struck the box cars and started them. Taylor discovered that the eleven steel cars were not coupled, and being so heavily laden they moved off with a fair start at a pretty good speed. Instead of adjusting the air brakes with which the cars were equipped, Taylor seems to have lost his head, and the presumption is that fearing they would be wrecked, he ran down, opened the switch and thus turn them into the main track, which, at this point, has a very heavy down grade.

In the meantime the heavy train with its three engines in charge of Conductor Collins, which had started from Eagle Rock at 2:55 p.m., was moving along at the rate of twelve or fifteen miles per hour. At starting it was drawn by engine 24, Burt Chapman, engineer, and engine 17, George Orem, engineer, but on account of its weight engine 50, George Flood, engineer, was ordered to hitch on at the mouth of Beaver Canyon and help to pull it through the heavy grade of the canyon, which was done, No. 50 being in the lead. The train was proceeding in good shape and Dry Creek had been nearly reached, when the eleven runaway cars were suddenly discovered turning a curve and coming at the rate of forty or fifty miles an hour. The sight was so sudden and the distance so short that it was impossible to do anything, and in a second or two the collision occurred, the shock being terrible, the steel rails on the runaway smashing through the boiler of No. 50. The concussion was so great that the three engines and nearly all the cars of both trains were derailed and they and their contents scattered in all directions. As soon as they recovered from the shock the railroad men began to look around to discover the extent of the accident. That the train was a complete wreck was apparent at a glance, and then came the search for the human victims, the casualties being finally summed up as follows:

JAMES CLARK, fireman No. 50, killed instantly, skull fractured.

GEORGE FLOOD, engineer No. 50, very badly scalded. Recovery doubtful.

ANDY KEACH, fireman No. 24, one leg mashed and amputated, the other broken in two places. Not expected to live.

BURT CHAPMAN, an engineer, No. 24, head badly cut, and otherwise bruised. Not serious.

GEORGE OREM, engineer No. 17, badly bruised.

BILL PURDY, fireman No. 17, several slight wounds.

HENRY HEWITT, head brakeman, who was riding on No. 17, was somewhat bruised, but nothing serious.

All the other hands were more or less shook up, but beyond a few bruises sustained no injuries.

As soon as the accident occurred Conductor Quinn telegraphed to Eagle Rock for assistance, and General Foreman C. S. Smith immediately ordered out a special relief train in charge of Conductor

Pocatello soon became the most important terminal on the entire line, and much freight had to be transshipped to or from the standard gauge at that point. To facilitate this chore, the Union Pacific installed a Ramsey Transfer — *an ingenious arrangement of raised and depressed tracks that permitted quick and easy exchange of standard gauge for narrow gauge trucks under a freight car, as shown above. Thus such commodities as coal coming from the UP's Wyoming mines to Butte smelters could be shipped through in the same car, rather than be subjected to costly and damaging car-to-car transfer. Facilities were needed for transferring passengers, too, so the impressive frame Pacific Hotel was erected adjacent to the depot (below, in August, 1884). (Both, C. H. Peake Collection)*

Cathcart, and having on board Dr. Bean, the Company Surgeon, at Eagle Rock, and other assistance, it at once proceeded to the scene. The wounded were immediately cared for and after being made as comfortable as possible were taken to Eagle Rock for treatment. Subsequently a wrecking train was sent to the point and the men are busily engaged in clearing the track.

Since he was sent forward by the conductor to attend to the cars on the side track the brakeman Taylor has not been seen and it is supposed that he became frightened at the result of his ignorance or carelessness and ran away. He is one of the new brakemen having entered upon his duties about the seventh of the month. He comes from Payette, Idaho, on the Short Line, and claims to have been an old brakeman.

JAMES CLARK who was instantly killed has been in the employ of the company about one year. He came here from California where he was in the employ of the Central Pacific. He is a young man, unmarried, and a member of the Brotherhood of Firemen.

ANDY KEACH, who was so badly injured, has been for some time in the employ of the company. He lives at Eagle Rock and has a wife and one child.

GEORGE FLOOD, who was seriously scalded was formerly an employe of the Rock Island and resided at Davenport, Iowa. He has been on the Utah Northern about one year. He is unmarried.

The next day's paper reported further that "the brakeman, Taylor, who turned the cars on the main line, is nearly crazy, and it is expected he will be a raving maniac by morning." Further reports on "condition of the wounded" from the wreck did not provide any additional details on Taylor, but did reveal that Keach, the fireman, died that Sunday morning, May 16. As the newspaper commented in a follow-up story, "the accident on the Utah & Northern yesterday was an expensive one . . . The loss of life and limb cannot be estimated, but that of property can, as the company will discover to its sorrow." The newspaper went on to point out that it "fully demonstrates the necessity of having skilled and experienced employees to handle trains."

It was not long before the Union Pacific discovered the limitations of handling large volumes of business over a *narrow gauge* railroad — especially a difficult line like the Utah & Northern. As early as 1885 the trade press was reporting plans to standard gauge the line from Butte to Pocatello. Bridge work was being done north of Pocatello with possible standard gauging in mind by this time. South of McCammon to Ogden, however, traffic was said to be mainly local in nature and thus there was no immediate need for standard gauging that section.

Transferring freight from narrow gauge to standard gauge cars, or vice versa, at Pocatello was a major bottleneck and created added costs. To alleviate this problem the Union Pacific installed a Ramsey Transfer. This ingenious affair permitted the changing of the trucks under cars from narrow to standard gauge and back again, so that the lading would not have to be transferred from one carbody to another. However, the Ramsey Transfer did not solve the problems of the Utah & Northern inherent in the narrow gauge operation.

The first section of the U&N to be converted was the Butte-Silver Bow-Garrison line. By 1886 the Union Pacific had lost interest in extending this line to Helena, or anywhere else in Montana. Not only had the Northern Pacific become too well established in that area, but still another competitor was invading central Montana — Jim Hill's Great Northern, through the agencies of the St. Paul, Minnesota & Manitoba and the Montana Central, building a line in 1886 and 1887 between St. Paul and Great Falls and Helena. Further, the Northern Pacific was now to build an alternate line from Logan west to Butte, with the intention of paralleling the U&N line from Butte to Garrison. The two roads soon reached an agreement whereby the U&N line would be transferred by lease to a new, jointly owned railroad — the Montana Union Railway Company — on August 1, 1886, and standard gauging followed shortly thereafter. This arrangement was terminated in 1898 and the Northern Pacific took over the line, granting trackage rights to the Union Pacific between Silver Bow and Butte.

By 1887 the Union Pacific was ready to standard gauge its long narrow gauge from Pocatello to Butte. One of the last important steps came when a new bridge was constructed over the Snake River at Eagle Rock, Idaho Territory, in preparation for standard gauging. The entire main line was relaid with 55-pound steel during 1885-87. The shopmen at Eagle Rock had been presenting labor problems for the Utah & Northern management by organizing a labor union and staging strikes, so when the shop was badly damaged by a windstorm in May 1886, the railroad made preparations to move the division point and shops to Pocatello. A new roundhouse was built at Pocatello and watering and coaling facilities enlarged. The move from Eagle Rock to Pocatello was effected on August 21, 1887. Company houses were lifted from their foundations and loaded aboard flat cars for the trip. Anything that could be moved, was moved. In Pocatello these houses were known as the Eagle Rock Row.

The move was a serious blow for Eagle Rock. Overnight Pocatello became a small city and Eagle Rock passed from importance, being renamed Idaho Falls in 1890. Today it is even difficult to locate the old Eagle Rock townsite.

The "narrow gauge to nowhere" gave up its identity on a single day. July 24, 1887, was selected as the date when the entire 262 miles from Pocatello to Butte would be relaid to standard gauge. Preparations had been going on for many months. New standard gauge ties had been inserted along most of the way, while 55-pound steel rails had replaced the aging 30 and 45-pound iron rails. One of the narrow gauge rails was already spiked in place for the standard gauging, so that it would be necessary to move only one rail.

Section crews had already marked the location for the standard gauge rail. In Pocatello, new engines and cars were ready and waiting, having been brought in over the Oregon Short Line. The Utah & Northern had organized the changeover well. It would be accomplished with minimum interruption in train service. The 262-mile section was divided into 40 segments of 6 miles each. Ten workmen were assigned to each section, with over 400 extra men having been hired for the changeover. As soon as it was light enough to see, the men set to work. One group went ahead removing the spikes, while the second group followed behind, moving and respiking the trackage to 4′ 8½″ gauge. It took most of the entire day for each six mile segment to be completed and the railroad paid each man four silver dollars for their efforts. The first standard gauge passenger train left Pocatello for Eagle Rock only three hours behind schedule. The seemingly impossible had been accomplished in just one working day! Engineer on the first train was George Orem aboard No. 727.

The Ogden to Pocatello line was rebuilt and changed to standard gauge during the summer of 1890. Standard gauge tracks were built alongside the old narrow gauge for a distance of 27 miles from McCammon south toward Ogden in July 1890. From Ogden to Deweyville a distance of 35 miles, the standard gauge line followed a new location. The entire road was shortened a full 20 miles and the grades reduced from 115 to 35 feet per mile. The last standard gauge rail was placed on October 1, 1890, making the entire line from Ogden to Butte (452 miles) all standard gauge.

On July 27, 1889, the Utah & Northern was consolidated with the Oregon Short Line Ry. Co., the Utah Central Ry Co., the Salt Lake & Western Railway Co., the Utah & Nevada Ry. Co., the Ogden & Syracuse Ry. Co., the Idaho Central Ry. Co. and the Nevada Pacific Ry. Co. to form the Oregon Short Line & Utah Northern Railway Company.

Following the standard gauging of the Utah & Northern in 1887-90, the narrow gauge locomotives were sent to the four winds, along with the rolling stock. The newest group of engines went to the Union Pacific's Colorado narrow gauge subsidiary, the Denver, Leadville & Gunnison. The entire Sumpter Valley Railway, in Oregon, was initially equipped with former Utah & Northern cars and locomotives, as well as rail, switches and switchstands. Other Utah & Northern locomotives saw service on the Union Pacific's Ilwaco Railway & Navigation Company line, the Portland & Willamette Valley Railroads, San Pete Valley, Salt Lake & Eastern, Utah Central, Nevada Short Line, Nevada Central, Eureka-Nevada, Kansas Central and even the White Pass & Yukon in Alaska and the Yukon. Several former Utah & Northern engines still exist in such places as Idaho Springs, Colorado; Sacramento, California; White Horse in the Yukon and Skagway, Alaska. A rather amazing record for a railroad that went out of business in 1889!

Today heavy diesels still roar through Pocatello over the Union Pacific's mainline to the Pacific Northwest and over portions of the Utah & Northern. In Beaver Canyon there is still a spike to be found from the narrow gauge, but for the most part the Utah & Northern, the narrow gauge that opened a frontier, has disappeared from the high country in which it was such a conspicuous pioneer.

In this rare view of U&N narrow gauge operations in Beaver Canyon, just south of the Idaho-Montana line, two helpers—U&N 85 and leased South Park 158, both Brooks moguls — are dropping down to Dry Creek after helping a freight up the long grade. (Montana Historical Society Collection)

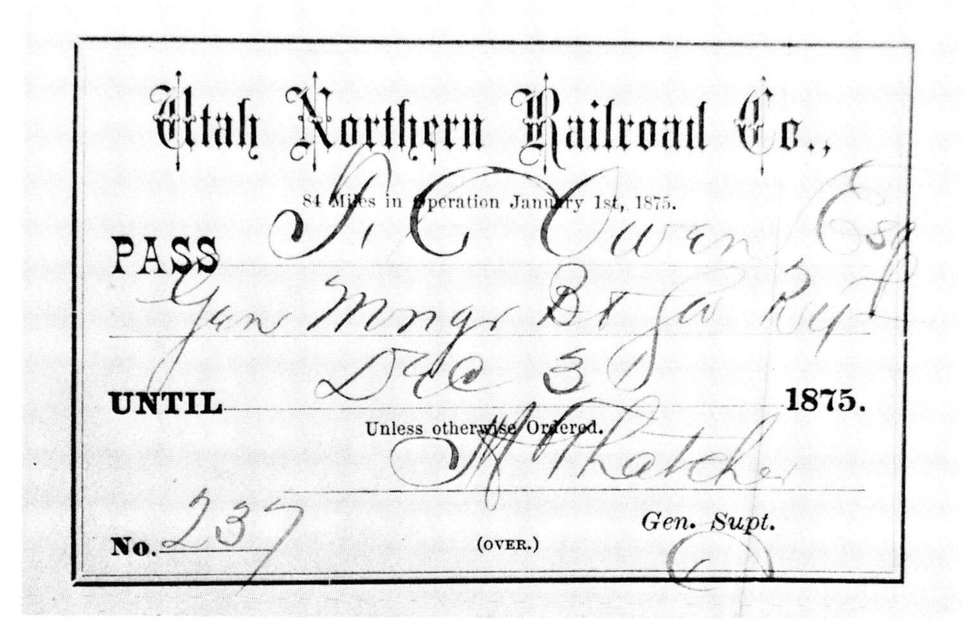
Utah Northern Railroad Co.,

84 Miles in Operation January 1st, 1875.

PASS S. C. Owen Esq

UNTIL Dec 31 1875.

Unless otherwise Ordered.

M. Thatcher

Gen. Supt.

No. 237 (OVER.)

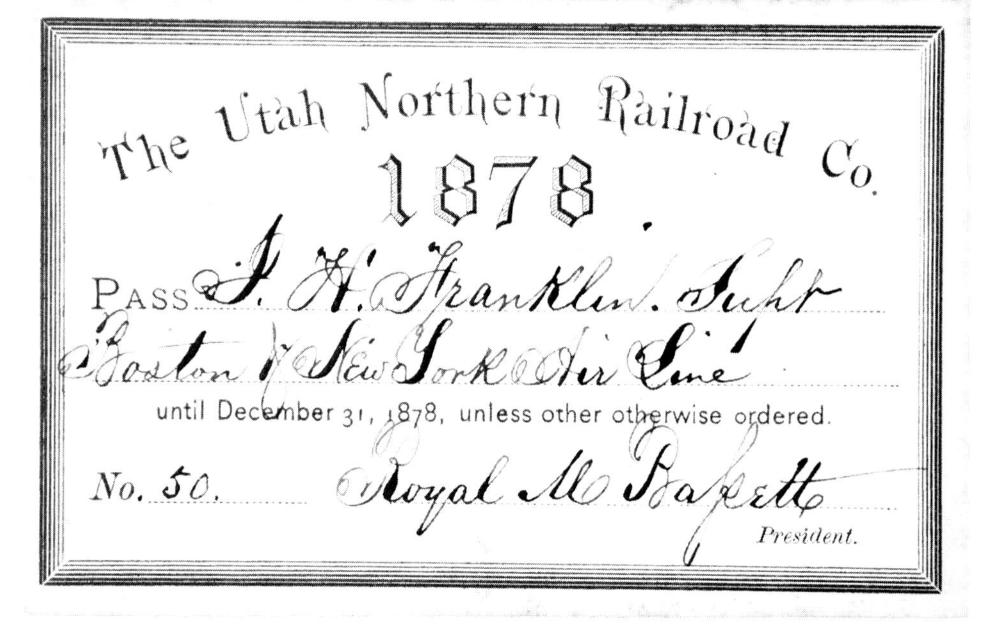
The Utah Northern Railroad Co.

1878

PASS J. H. Franklin Supt

Boston & New York Air Line

until December 31, 1878, unless other otherwise ordered.

No. 50. Royal M Bassett

President.

1898 Montana Union Railway Co.

Pass Mr. J. D. Rhodes

Until December 31st Unless Revoked.

No 150

HOSFORD & SONS ENG & PTG CO. N.Y.

President & General Manager

Passes issued by the Utah Northern (1875 and 1878) and the Montana Union, which succeeded to the Utah & Northern's Silver Bow-Garrison line. (Center, Museum Collection; others, Author's Collection)

Attracting Tourists to the Utah & Northern

The Union Pacific went to great lengths to promote tourism, emigration and development along the U&N's route, publishing numerous elaborate timetable and descriptive folders and brochures. The excerpts on this page are from a September, 1879 folder issued when the line reached Camas, Idaho. (Museum Collection)

THE NEW NORTHWEST.

IDAHO, OREGON AND WASHINGTON.

The Utah & Northern Railway already crosses a wide belt of Eastern Idaho, every mile of which is valuable either for its pasturage, its agricultural, timber or mineral lands. This region is only in the infancy of development, and is a promising field for the home-seeker, mining prospector or capitalist. Idaho is called the "Gem of the Mountains," on account of its great diversity of resources, its mild and healthful climate, its wonderful mineral springs, and its fine scenery. It is 400 miles long by 300 wide, contains some 20,000 inhabitants, and its mines have yielded $65,000,000. Wide areas of grazing lands sustain cattle, horses and sheep winter and summer, while the valleys produce all cereals and vegetables of the temperate zone, besides apples, pears, grapes, peaches, plums, apricots and other fruits. Good stage and wagon roads lead to different parts of Idaho from stations on the Utah & Northern Railway.

It is now demonstrated beyond a doubt that hundreds of miles of gravel bars along Snake River, Eastern Idaho—some of which are directly on the line of the Utah & Northern Railway—are rich in deposits of fine gold. Several companies are regularly taking out from $20 to $40 per day to the man, and good "prospects" of gold are found along the river for a distance of 400 miles.

The extension of the Utah & Northern Railway gives easy access to the hitherto isolated Salmon River region. Covering an area of 10,000 square miles, in every corner of which gold and silver mines are being discovered, this locality offers one of the very best fields for the capitalist or prospector. Hundreds of tons of ore, worth from $500 to $2,000 per ton, have been packed out on mules and shipped to the Salt Lake Smelting Works.

Superb Concord Coaches of the Gilmer & Salisbury Line run to Salmon City tri-weekly, and of the Terminus & Challis Line each alternate day. Stage distances and time from Eagle Rock, are, to Salmon City, 160 miles—stage time, 2 days; Eagle Rock to Challis, 175 miles—time, 2 days. Rates of Fare are given on another page of this folder.

Oregon and Washington, lying west of Idaho, contain an area, in round numbers, of 200,000 square miles—a vast empire, within whose bounds almost every variety of climate can be found—and whose mountains, plains and valleys send forth a greater diversity of products than any section of the globe. Together they boast a coast line of 700 miles, have 1,000 miles of navigable rivers, and contains 200,000 inhabitants. Gold, silver, iron, coal, copper and other minerals abound. Oregon and Washington contain grazing lands which will sustain 40,000,000 sheep and 10,000,000 cattle, not one-tenth of which are utilized, and with one-fifth of their arable lands under cultivation, produce 15,000,000 bushels of wheat annually. The climate is much milder and much more desirable in every way than that of Iowa or Illinois, and the rainfall being abundant in the western half of these commonwealths, farmers are surrounded by more favorable conditions than are enjoyed almost anywhere in the East.

Oregon and Washington are reached via Union and Central Pacific Railroads to Kelton, Utah, and thence by stage via Boise City, Idaho; or by the same rail line to Redding, California, and thence by stage; and also by steamer from San Francisco in connection with the Overland Route. Rates by all of these lines are given elsewhere in this folder.

UTAH & NORTHERN R'Y TIME TABLE.

NORTHWARD. SOUTHWARD.

No. 5. Freight	No. 3. Mixed.	No. 1. Passenger.	Distan. from Ogden.	STATIONS.	No. 2. Passenger.	No. 4. Mixed.	No. 6. Freight.
....	9.25 am	6.30 pm	......	Lv...Ogden...Ar	8 55 am	5.35 pm	....
....	10.10 "	7.10 "	9	..Hot Springs..	8.23 "	4.52 "	....
....	10 35 "	7.28 "	14	.... Willard	8.05 "	4.30 "	....
....	11 30 "	8.00 "	22	....Brigham....	7 40 "	3.55 "	....
....	12.10 pm	8.26 "	30	.. Call's Fort...	7.18 "	3.15 "	....
....	12 45 "	8.50 "	37	...Deweyville..	6 55 "	2.45 "	....
....	1.22 "	9.25 "	43	...Collinston ..	6.33 "	2.20 "	....
....	2 25 "	10.12 "	53	.....Mendon....	5.50 "	1.05 "	....
....	3.30 "	10.55 "	60	..... Logan.....	5.10 "	11.00 am	....
....	4 00 "	11.15 "	65	...Hyde Park...	4.50 "	10.35 "	....
....	5.00 "	11.47 "	74	...Richmond .	4.17 "	9.45 "	....
....	5.40 "	12.10 am	80	....Franklin ...	3.55 "	9.10 "	....
....	7.10 pm	1.05 "	92	Ar Battle Cre'k Lv	3.00 "	7.45 am	....
6.30 am	....		......	Lv Battle Cre'k Ar		....	7.40 pm
7.50 "	....	2.05 "	106	...Swan Lake ..	2 05 "	....	6.35 "
8.25 "	....	2.35 "	113	....Nine Mile...	1 30 "	....	5.45 "
9.40 "	....	3.27 "	127	.....Oneida	2 40 "	....	4.35 "
11.35 am	....	5.00 "	148	Ar. Portneuf .Lv	11.05 pm	....	2.20 "
12.10 pm	....		......	Lv. Portneuf .Ar		....	1.45 "
1.00 "	....	5.40 "	158	....Pocatello...	10.25 "	....	1.00 "
1.45 "	....	6.15 "	168	...Ross Fork...	9.45 "	....	12.10 "
2.45 "	....	7.00 "	181	Ar Blackfoot.Lv	9.00 "	....	11.10 am
2.55 "	....	7.30 "	......	Lv.Blackfoot.Ar	8 35 "	....	....
4.55 "	....	9.00 "	207	.. Eagle Rock..	7.05 "	....	9.00 "
6.10 "	....	10.00 "	221	..Market Lake.	6.10 "	....	7.30 "
7.50 pm	....	11 10 am	245	Ar... Camas...Lv	4.50 pm	....	5 50 am

PULLMAN'S PALACE CARS
On the Union Pacific R. R., and
SILVER PALACE CARS
On the Central Pacific Railroad,

Are the FINEST DAY & SLEEPING COACHES in the World.

Are the FINEST DAY & SLEEPING COACHES in the World.

These cars are so constructed as to combine the convenience and elegance of a private parlor by day, and the comforts of a well-furnished bed chamber by night—clean bedding, thick hair mattresses, thorough ventilation, etc., etc. Conductors and porters accompany each car, to provide for the wants of passengers. **Only first class** passengers are admitted to sleeping cars, or have stop-over privileges.

MONTANA.

THE UTAH & NORTHERN RAILWAY, which is now in operation from Ogden, Utah, to Camas, Idaho—245 miles—is being rapidly extended northward into Montana. Probably 200 miles will be built during the present year. All the important cities of the territory will thus be brought within easy reach of the railroad, and the stage trip to the most remote settlements will be reduced to little more than one day's time.

No section of our country at the present time offers **greater inducements** to immigrants than Montana. Its mineral resources, although as yet but imperfectly explored, are known to be inexhaustible. Its gold and silver mines have yielded $150,000,000, and the annual yield since 1864 has averaged $8,500,000. Over 10,000 lodes and 1,000 placer mines have been recorded. Alder Gulch, in which Virginia City is located, has alone poured out $40,000,000 in glittering dust, and is still yielding at the rate of $1,000,000 per year. Ores in many of the mines are so rich that they pay handsomely after being hauled 500 miles to the railway, and thence to Europe for reduction. Iron, coal, copper, cinnabar, etc., are equally plentiful; in fact, Montana's mountains are literal storehouses of mineral riches, only waiting the magic touch of capital to add lavishly to our nation's wealth.

An immense area of the finest pasture lands, now trodden only by the hoof of the buffalo, the deer or the antelope, can be made to support vast herds of cattle and sheep, while numerous fertile valleys only await the hand of the farmer to produce abundant crops, for which, the large mining population will always furnish a home market, not to be over-supplied. Although the lack of railroad communication, the difficulties and expense of travel, and the great cost attendant upon the shipment of stock and mineral products to market, have hitherto been almost insuperable obstacles in the way of this territory's development, yet its bountiful resources have already drawn thither a population of some 30,000 people. The low rates of passenger and freight transportation now offered, will, in a large measure, remove those obstacles, promote its development, and inaugurate an era of general prosperity which the completion of the railroad will increase and render permanent.

Now is the time for enterprising men to go and gain a foothold, establish themselves in business and acquire property, which the advent of the railroad will rapidly enhance in value. Mines can now be bought at low figures, which, with railroad communication, will become exceedingly valuable. New mines may be opened and farms located. Herds of stock can now be cheaply acquired, which can then be marketed at small expense and will yield large returns.

The **RATES OF FARE** now in force from Omaha to the most important places in Montana are given below, with the Distance and Time by Gilmer, Salisbury & Co.'s Stage Line, from Camas, present terminus of the Utah & Northern Ry.

	1st Class.	2d Class.	Emig't.	Distance.	Stage Time.
Lovell's, Mon.,	**$100.00**	**$75.00**	**$45.00**	**155 miles.**	**25 hrs.**
Virg'a City, "	**100.00**	**75.00**	**45.00**	**220 "**	**35 "**
Butte, "	**100.00**	**75.00**	**45.00**	**245 "**	**40 "**
Deer Lodge, "	**100.00**	**75.00**	**45.00**	**272 "**	**46 "**
Helena, "	**100.00**	**75.00**	**45.00**	**282 "**	**48 "**

Holders of Second Class and Emigrant Tickets, via Gilmer, Salisbury & Co.'s line, will both be carried from the railway terminus to destination in Covered Mail Wagons. One hundred pounds baggage free by rail; forty pounds free by stage, on first class; 50 pounds free by wagon on second class and emigrant; extra baggage on stage and wagon lines, 15c per lb. **Stages and Wagons run Daily.**

Freight Rates Proportionately Low.

All should remember that by entering Montana via the Union Pacific and Utah & Northern R. R., at the South, they traverse or pass **within a day's Stage ride of all the best mining regions and the finest agricultural valleys**—an advantage possessed by **no other route.** Emigrants, prospectors and employment seekers thus have a wide choice of localities, before finally reaching Helena and other northern cities

The material on these two pages is from a folder published in the winter of 1879-1880, after the line had progressed another 29 miles to Beaver Canyon. The folder was full of information — some useful, some rhetorical. (Museum Collection)

NEW RAIL ROUTE

To MONTANA

VIA THE

UNION PACIFIC

AND

UPPER FALLS OF THE YELLOWSTONE.
Reached via Union Pacific and Utah & Northern Railroads.

UTAH & NORTHERN

RAILROADS.

Save Money, Time and 1,000 Miles of Distance

TO ALL POINTS IN

MONTANA AND YELLOWSTONE PARK

And avoid the perils and delays of River Navigation by going via the only Direct and Desirable Route, the

Union Pacific and Utah & Northern Railroads

And their closely connecting and well equipped stage lines.

For valuable information call upon or address,

THOS. L. KIMBALL,
Gen'l Passenger and Ticket Agent, Omaha, Neb.

Omaha Daily Republican Print.

VALUABLE INFORMATION.

Distances, Time, Fare, Baggage Allowed, Extra Baggage and Household Goods.

Fares from Omaha to Lovell's, Virginia City, Butte, Deer Lodge, Helena and other central points in Montana are as follows: First class $100; Second class $75; Emigrant $45. On the cars children five years old and under twelve, half fare in any of these classes; under five years old, free; on stages children under twelve and over three years old, half fare; under three, free. Passengers holding first class tickets will be carried from the Utah & Northern Railway terminus by Gilmer, Salisbury & Co.'s stage line with 40 pounds of baggage free. Holders of second class and emigrant tickets will both be transported from the Utah & Northern terminus by Gilmer, Salisbury & Co.'s line of covered wagons—carrying the United States mail—and will be allowed 50 pounds of baggage free.

Extra Baggage and Household Goods.—Extra baggage by stage or mail wagon from the terminus of the Utah & Northern Railway to points named above will be charged 15 cents per pound, but it may be forwarded by freight wagons at a cost of from two to three cents, its transportation in this way, however, requiring considerably more time. Freights on household goods (*well boxed*) from Omaha to Utah & Northern Railway terminus $4 05 per hundred pounds, or double that rate if carried in trunks. Freight rates from the railway terminus to Montana points above named are from $1.50 to $2.50 per hundred pounds.

Stages run Day and Night making connections with Utah & Northern Railway trains daily. Mail wagons also run daily. First class eating stations along the stage road furnish meals or lunch at reasonable rates. Telegraphic stations are established at frequent intervals along the stage road. All streams are well bridged and the entire equipment of the stage line is the finest in the west. The Utah & Northern Railway, completed to Beaver Cañon, Idaho, 274 miles north of Ogden, in September, 1879, is being rapidly extended northward into Montana. Unless winter opens unusually early, it will, no doubt, reach Red Rock, Montana, 30 miles north of Beaver Cañon, in December, 1879, reducing stage travel to the more distant points named below to 36 hours. Following are distances and stage time from Beaver Cañon to principal points as well as rates of fare from Omaha in force November 1, 1879:

	1st Class.	2d Class.	Emigr't.	Distance.	Stage Time.
Lovell's, Montana,	$100.00	$75.00	$45.00	118 miles	23 hours.
Virginia City, "	100.00	75.00	45.00	193 "	28 "
Butte, "	100.00	75 00	45.00	208 "	32 "
Deer Lodge, "	100.00	75.00	45 00	235 "	38 "
Helena, "	100.00	75.00	45.00	245 "	40 "

DISTANCES AND FARES IN MONTANA.

Following are carefully compiled tables of distances from Helena, Deer Lodge and other points to all stations in Montana with stage fares in effect in June, 1879. Stages on nearly all routes run daily, making an average of over 100 miles in 24 hours.

ROUTE TO UTAH & NORTHERN R'Y—*Gilmer & Salisbury Stages.*

From Helena to	Miles	Fare.	From Helena to	Miles.	Fare.
Clancy	18	$1 50	Salisbury	90	$13 00
Jefferson	22	2 00	Virginia City	120	16 00
Whitehall	60	8 00	Lovell's	135	20 00
Silver Star	85	12 00	Railroad Terminus	294	

DEER LODGE, BUTTE & MISSOULA ROUTE—*Gilmer & Salisbury Stages.*

From Helena to	Miles.	Fare.	From Helena to	Miles.	Fare.
Sweetlands	25	$2 00	Pioneer	61	$8 00
Blackfoot	29	3 00	New Chicago	77	11 00
Deer Lodge	45	6 00	Phillipsburg	102	12 00
Butte, via Deer Lodge	80	8 00	Missoula	150	17 00

DEER LODGE AND LOVELL'S ROUTE—*Gilmer & Salisbury's Stages.*

From Deer Lodge to	Miles.	Fare.	From Deer Lodge to	Miles.	Fare.
Warm Springs	18	$1 50	Camp Creek	75	$10 00
Silver Bow	35	2 00	Lovell's	115	
Butte	40	3 00	Eagle Rock	284	

BOZEMAN ROUTE—*H. F. Galen Stages.*

From Helena to	Miles.	Fare.	From Helena to	Miles.	Fare.
Radersburg	48	$5 00	Central Park	86	$10 00
Gallatin City	65	7 50	Bozeman	101	12 00
Hamilton	75	[illegible]	Virginia City	100	12 00

BOZEMAN & TONGUE RIVER ROUTE—*Salisbury & Piatt's Stages.*

From Bozeman to	Miles.	Fare	From Bozeman to	Miles.	Fare.
Benson's Landing	30	$3 50	Etchetah	239	$28 50
Stillwater	102	12 00	Rock Springs	283	35 00
Huntley	163	19 50	Ft. Keogh and Miles City	337	42 00

DIAMOND CITY AND WHITE SULPHUR SPRINGS.
Marks & Patterson's Stages.

From Helena to	Miles.	Fare.	From Helena to	Miles.	Fare.
Cañon Ferry	18	$2 50	Camp Baker	60	$7 50
Diamond City	35	5 00	White Sulphur Springs	78	10 00

BITTER ROOT VALLEY ROUTE.
J. A. Robinson Stage Line.

Missoula to	Miles.	Fare.
Stevenville	28	$3 00
Corvallis	43	4 50
Skalkaho	51	6 00

VIRGINIA CITY AND BOZEMAN.
H. F. Galen Stages.

Virginia to	Miles.	Fare.
Sterling	30	$4 00
Central Park	60	8 00
Bozeman	75	12 00

BEWARE OF

MISSOURI RIVER NAVIGATION

AND THE BENTON STAGE ROAD!

After braving the hardships, perils and delays of Missouri River navigation—the trip from Omaha or Bismarck usually consuming several weeks (sometimes months)—the traveler by that route still has 150 to 300 miles of staging from Fort Benton to the Montana settlements. Before embarking on such a roundabout line, all should read the following extracts from Montana papers concerning the Fort Benton Stage Road:

"Road Flooded and Impassable!"

The late rains have made the Benton Road almost impassable. The freight teams scattered all along the road find it useless to attempt to move, and are patiently awaiting fine weather. At low places the road is flooded. —*Helena Independent*, *June*, 1878.

"Stages Taken Off!"

Freight has entirely ceased coming over the Benton Road, and even stages have been taken off on account of the impassable roads through the Sun River bottom. We are told that it is even considered dangerous to attempt the route with an empty wagon, or to lead a mule through.—*Helena Herald*, *July*, 1878.

"One Bottomless Mudhole!"

Teams have been from 40 to 50 days in making the round trip (between Helena and Fort Benton), and freights have ranged from $25 to $60 per ton. The road beyond Sun River for 20 miles is *one bottomless mudhole*, that must be corduroyed or macadamized. Every team that now goes to Benton pays in the spring tolls to the amount of $17 per team for the round trip.—*Address before the Helena Board of Trade*, *September* 6, 1878.

"In a Most Deplorable Condition!"

The road has truly been in a most deplorable condition during the past season. The road leading from Sun River bridge was impassable for at least ten days, and freighters during this time were paying a toll of $2 per team, for the privilege of passing through a farmer's field.—*Fort Benton Record*, *September*, 1878.

"Another Steamboat Sunk."

Another steamer (the Helena) has been wrecked on the Missouri river, and now lies at Bon Homme Bend, in view of the ill-fated Peninah, which went down with a valuable cargo only a few weeks ago. This makes four bad steamboat disasters on the upper Missouri and Yellowstone rivers this season. The moral seems plain: Travel and ship goods by rail until the millenium or some other period in the mysterious future when the navigation of the Missouri is attended with an average degree of safety.—*Omaha Republican*, *October*, 1879.

Avoid these Dangers and Delays to Travel and Shipments, by using only the

UNION PACIFIC RAILROAD ROUTE!

Always Safe, Speedy and Pleasant!

UTAH & NORTHERN RAILWAY CONDENSED TIME TABLE.

NORTHWARD.			Distance f'm Ogden	STATIONS.	SOUTHWARD.		
No. 5. Freight.	No. 3. Mixed.	No. 1. Pass'gr.			No. 2. Pass'gr.	No. 4. Mixed.	No. 6. Freight.
....	9.25 am	6.30pm	...	Lv... Ogden ... Ar	8.55 am	5.35pm	....
....	10.10	7.10	9	... Hot Springs ...	8.23	4.52	....
....	10.35	7.28	14	.... Willard	8.05	4.30	....
....	11.30 am	8.00	22	..... Brigham	7.40	3.55	....
....	3.30pm	10.55	60	..... Logan	5.25	12 30pm	....
....	5.00	11.47pm	74	.... Richmond	4.17	9.45 am	....
....	5.40	12.10 am	80	..... Franklin	3.55	9.10	....
6 30 am	7.10pm	1.05	92	... Battle Creek ...	3.00	7.45 am	†7.40pm
7.50	....	2.05	106	.... Swan Lake ...	2.05	....	6.25
9.40	....	3.27	127	..... Oneida	12.40 am	....	4.35
1.45pm	....	6.15	168	.... Ross Fork	9.45pm	....	12.10pm
2.55	....	7.30	181	.... Blackfoot	9.00 †	....	11.10 am
4.55	....	9.00	207	.... Eagle Rock	7.05	....	9.00
6.10	....	10.00	224	... Market Lake ...	6.10	....	7.30
7.50	....	11.10 am	245	..... Camas	4.50	....	5.50
10.30pm	....	†1.10pm	274	Ar BeaverCañon Lv	2.55pm	....	8.40 am

The Union Pacific and Utah & Northern Railroads constitute the Only Route to Montana in Fall, Winter or Early Spring.

ROOM FOR ALL!

THE SNAKE RIVER GOLD FIELDS

Hundreds of Miles of Placer Diggings within Sight of the Utah & Northern Railway, Paying from $20 to $40 a Day to the Man.

It is now demonstrated, beyond a doubt, that hundreds of miles of gravel bars along Snake River, Eastern Idaho - some of which are directly on the line of the Utah & Northern Railway—are rich in deposits of fine gold. Several companies are regularly taking out from $20 to $40 per day to the man. Their large and regular shipments of dust to San Francisco have created great excitements in mining circles, and western journals already pronounce these the most

EXTENSIVE PLACER DIGGINGS

in the world, as good "prospects" of gold are found all along the river for a distance of 400 miles. It is generally believed that the Snake River Gold Fields will be operated by thousands of miners during 1880.

OUTFITTING

can be done at Eagle Rock, the point at which the Utah & Northern crosses Snake River, 206 miles north of Ogden, and within an hour's walk of some of these great bars **Now is the time** to strike for fortune in this vast new region, which will soon be over-run by miners from every State and Territory.

PASSENGER RATES

from Omaha to Eagle Rock are:

Regular First Class, -	**$93 50**	**Second Class, -**	**$70 00**
Limited First Class, -	**81 00**	**Emigrant, - -**	**40 00**

UNION PACIFIC EXPRESS

THE ONLY FAST EXPRESS LINE FROM THE EAST TO

Helena, Deer Lodge, Virginia City, Butte City

AND ALL PRINCIPAL POINTS IN

MONTANA.

Connections made with responsible Express Companies for all parts of the world. Direct lines to

Denver, Col., Leadville, Col., Central City, Col., Georgetown, Col., Deadwood, Dakota,

And all points in the **BLACK HILLS, COLORADO, WYOMING, UTAH, NEVADA, IDAHO, OREGON** and **CALIFORNIA.**

All kinds of express matter forwarded with safety and utmost despatch by passenger trains and fast stages.

Mark all consignments Care of Union Pacific Express. For rates or information apply to

E. M. MORSMAN, Supt.,
OMAHA, NEB.

Write for Information.

Further detailed and reliable information in relation to the different districts of Montana, the routes thereto, rates, etc., will be furnished on application to any of the officers or agents named below:

D. W. FULLER, New England Agent, } 228 Washington street,
WM. KNOWLAND, Traveling Agent, } Boston, Mass.

F. KNOWLAND, General Eastern Agent, } 287 Broadway,
WM. L. GREENE, Traveling Agent. } New York City.

F. M. FUNK, Traveling Agent, 116 Market st., Philadelphia, Pa.

D. E. BURLEY, Traveling Agent, 143 W. Baltimore st., Baltimore, Md.

D. C. BLACKMAN, Traveling Agent, 40½ Exchange st., Buffalo, N. Y.

J. W MORSE, General Agent, } 57 Clark st., Chicago, Ill.
W. P. COOLEY, Traveling Agent, }

JAS. D. WELSH, General Agent, No. 4 Burnet House, Cincinnati, O.

JAS. F. AGLAR, General Agent, } 406 Pine st. (Planters' House).
N. HAIGHT, Traveling Agent, } St Louis, Mo.

A. O. GRISWOLD, General Agt., 9 Atwater Block, Cleveland, Ohio.

M. H. JUDD, Traveling Agent, Omaha, Neb., and Council Bluffs, Ia.

Or THOS. L. KIMBALL,
General Passenger and Ticket Agent, **OMAHA, NEB.**

UTAH & NORTHERN BRANCH,

Running from Ogden to Butte City.—The Pioneer Montana Line.

TIME TABLE.

NORTHWARD DAILY. No. 7. Freight	No. 5. Freight	No. 3. Passg'r	Dist. from Ogden.	STATIONS. (Salt Lake City Time) †Meals.	Population.	SOUTHWARD DAILY. No. 4. Passg'r.	No. 6. Freight	No. 8. Freight
P M	A M	P M				A M	P M	A M
6 00	9 00	†7 00	....	Lv...Ogden....Ar	6210	†7 45	4 30	5 00
6 45	9 45	7 30	9	.....Hot Springs.....	50	7 10	3 45	4 15
7 10	10 10	7 50	14	.......Willard.......	1000	6 52	3 20	3 45
7 45	11 05	8 15	21	.......Brigham......	2000	6 30	2 45	3 15
8 16	11 38	8 38	28	.....Call's Fort.....	....	6 05	2 05	2 40
9 10	12 15	9 05	36	.....Deweyville......	100	5 40	1 30	2 00
10 00	1 00	9 40	42	......Collinston......	....	5 17	1 00	1 25
11 00	2 05	10 30	51	.......Mendon	1000	4 25	11 40	12 10
12 20	3 30	11 20	58	........Logan........	4000	4 00	11 05	11 35
12 45	3 55	11 37	63	..... Hyde Park	1200	3 20	10 02	10 05
1 05	4 20	11 50	65	.....Smithfield......	500	3 09	9 50	9 50
1 40	5 00	12 15	71	.....Richmond......	1000	2 45	9 20	9 15
2 20	5 50	12 40	78	.......Franklin......	1000	2 20	8 50	8 35
4 15	7 30	1 35	90	.....Battle Creek	....	1 30	7 35	7 20
5 30	8 55	2 30	101	........Oxford.......	50	12 35	6 05	5 45
5 50	9 10	2 45	104	.....Swan Lake.. ..	50	12 20	5 50	5 25
8 00	11 00	4 00	125	.........Arimo	50	11 00	4 00	3 30
10 00	12 45	5 15	147	......Portneuf.......	. . .	9 40	2 15	1 05
10 50	1 25	5 45	156	......Pocatello	100	9 08	1 25	12 17
11 35	2 05	6 15	166	......Ross Fork......	50	8 40	12 25	11 35
12 45	3 00	†7 25	179	....Blackfoot	500	†8 00	11 30	10 40
3 30	5 30	8 55	204	......Eagle Rock.....	200	6 10	9 30	8 45
5 10	6 50	9 45	222	... Market Lake	....	5 10	6 50	6 50
6 45	8 30	10 50	243	........Camas	50	4 00	5 00	5 15
8 40	10 20	Noon	263	....High Bridge.....	....	2 57	3 25	3 45
9 35	11 55	12 40	272	... .Beaver Cañon ...	50	2 25	2 35	3 05
11 00	1 45	1 35	284	.......Monida.......	....	1 35	12 05	2 00
12 30	3 35	2 55	302	.....Spring Hill.....	....	12 30	10 25	12 15
2 10	5 10	4 05	322	..... Red Rock.....	50	10 50	8 25	10 00
3 25	6 25	4 55	340	.....Barratt's.......		10 00	7 10	8 40
4 15	7 40	5 30	348	.... Dillon	50	9 35	6 35	8 00
5 55	9 30	6 40	366	.... Glen	....	8 15	4 40	5 15
7 20	11 00	†7 50	378	.......Melrose	300	†7 35	3 30	4 15
8 15	11 55	8 30	388	........Lavell........	....	6 30	2 15	3 20
9 30	1 10	9 15	400	........Feely........	....	5 45	1 10	2 15
9 55	1 33	9 32	404	..... .Buxton........	....	5 20	12 40	1 45
10 40	2 20	10 00	409	Silver Bow Junction	....	5 00	12 10	1 10
11 20	3 00	10 30	416	Lv. Butte City. Ar	6000	4 20	11 10	12 10
A M	A M	P M				A M	P M	P M

Trains of this Line connect with stages for all points of Montana and Idaho.

The evolving pattern of train schedules on the U&N is shown in the timetable reprints on these pages — beginning with the May, 1882 schedule on this page, one of the last (June 1886) narrow gauge schedules top right, and first standard gauge arrangement (August 1887) bottom right. Scheduled passenger time was reduced from nearly 17 hours Pocatello-Butte in 1882 to about 14 hours in final narrow gauge days, to the standard gauge schedule of 12 hours 25 minutes northbound and only 11 hours southbound — the latter marking an improvement in miles per hour average from about 15 to 23½. The map below is also from the May, 1882 timetable and shows both lines in operation at that time and projected extensions—including the U&N main line west to Missoula, with a branch to Helena via Melrose and Radersburg — neither of which was ever undertaken. (Museum Collection)

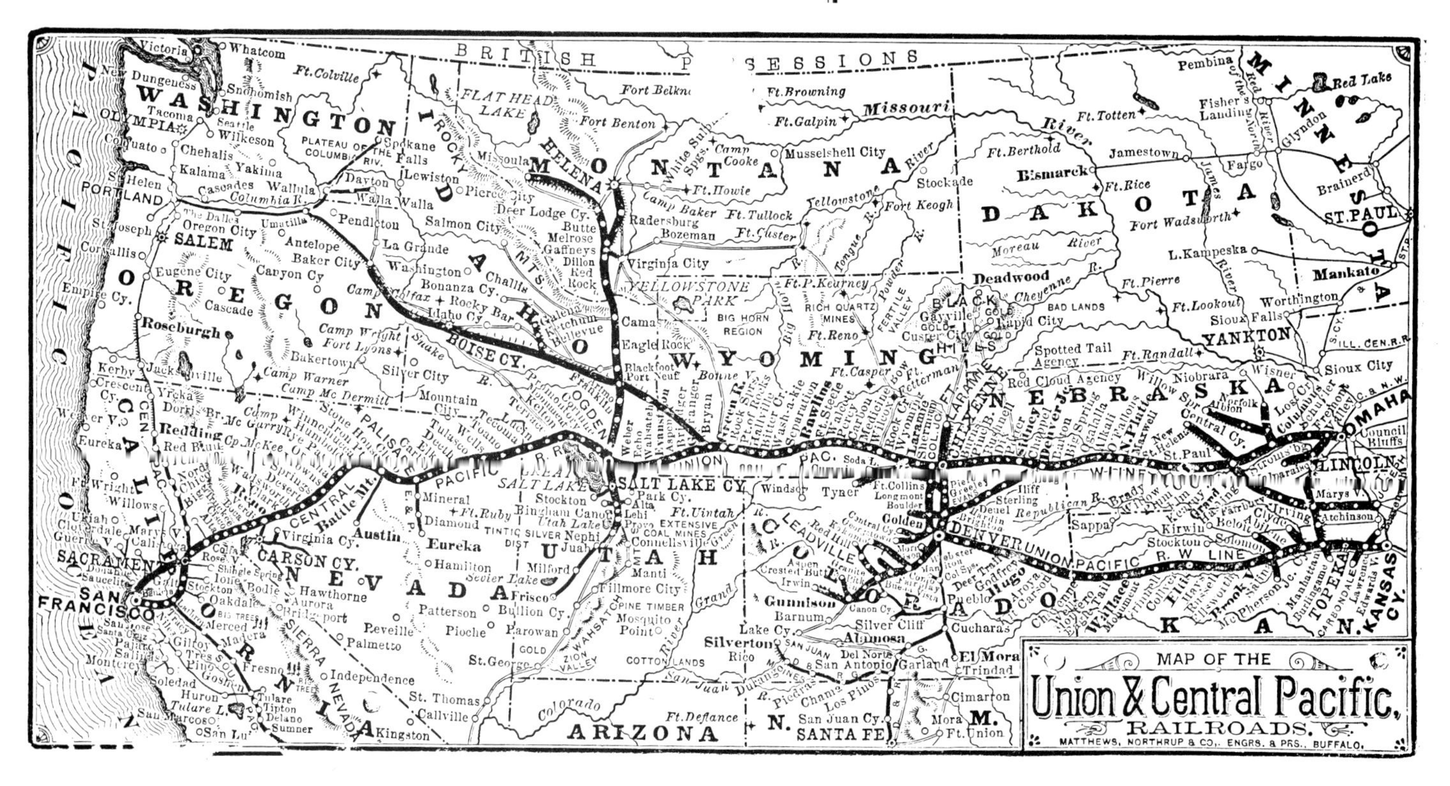

UNION PACIFIC RAILWAY.

UTAH AND NORTHERN DIVISION.

Trains Between OGDEN and BUTTE.

TIME TABLE.

No. 611 Freight.	No. 605 Passen'r	No. 601 Express.	Miles.	STATIONS.	Miles.	No. 602 Express.	No. 606 Passen'r	No. 612 Freight.
A	B	A				A	B	A
9 30	**6 00**	10 35	0	Lv........Ogden........Ar	417	**4 50**	9 30	**1 20**
10 10	**6 24**	*11 02	9	........Hot Springs........	408	***4 23**	9 04	**12 38**
10 37	**6 38**	*11 19	14	..........Willard..........	403	***4 08**	8 49	**12 12**
11 38	**6 56**	11 38	21	..........Brigham..........	396	**3 50**	8 32	11 38
12 20	**7 20**	***12 06**	31	........Honeyville........	386	***3 20**	8 10	10 10
1 35	**7 50**	***12 45**	42	........Collinston........	375	***2 42**	7 42	9 00
3 00	**8 20**	***1 19**	51	..........Mendon..........	366	***2 00**	7 12	7 50
4 15	**8 40**	**‡2 00**	58	............Logan............	359	**‡1 40**	6 55	7 20
4 40	**8 50**	***2 13**	63	.... Hyde Park........	354	***1 00**	6 43	6 18
4 48	**8 56**	***2 20**	65	.... Smithfield	351	***12 52**	6 35	6 05
5 25	**9 0**	***2 36**	71	..........Richmond..........	346	***12 32**	6 21	5 25
5 55	**9 27**	***2 55**	78	..........Franklin..........	339	***12 10**	6 05	5 00
7 20 **7 55**	**10 0**	**3 35** **3 45**	90	Ar. ....Battle Creek.... Lv. Lv. Ar.	327	11 25 11 12	5 30	3 30 2 20
9 00	....	***4 20**	101	..........Oxford..........	316	10 41	....	1 25
10 45	....	***5 15**	119	..........Thatcher	297	*9 54	....	**11 40**
11 59	....	**5 46**	132	....McCammon........	285	9 24	....	**10 35**
12 45	....	***6 14**	143	...........Inkom...........	274	*8 57	....	**9 25**
1 35 9 10	....	**‡6 45** **7 30**	153	Ar. ......Pocatello...... Lv. Lv. Ar.	262	8 25 ‡7 45	....	**8 10** **7 20**
10 45	....	**8 32**	179	..........Blackfoot..........	238	6 41	....	**5 30**
12 30 8 45	....	**9 40** **9 55**	205	Ar. .....Eagle Rock..... Lv. Lv. Ar.	212	5 35 5 25	....	**3 00** **1 45**
10 20	....	***10 40**	222	.......Market Lake........	195	*4 40	....	**12 10**
12 40	....	**11 40**	243	...........Camas...........	174	3 42	....	10 25
1 45	....	*12 15	255	.........Dry Creek..........	162	*3 10	....	9 30
2 45	....	*12 50	264	.........High Bridge.........	153	*2 42	....	8 50
4 15	....	1 25	272	........Beaver Canon........	145	2 15	....	8 05
5 55	....	*2 30	284	...........Monida...........	133	*1 35	....	6 45
7 30 11 30	....	3 20 3 30	300	Ar. ....Spring Hill.... Lv. Lv. Ar.	117	12 45 12 35	....	4 30 5 10
1 20	....	*4 35	323	..........Red Rock..........	94	**11 15**	....	2 50
3 40	....	5 45	348	............Dillon............	69	**9 50**	....	12 25
7 45	....	‡7 45	379	...........Melrose...........	38	**‡8 05**	....	9 25
9 55	....	*8 45	399	............Feely............	16	***6 55**	....	9 00
10 50	....	9 20	410	.........Silver Bow.........	7	**6 00**	....	5 35
11 25	....	9 40	417	Ar......... Butte.........Lv	0	**5 35**	....	5 00

UTAH & NORTHERN DIVISION.

Ogden to Butte City and Garrison—The Pioneer Montana Line. Through Broad Gauge Route from Kansas City, Council Bluffs, and Omaha, via Granger and Pocatello.

NORTHWARD.		Dist. fr Ogden	STATIONS (Mountain Time)	Popula'n	Elevat'n	SOUTHWARD.	
	No. 601 Pass. A					No. 602 Pass. A	
	A M					P M	
....	10 55	....	Lv..........**Ogden**..........Ar	10,000	4294	**4 00**	....
....	11 20	9	..........**Hot Springs**..........	50	4278	**3 35**	....
....	11 55	21	..........**Brigham**..........	2,500	4318	**3 00**	....
....	**12 22**	31	....Honeyvile..........	......	....	**2 32**	....
....	**12 58**	41	..........Collinston..........	600	....	**2 05**	....
....	**1 30**	51	..........**Mendon**..........	600	4456	**1 30**	....
....	† **2 10**	58	...........**Logan**...........	5,500	4504	† **1 10**	....
....	**2 23**	63	..........**Hyde Park**..........	1,200	....	12 37	....
....	**2 30**	65	..........**Smithfield**..........	1,500	4559	12 30	....
....	**2 48**	71	..........**Richmond**..........	1,300	4533	12 20	....
....	**3 05**	78	..........**Franklin**..........	1,400	4510	11 57	....
....	**3 35**	90	..........**Battle Creek**..........	75	4497	11 20	....
....	**4 10**	101	..........**Oxford**..	500	4771	10 50	....
....	**4 17**	104	..........Swan Lake..........	......	....	10 40	....
....	**4 55**	119	.... Hatcher	10	....	9 57	....
....	**5 05**	125	..........**Arimo**..........	......	4656	9 45	....
....	**5 20**	132	..........**McCammon**..........	25	....	9 25	....
....	† **6 25** **7 30**	154	Ar ..... **Pocatello**........ Lv Lv Ar	1,200	4492	8 20 †7 25	....
....	**7 58**	166	..........**Ross Fork**..........	......	....	7 00	....
....	**8 27**	179	..........**Blackfoot**..........	800	4512	6 30	....
....	**9 30**	205	..........**Eagle Rock**..........	1,100	4720	5 35	....
....	**10 20**	222	..........**Market Lake**..........	50	4789	4 57	....
....	**11 15**	243	..........**Camas**..	300	....	4 15	....
....	12 52	272	..........**Beaver Canon**..........	300	6035	3 05	....
....	1 35	283	..........Monida..........	......	....	2 20	....
....	1 55	292	..........Williams..........	......	....	1 55	....
....	2 20	300	..........**Spring Hill**..........	250	6196	1 35	....
....	3 10	323	..........**Red Rock**..	30	5610	12 28	....
....	4 10	348	..........**Dillon**..........	1,600	5110	**11 40**	....
....	5 45	378	..........**Melrose**..........	150	5195	**10 23**	....
....	7 35	410	..........**Silver Bow**..........	100	5349	**9 00**	....
....	†7 55	417	Ar.......**Butte City**...... .Lv	20,000	5492	† **8 30**	....
	A M					P M	

This 1883 employees' timetable provides much information about the scheduling of trains during the narrow gauge era. Freight times of from 10 to 12 hours for the 95 miles between Eagle Rock (now Idaho Falls) and Spring Hill (now Lima) provide some idea of the problems experienced in operating a narrow gauge railroad over such terrain — an average of 8 mph for a through freight over an entire division suggests a labor-intensive operation. (Museum Collection)

UNION PACIFIC RAILWAY.

IDAHO DIVISION.

SOUTHERN DISTRICT, UTAH AND NORTHERN RAILWAY.

OGDEN TO EAGLE ROCK.

TIME SCHEDULE NO. 2.

To take Effect Sunday, July 1st, 1883, at 12:05 A. M

For the Government and Information of Employes only. The Company reserves the right to vary therefrom at pleasure.

ALL TRAINS WILL RUN DAILY.

BOUND NORTH.									BOUND SOUTH.					
SECOND CLASS. No. 7 U. & N. Freight.	SECOND CLASS. No. 11 O. S. L. Freight.	FIRST CLASS. No. 1 O. S. L. Express.	SECOND CLASS. No. 9 U. & N. Freight.	SECOND CLASS. No. 5 U. & N. Freight.	FIRST CLASS. No. 3 U. & N. Express.	Distances from Ogden.	STATIONS.	Distances from Eagle Rock.	FIRST CLASS. No. 4 U. & N. Express.	SECOND CLASS. No. 6 U. & N. Freight.	SECOND CLASS. No. 10 U. & N. Freight.	FIRST CLASS. No. 2 O. S. L. Express.	SECOND CLASS. No. 12 O. S. L. Freight.	SECOND CLASS. No. 8 U. & N. Freight.
			Dep 7.40 P.M	Dep 6.10 A.M	Dep. 10.30 A.M		Ogden	204.8	Arr 4.30 P.M	Arr 1.55 P.M	Arr 2.40 A.M			
			8.35	7.05	11.05	9.0	Hot Springs	195.8	3.55	1.00	1.45			
			8.45	7.17	* 11.12	10.4	Woodland	194.4	* 3.48	12.50	1.35			
			9.05	7.35	11.25	14.0	Willard	190.8	3.35	12.30 P.M	1.15			
			9.45	Arr 8.15 Dep 8.25	**11.50** A.M	21.0	Brigham	183.8	3.10	Dep 11.50 Arr 11.35 A.M	12.35 A.M			
			10.40	9.20	* 12.30 P.M	30.5	Honeyville	174.3	* 2.30	10.30	11.40 P.M			
			11.10 P.M	**9.50**	* 12.50	35.5	Dewey	169.3	* 2.10	**9.50**	**11.10**			
			12.00 Night	10.40	* 1.17	41.5	Collinston	163.3	1.50	9.15	10.35			
			12.30 A.M	11.10	**1.35**	45.5	Cachill	159.3	**1.35**	8.50	10.10			
			1.00	11.40 A.M	1.55	51.0	Mendon	153.8	1.00	8.00	9.20			
			Arr 1.40 Dep 2.30	Arr 12.25 Dep 1.30 P.M	Arr 2.15 Dep 2.35	58.0	Logan	146.8	Dep 12.35 Arr 12.15 P.M	Dep 7.20 Arr 6.25	Dep 8.10 Arr 7.55			
			2.57	1.57	* 2.50	62.7	Hyde Park	142.1	* 12.00 Noon	6.00	7.30			
			3.15	2.15	2.58	65.4	Smithfield	139.4	11.51 A.M	5.45	7.15			
			3.50	2.50	3.19	71.2	Richmond	133.6	11.32	5.10	6.40			
			4.30	Arr 3.30 Dep 3.40	**3.40**	78.0	Franklin	126.8	11.10	**4.30**	6.00			
			5.10	4.20	* 4.05	85.0	[illegible]ston	119.8	* 10.47	3.45	5.20			
			Arr 5.40 A.M	Arr **4.50** P.M	Arr. **4.20** P.M	90.0	Battle Creek	114.8	Dep. 10.30 A.M	Dep 3.15 A.M	Dep **4.50** P.M			
			Dep 5.55 A.M	Dep **5.10** P.M	Dep **4.30** P.M	90.0	Battle Creek	114.8	Arr. 10.20 A.M	Arr. 2.20 A.M	Arr. **3.30** P.M			
			6.25	5.40	* 4.45	93.7	Morrell	111.1	* 10.05	1.50	3.00			
			7.10	6.25	5.14	100.8	Oxford	104.0	9.37	1.00	2.10			
			7.30	6.50	* 5.27	104.3	Swan Lake	100.5	* 9.24	12.35 A.M	1.45			
			8.15	7.35	* 5.55	110.8	Calvin	94.0	* 8.55	11.50 P.M	1.00			
			Arr 8.35 Dep 8.45	7.55	* 6.05	114.0	Downey	90.8	**8.45**	11.30	12.40 P.M			
			9.30	8.40	* 6.32	121.0	Toombs	83.8	* 8.19	10.42	11.53 A.M			
			Arr 9.50 A.M	Arr 9.00 P.M	Arr 6.45 P.M	124.5	Arimo	80.3	Dep 8.05 A.M	Dep 10.20 P.M	Dep. 11.30 A.M			
Dep 2.55 A.M	Dep 7.27 P.M	Arr 10.30 Dep 10.40 A.M	Arr 9.40 Dep 9.50 P.M	Dep 7.05 P.M		131.5	McCammon (JOINT TRACK.)	73.8	Dep 7.45 A.M	Dep. **9.40** P.M	Dep 10.50 Arr 10.40 A.M	Arr 7.25 A.M	Arr. 4.50 P.M	
3.22	7.40	11.10	10.20	7.20		136.5	Onyx (JOINT TRACK.)	68.3	7.30	9.10	10.10	7.12	4.22	
3.52	7.54	11.45 A.M	10.55	7.38		142.5	Inkom (JOINT TRACK.)	62.3	7.12	8.35	9.35	6.57	3.50	
4.15	**8.05**	12.17 P.M	11.27 P.M	**7.55**		148.3	Portneuf (JOINT TRACK.)	56.5	6.55	Dep 8.05 Arr 7.45	9.08	6.45	3.28	
Arr **5.00** A.M	Arr. 8.25 P.M	Arr 12.55 Dep 1.45 P.M	Arr 12.05 Dep 12.40 A.M	Arr 8.15 Dep 8.45 P.M		154.7	Pocatello (JOINT TRACK.)	50.1	Dep 6.33 Arr 6.05 A.M	Dep 7.05 Arr 6.15 P.M	Dep 8.25 Arr 7.40 A.M	Dep **6.25** A.M	Dep 2.45 P.M	
			Dep 2.50 P.M	Dep 1.45 A.M	* Dep. 9.20 P.M	166.3	Ross Fork	38.5	* Dep 5.30 A.M	Dep 5.10 P.M	Dep 6.35 A.M			
			4.00	2.55	9.58	178.9	Blackfoot	25.9	4.52	**4.00**	5.25			
			5.10	Arr 4.07 Dep 4.17	* 10.33	191.1	Basalt	13.7	* **4.17**	2.50	Dep 4.17 Arr 4.07			
			Arr 6.30 P.M	Arr 5.40 A.M	Arr 11.15 P.M	204.8	Eagle Rock		Dep 3.35 A.M	Dep 1.30 P.M	Dep 2.45 A.M			
			Dep [illegible]	Dep [illegible] A.M	Dep 7.15 A.M	348.0	Dillon		Dep 7.45 P.M	Dep 7.10 P.M	Dep 9.20 A.M			
			Arr 10.40 P.M	Arr. 10.35 A.M	Arr 11.25 A.M	416.8	Butte		Dep. 3.30 P.M	Dep 11.25 A.M	Dep 1.20 A.M			
					Arr 12.40 P.M	442.9	Deer Lodge		Dep 2.15 P.M					

F. S. RAWLINS, Train Dispatcher, EAGLE ROCK.

W. P. P. ST. CLAIR, Superintendent, EAGLE ROCK.

W. B. DODDRIDGE, Gen'l Sup't, OGDEN.

THOS. L. KIMBALL, Ass't Gen'l Manager, OMAHA.

S. H. H. CLARK, Gen'l Manager, OMAHA.

SPECIAL RULE NO. 1.—Study rules well and know that you understand them. IMPORTANT CHANGES HAVE BEEN MADE.
SPECIAL RULE NO. 2.—FULL-FACED FIGURES indicate MEETING and PASSING POINTS.
SPECIAL RULE NO. 3.—U. & N. Trains on this schedule will take their date at OGDEN and EAGLE ROCK.
SPECIAL RULE NO. 4.—Conductors and engineers when MEETING or PASSING trains must STOP and ascertain the numbers or names of such trains met or passed.
SPECIAL RULE NO. 5.—All trains and light engines passing side tracks at night where work or other trains are stationed, and no night operator, will notify such trains by leaving message with watchman what they are and time they passed.
SPECIAL RULE NO. 6.—Trains will not exceed schedule time except by special orders.
SPECIAL RULE NO. 7.—Trains will come to a full STOP before reaching U. C. crossing at Ogden.

SPECIAL RULE NO. 8.—Passenger trains must positively reduce speed over all switches to Ten (10) Miles an hour, and Freight Trains to Six (6) Miles an hour.
SPECIAL RULE NO. 9.—South Bound Trains will look out carefully for Helping Engines returning from MORRELL to BATTLE CREEK ahead of them.
SPECIAL RULE NO. 10.—Engines running without trains, or backing up pulling trains, will carry one Red Light at night, on rear of tank.
SPECIAL RULE NO. 11.—Engines helping trains carrying signals will duplicate the signals while helping the train. Conductors must notify Engineers of helping engines on their trains of any orders they may have.

*Trains do not stop except on SIGNAL.

NOTE.—Passengers may be carried upon trains five (5) and six (6) between Ogden and Oxford without permits.

JOINT TRACK.—All trains on joint track take their date at McCammon and Pocatello. Junction switches at McCammon and Pocatello will be set for standard gauge. All trains will register at McCammon and Pocatello. Oregon Short Line Dispatcher will give all orders concerning the movement of trains between McCammon and Pocatello.

UNION PACIFIC RAILWAY.

IDAHO DIVISION.

NORTHERN DISTRICT, UTAH AND NORTHERN RAILWAY.

EAGLE ROCK TO BUTTE.

TIME SCHEDULE NO. 2.

THIRD EDITION.

To take Effect Sunday, September 30, 1883, at 12:05 A. M

For the Government and Information of Employes only.

The Company reserves the right to vary therefrom at pleasure.

ALL TRAINS WILL RUN DAILY.

BOUND NORTH. Second Class. No. 11 Mixed.	Second Class. No. 9 Freight.	Second Class. No. 5 Freight.	First Class. No. 3 Express.	First Class. No. 1 Express.	Distances from Eagle Rock.	STATIONS.	Distances from Garrison.	BOUND SOUTH. First Class. No. 2 Express.	First Class. No. 4 Express.	Second Class. No. 6 Freight.	Second Class. No. 10 Freight.	Second Class. No. 12 Mixed.
	Dep... 7.40P.M	Dep... 6.10A.M	Dep... 10.30A.M			**Ogden**	454.3		Arr. 4.30 P.M	Arr 1.55P.M	Arr 2.40A.M	
	Dep... 2.30A.M	Dep... 1.30P.M	Dep.. 2.35P.M			**Logan**	396.3		Dep. 12.35P.M	Dep. 7.20A.M	Dep. 8.40P.M	
	Dep... 9.05P.M	Dep... 10.20A.M	Dep.. 11.30P.M			**Eagle Rock**	249.5		Arr. 3.20A.M	Arr. 12.00noon	Arr 12.45A.M	
	10.00	**11.10**A.M	**11.55**P.M		8.5	**Payne**	241.0		2.55	**11.10**A.M	Dep. **11.55** / Arr **11.45** P.M	
	10.55P.M	12.00 Noon	12.20A.M		17.1	**Market Lake**	232.4		2.30	10.20	**10.55**	
	12.05A.M	1.05P.M	* 12.52		27.6	**Hawgood**	221.9		* 1.58	9.15	9.55	
	Arr. **1.15** / Dep. **1.35**	2.10	**1.25**		38.4	**Camas**	211.1		**1.25**	8.10	8.50	
	3.00	3.20	2.00		50.1	**Dry Creek**	199.4		12.50	7.00	7.40	
	4.00	4.20	* 2.30		58.9	**High Bridge**	190.6		* 12.23	6.05	6.45	
	4.25	4.45	* 2.42		62.1	**China Point**	187.4		* 12.12A.M	5.45	6.25	
	Arr. **5.00** / Dep. **6.00**	Arr. **5.15** / Dep. **6.15**	3.00		67.4	**Beaver Canon**	182.1		11.55P.M	**5.15**	Dep. **5.55** / Arr. **5.35**	
	6.50	7.05	3.30		72.9	**Pleasant Valley**	176.6		11.30	4.35	4.55	
	7.35	7.50	**3.50**		79.4	**Monida**	170.1		11.10	Dep. **3.50** / Arr. **3.40**	4.15	
	8.30	8.45	* 4.17		88.2	**Williams**	161.3		* 10.42	2.45	3.20	
	Arr. 9.15A.M	Arr. **9.30**P.M	Arr. 4.40A.M		95.2	**Spring Hill**	154.3		Dep. **10.20**P.M	Dep. 1.55A.M	Dep. 2.30P.M	
	Dep. 9.35A.M	Dep. **10.10**P.M	Dep. 4.50A.M		95.2	**Spring Hill**	154.3		Arr. **10.10**P.M	Arr. 12.15A.M	Arr. 2.10P.M	
	10.30	**11.10**P.M	* 5.22		105.7	**Dell**	143.8		* 9.38	**11.10**P.M	1.07P.M	
	11.50A.M	12.20A.M	6.00		118.0	**Red Rock**	131.5		9.00	9.55	**11.50**A.M	
	12.40P.M	1.10	* 6.27		126.7	**Grayling**	122.8		* 8.35	9.03	11.00	
	1.30	2.00	* 6.55		135.4	**Barratt's**	114.1		**8.08**	Dep. **8.08** / Arr. **7.58**	10.10	
	Arr. 2.20 / Dep. 2.35	Arr. 2.45 / Dep. 2.55	7.15		143.2	**Dillon**	106.3		7.45	Dep. 7.10 / Arr. 6.45	Dep. 9.20 / Arr. 9.05	
	4.05	4.15	**7.55**		155.2	**Apex**	94.3		* 7.10	5.30	Dep. **7.55** / Arr. **7.45**	
	4.45	4.55	* 8.15		161.7	**Glen**	87.8		* 6.45	**4.45**	7.00	
	Arr. **5.55** / Dep. **6.25**	Arr. **6.00** / Dep. **6.20**	Arr. 8.55 / Dep. 9.15		174.0	**Melrose**	75.5		Dep. **6.05** / Arr. **5.45**	3.35	Dep. **6.00** / Arr. **5.30**	
	7.25	7.20	* 9.45		183.8	**Lavell**	65.7		* 5.15	2.35	4.30	
	8.45	8.40	* 10.25		195.9	**Feely**	53.6		* 4.35	1.25	3.20	
	9.15	9.10	* 10.40		199.9	**Buxton**	49.6		* 4.17	12.50	2.45	
Dep... 11.40P.M	Arr. 9.45 / Dep. 9.55	Arr. 9.40 / Dep. 9.50	Arr. **10.55** / Dep. **11.05**	Dep.. **4.00**P.M	205.0	**Silver Bow**	44.5	Arr **10.55**A.M	Dep **4.00** / Arr **3.50**	Dep 12.20 / Arr 12.10 P.M	Dep. 2.15 / Arr 2.05	Arr... 1.00P.M
Arr. 12.25A.M	Arr... 10.40P.M	Arr. **10.30**A.M	Arr.. **11.25**A.M	Arr.. 4.25P.M	212.0	**Butte**	51.5	Dep **10.30**A.M	Dep. 3.30P.M	Dep **11.25**A.M	Dep. 1.20A.M	Dep 12.20P.M

DEER LODGE BRANCH.

BOUND NORTH. Second Class. No. 15 Mixed.	First Class. No. 13 Express.	Distances from Eagle Rock	STATIONS.	Distances from Garrison.	BOUND SOUTH. First Clas. No. 14 Express.	Second Class. No. 16 Mixed.
Dep... 1.10P.M	Dep... 11.05A.M	205.0	**Silver Bow**	44.5	Arr 3.50P.M	Arr 11.30P.M
2.15	11.40A.M	216.3	**Stuart**	33.2	3.15	10.25
2.55	12.02P.M	223.6	**Warm Springs**	25.9	**2.55**	9.45
3.30	* 12.18	229.6	**Race Track**	19.9	* 2.38	9.10
Arr 4.15 / Dep 4.30	12.40	238.1	**Deer Lodge**	11.4	2.15	Dep. 8.25 / Arr 7.25
5.25	12.57	243.8	**Mullen**	5.7	1.58	6.50
Arr... **6.00**P.M	Arr **1.15**P.M	249.5	**Garrison**		Dep **1.40**P.M	Dep. **6.15**P.M

F. S. RAWLINS, Train Dispatcher, Eagle Rock.

W. P. P. St. CLAIR, Superintendent, Eagle Rock.

W. B. DODDRIDGE, Gen'l Superintendent, Ogden.

THOS. L. KIMBALL, Ass't Gen'l Manager, Omaha.

S. H. H. CLARK, Gen'l Manager, Omaha.

SPECIAL RULE NO. 1.—Study rules well and know that you understand them. **Important changes have been made.**

SPECIAL RULE NO. 2.—FULL-FACED FIGURES indicate MEETING and PASSING POINTS.

SPECIAL RULE NO. 3.—Train 3 will wait at Silver Bow until Train 2 arrives.

SPECIAL RULE NO. 4.—Conductors and Engineers when MEETING or PASSING trains must STOP and ascertain the numbers or names of such trains met or passed.

SPECIAL RULE NO. 5.—All trains and light engines passing side tracks at night where work or other trains are stationed, and no night operator, will notify such trains by leaving message with watchman, what they are and time they passed.

SPECIAL RULE NO. 6.—Trains 13 14, 15 and 16 will take their date at SILVER BOW and GARRISON.

SPECIAL RULE NO. 7.—Trains 1, 2, 11 and 12 will take their date at SILVER BOW and BUTTE.

SPECIAL RULE NO. 8.—Trains 3, 4, 5, 6, 9 and 10 will take their date at EAGLE ROCK and BUTTE.

SPECIAL RULE NO. 9.—Trains will not exceed schedule time except by special order.

* Trains do not stop except on signal.

SPECIAL RULE NO. 10.—Passenger Trains must positively reduce speed over all switches to Ten (10) Miles per hour, and Freight Trains to Six (6) Miles per hour.

SPECIAL RULE NO. 11.—South Bound Trains will look out carefully for helping Engines running ahead MONIDA to CAMAS.

SPECIAL RULE NO. 12.—Engines running without trains, or backing pulling trains, will carry one Red Light at night, on rear of tank.

SPECIAL RULE NO. 13.—Engines helping trains carrying signals will duplicate the signals while helping the train. Conductors must notify Engineers of helping engines on their trains of any orders they may have.

SPECIAL RULE NO. 14.—All trains, or engines without trains, will register at SILVER BOW.

SPECIAL RULE NO. 15.—All trains must come to a full stop within 200 feet of SILVER BOW JUNCTION SWITCH.

SPECIAL RULE NO. 16.—The line from SILVER BOW to DEER LODGE will be known as the Deer Lodge branch, BUTTE will be known as the Northern Terminus of Main Line. Trains on Deer Lodge branch will leave switches RIGHT for Main line, at SILVER BOW.

HERALD PRINT, OMAHA.

Motive Power and Rolling Stock

The equipment roster of the Utah & Northern provides railroad historians with an interesting study in the development of narrow gauge motive power and rolling stock. From a simple beginning in 1872 of five Grant Locomotive Works engines (a diminutive Eightwheeler and Mogul, and three only slightly larger Tenwheelers), the locomotive roster expanded to an all time total of 54 engines, ranging in size from a second-hand Mason 0-4-2T (built originally as Mason's first Forney-type) to the powerful Rhode Island-built 2-8-0's that later saw another half century of service on Colorado's South Park narrow gauge. Rolling stock expanded from 4 passenger cars to 37, and 42 freight cars to 1,564 — excluding cars borrowed temporarily from the Denver, South Park & Pacific RR and other Union Pacific subsidiaries.

With the takeover of the Utah Northern RR in 1878 by the Union Pacific, a period of expansion occurred and the equipment of the line was added to greatly. One of the first orders of business was the acquisition from the Baldwin Locomotive Works of 10 new 2-6-0 locomotives in 1878-79, followed by an additional 6 engines in 1880. These engines were of standard Baldwin pattern and weighed about 20 tons, only slightly more than the Grant Tenwheelers. In 1881 the first of 23 larger (23 tons) Moguls arrived from the Brooks Locomotive Works. These engines were part of an order placed with Brooks by the Union Pacific for identical locomotives for the subsidiary narrow gauge lines of its system throughout the West.

The last major addition to the Utah & Northern's narrow gauge roster occurred in 1886, when six large (35½ ton) 2-8-0's arrived to handle the heavy traffic from Pocatello north into the Montana silver camps. Even though standard gauging of the line was by then imminent, the motive power situation had become sufficiently critical that management felt the added heavier power was needed. Locomotives had been borrowed from the Union Pacific's South Park (DSP&P) line in Colorado to relieve the shortage; at least four Mason Bogie 2-6-6T's and three Brooks Moguls from the South Park were noted in service on the U&N. At the same time, freight cars from the South Park were pressed into service on the U&N, moving on their own wheels from Gunnison, Colorado, to Salt Lake City via the Rio Grande.

The first freight cars on the Utah Northern RR were built by Billmeyer & Small's York Car Works, of York, Pennsylvania, and were small, four-wheel affairs similar to the first cars built for the Denver & Rio Grande narrow gauge. Union Pacific control and expansion brought a flood of cars to the line, all eight wheel cars of much greater capacity. An interesting note is the fact that a number of coal cars (9150 through 9399, 9697 through 9699, and 10400 through 10449 — a total of 303 cars) were equipped as built with "interchangeable trucks," for use on narrow or standard gauge tracks. A Ramsey Transfer was in use at Pocatello for changing the trucks from one gauge to the other.

The first four UN RR passenger cars also were provided by Billmeyer & Small, and the fleet eventually expanded to 37 cars. Among the cars ordered by the Union Pacific for use on the U&N were five Pullman sleepers from Jackson & Sharp in 1881.

With the standard gauging of the Pocatello-Butte line in 1887, and the Ogden line in 1890, the Union Pacific was faced with the need to dispose of some 43 narrow gauge locomotives (excluding those returned to the South Park Division). The smallest and oldest were scrapped; one served out the years as a tie-planing machine at Eagle Rock. The two newest Brooks Moguls were already gone; one had been diverted to the Kansas Central early; the other was sent to the South Park in exchange for a wrecked Mason Bogie. The six big Rhode Islands were also sent to the South Park (now Denver, Leadville & Gunnison Ry.) in 1890, and one of these is still in existence and on display at Idaho Springs, Colorado (as Colorado & Southern no. 60).

Other Utah & Northern engines were scattered to the four winds. As the Union Pacific had little use for the smaller, older power, the Baldwin and Brooks Moguls were thrown on the used locomotive market at a time when buyers were scarce. It is said that they were offered to sugar factories, smelters, lumber firms and short line railroads for as little as $250 apiece. Large portions of discarded U&N rail, hardware, locomotives and cars went into the building of Oregon's Sumpter Valley Railway in 1890. Other locomotives saw service on the Nevada Central, Ilwaco Railway & Navigation, Portland & Willamette Valley, Salt Lake & Fort Douglas, Utah Central, San Pete Valley, Columbia & Puget Sound, Golconda & Adelaide and Eureka-Nevada. Several made their way to midwest shortlines and deep-south lumber lines. Still others went north of the border — to obscure roads like the Columbia & Western and Tanana Mines. Two Brooks Moguls ended up on the White Pass & Yukon Route, where they can still be viewed today — if heavily rebuilt — at Skagway and Whitehorse. (One identical Brooks, a sister engine from the Kansas Central, can also be seen as Klondike Mines Ry. No. 1 at Dawson City; this locomotive is deteriorated but does appear entirely original.) And finally, one Baldwin Mogul — former U&N 13 — is displayed in the new California State Railroad Museum at Sacramento as Nevada Short Line No. 1.

That any reminder of the narrow gauge Utah & Northern should exist, nearly a century after the railroad's demise, is at best pure chance.

Initial UP purchases of motive power for the U&N were Baldwin Moguls like these. No. 19 (later 23) became Portland & Willamette Valley no. 1 (left); another became Oregon Short Line no. 1 on the Salt Lake City-Stockton line; and no. 14 (later 18) passed through the Southern Iron & Equipment Co. (bottom) to Noble Lumber Company ownership. (Bottom, Edward Bond Collection; others, Arthur Petersen Collection)

The Rosters: Presented first is our reconstruction of the all-time record of Utah Northern — Utah & Northern motive power, giving sources, dates and dispositions as completely and accurately as possible in light of available data. Following, second, is a reprinting of the 1885 Union Pacific official record of all equipment assigned to the Utah & Northern, with specifications, reflecting with reasonable accuracy the locomotive and car equipment in use at that time.

LOCOMOTIVE ROSTER

Utah & Northern Ry. — Oregon Short Line & Utah Northern Ry.

1878 NO.	1885 NO.	TYPE	BUILDER	C/N	DATE	NOTES
1	—	4-6-0	Grant	—	1872	*Franklin* (see Note A)
1	290	2-6-0	Baldwin	3663	11/1874	2nd #1, 1881; from Summit County RR #2; off roster by 1889.
2	—	4-4-0	Grant	—	1871	*John W. Young* (see Note A)
3	297	2-6-0	Grant	—	1871	*Logan;* scrapped by 1887
4	285	4-6-0	Grant	—	1872	*Utah;* scrapped by 1887
5	286	4-6-0	Grant	—	1872	*Idaho;* scrapped by 1887
6	10	2-6-0	Baldwin	4425	9/1878	
7	11	2-6-0	Baldwin	4429	9/1878	On Utah & Nevada Ry. ca. 1890-91 per UP records; to Sumpter Valley Ry. #11 ca. 1902, reno. #12 1906; presented to University of Idaho; scrapped, 1942.
8	12	2-6-0	Baldwin	4430	9/1878	
9	13	2-6-0	Baldwin	4555	3/1879	
10	14	2-6-0	Baldwin	4558	3/1879	
11	15	2-6-0	Baldwin	4559	3/1879	
12	16	2-6-0	Baldwin	4561	3/1879	
13	17	2-6-0	Baldwin	4562	3/1879	Sold - - - ; to Golconda & Adelaide RR #1 1898; to Nevada Short Line Ry. #1 1914; for sale 1920-24; to Nevada Central Ry. #6 1924; sold 1938 to Hyman-Michaels Co. and presented to Pacific Coast Chapter, Railway & Locomotive Historical Society for preservation; used in 1939 Exposition at Treasure Island, San Francisco, as UP RR #119; to California State Railroad Museum, Sacramento.
14	18	2-6-0	Baldwin	4563	3/1879	Sold - - - ; to Noble Lumber Co., Noble, La., 11/21/1903 (via Southern Iron & Equipment #111); to Swift Lumber Co.
15	19	2-6-0	Baldwin	4564	3/1879	Sold to Ilwaco Ry. & Nav. Co. #1, 1888, for $2,500; scrapped 1911.
16	20	2-6-0	Baldwin	4964	2/1880	
17	21	2-6-0	Baldwin	4966	2/1880	
18	22	2-6-0	Baldwin	4967	2/1880	
19	23	2-6-0	Baldwin	5121	5/1880	Sold - - - ; to Portland & Willamette Valley RR #1; to Ilwaco Ry. & Nav. Co. #4 in 1906 for $500, then #N2 and #2; scrapped 1931.
20	24	2-6-0	Baldwin	5122	5/1880	
21	25	2-6-0	Baldwin	5129	6/1880	
22	2	2-6-0	Baldwin	3113	1/1873	Orig. Summit County RR #1; in use on U&N ca. 1878; to U&N 2nd #2 in 1881; in service in 1889.
23	80	2-6-0	Brooks	494	1/1881	
24	81	2-6-0	Brooks	495	1/1881	
25	82	2-6-0	Brooks	504	2/1881	
26	83	2-6-0	Brooks	505	2/1881	
27	84	2-6-0	Brooks	514	3/1881	
28	85	2-6-0	Brooks	515	3/1881	

29	86	2-6-0	Brooks	520	4/1881	
30	87	2-6-0	Brooks	529	4/1881	
31	88	2-6-0	Brooks	530	4/1881	Sold to Sumpter Valley Ry. #1, 1892, then #5, 1906; sold to Eureka Nevada Ry. #5, 1912, rebuilt and reno. #9, 1919, scrapped 1927-1938.
32	89	2-6-0	Brooks	536	5/1881	
33	90	2-6-0	Brooks	554	7/1881	
34	91	2-6-0	Brooks	559	7/1881	
35	92	2-6-0	Brooks	562	7/1881	
36	93	2-6-0	Brooks	566	8/1881	
37	94	2-6-0	Brooks	567	8/1881	
38	95	2-6-0	Brooks	579	9/1881	
39	96	2-6-0	Brooks	587	9/1881	
40	97	2-6-0	Brooks	597	10/1881	
41	98	2-6-0	Brooks	605	11/1881	
42	99	2-6-0	Brooks	626	12/1881	
43	100	2-6-0	Brooks	627	12/1881	
44	—	2-6-0	Brooks	800	10/1882	Transferred to Kansas Central RR #13, reno. #106, 1885; sold to Mississippi River & Bonne Terre Ry. 1891.
45	101	2-6-0	Brooks	801	10/1882	To Denver, South Park & Pacific RR #101 in 1886, apparently in exchange for DSP&P #50 Mason 2-6-6T destroyed on U&N; probably sold to New York Equipmt. Co. 1893, to Kaaterskill Ry. #3 1893, to Catskill & Tannersville #1 ca. 1898, retired 1908. See Note C.
45	296	0-4-2T	Mason	461	7/1872	Orig. American Fork RR #1, sold 1873 - - -; rebuilt from 0-4-4T to 0-4-2T; scrapped by 1887. See Note B.
—	260	2-8-0	Rhode Is.	1592	2/1886	To Denver, Leadville & Gunnison Ry. #260, 9/1890; then Colorado & Southern #57, 1899; scrapped 1923.
—	261	2-8-0	Rhode Is.	1593	2/1886	To DL&G #261, then C&S #58 (as above); scrapped 1939.
—	262	2-8-0	Rhode Is.	1594	3/1886	To DL&G #262, then C&S #59; scrapped 1925.
—	263	2-8-0	Rhode Is.	1595	3/1886	To DL&G #263, then C&S #60; presented to Idaho Springs, Colo., for display in 1941.
—	264	2-8-0	Rhode Is.	1596	4/1886	To DL&G #264, then C&S #61; scrapped 1930.
—	265	2-8-0	Rhode Is.	1597	4/1886	To DL&G #265, then C&S #62; scrapped 1927.

Note A: Although the *Franklin* was the third engine received by the Utah Northern, six months after the *John W. Young* and the *Logan*, it appears to have been accorded the number 1 and the latter two numbered 2 and 3. This may have been due to an early (1872?) and unrecorded renumbering, or the locomotives may have originally only been identified by name (not unusual for that period). Both the *Franklin* and *John W. Young* were apparently destroyed in a roundhouse fire at Logan on March 31, 1881, and were replaced by two Summit County RR locomotives. One source contends that the *Franklin* was rebuilt to an 0-6-0T for further use, but this report has not been substantiated.

Note B: This locomotive was the first Mason Forney-type constructed, built to 3 foot gauge in 1871 on speculation; sold in April 1872 to the American Fork RR (and named *Onward*) after being converted to 3 foot 2 inch gauge and further modified, being shipped in July 1872. Found unsatisfactory, a Porter 0-6-0 was obtained as replacement and the Mason taken out of service (perhaps as early as 1873); it was said to have been stored at Sandy, Utah, for some time. At some point it found its way into the UP system, and was further rebuilt (into a 3 foot gauge 0-4-2T). This may be the same "dinky engine" said to have been rebuilt at the Omaha Shops in 1883 into DSP&P #75 and used as a switch engine briefly in 1883-84 on the South Park, before its appearance in 1885 on the Utah & Northern.

Note C: There appear to be some discrepancies in the record of engines 44, first 45 and second 45. In all likelihood, #44 was diverted to the Kansas Central early, and first 45 was then renumbered 44, thus making room on the roster by 1885 for the small Mason to be numbered 45.

Following is a reprinting of the 1885 Union Pacific official record of all equipment assigned to the Utah & Northern.

LOCOMOTIVES — UTAH NORTHERN, N. G.

NEW NO.	OLD NO.	CLASS	NAME OF BLD'R	DIA. OF CYL. & STROKE	AIR BRAKES	WHEEL	BOILER SHELL	WHEEL BASE RIGID FT & IN	WHEEL BASE TOTAL FT & IN	WHEEL BASE E & T FT & IN	LENGTH OVER ALL FT & IN	WEIGHT DRIV-ERS	WEIGHT TOTAL	TENDER WATER	TENDER COAL	REMARKS
2	22	D. F. 1	Bald.	11x16		38	38	8 7	11 2	32 2	38 6	27700	32900	1015	2	Mogul.
10	6	D. G. 2	Bald.	12x18		42	37	11 8	17 8	35 0	42 6	33000	39000	1200	3	
11	7	"	"	"		42	37	11 8	17 8	35 0	42 6	33000	39000	1200	3	
12	8	"	"	"		42	37	11 8	17 8	35 0	42 6	33000	39000	1200	3	
13	9	"	"	"		42	37	11 8	17 8	35 0	42 6	33000	39000	1200	3	
14	10	"	"	"		42	37	11 8	17 8	35 0	42 6	33000	39000	1200	3	
15	11	"	"	"		42	37	11 8	17 8	35 0	42 6	33000	39000	1200	3	
16	12	"	"	"	x	42	37	11 8	17 8	35 0	42 6	33000	39000	1200	3	
17	13	"	"	"		42	37	11 8	17 8	35 0	42 6	33000	39000	1200	3	
18	14	"	"	"		42	37	11 8	17 8	35 0	42 6	33000	39000	1200	3	
19	15	"	"	"		42	37	11 8	17 8	35 0	42 6	33000	39000	1200	3	
20	16	"	"	"		42	37	11 8	17 8	35 0	42 6	33000	39000	1200	3	
21	17	"	"	"		42	37	11 8	17 8	35 0	42 6	33000	39000	1200	3	
22	18	"	"	"	x	42	37	11 8	17 8	35 0	42 6	33000	39000	1200	3	
23	19	"	"	"		42	37	11 8	17 8	35 0	42 6	33000	39000	1200	3	
24	20	"	"	"	x	42	37	11 8	17 8	35 0	42 6	33000	39000	1200	3	
25	21	"	"	"		42	37	11 8	17 8	35 0	42 6	33000	39000	1200	3	
80	23	D. I. 2	Brooks	14x18	x	42	36	12 1	18 2	36 6	44 8	39700	45800	1358	3	
81	24	"	"	"	x	42	36	12 1	18 2	36 6	44 8	39700	45800	1358	3	
82	25	"	"	"		42	36	12 1	18 2	36 6	44 8	39700	45800	1358	3	
83	26	"	"	"		42	36	12 1	18 2	36 6	44 8	39700	45800	1358	3	
84	27	"	"	"	x	42	36	12 1	18 2	36 6	44 8	39700	45800	1358	3	
85	28	"	"	"	x	42	36	12 1	18 2	36 6	44 8	39700	45800	1358	3	
86	29	"	"	"	x	42	36	12 1	18 2	36 6	44 8	39700	45800	1358	3	
87	30	"	"	"	x	42	36	12 1	18 2	36 6	44 8	39700	45800	1358	3	
88	31	"	"	"	x	42	36	12 1	18 2	36 6	44 8	39700	45800	1358	3	
89	32	"	"	"	x	42	36	12 1	18 2	36 6	44 8	39700	45800	1358	3	
90	33	"	"	"	x	42	36	12 1	18 2	36 6	44 8	39700	45800	1358	3	
91	34	"	"	"	x	42	36	12 1	18 2	36 6	44 8	39700	45800	1358	3	
92	35	"	"	"		42	36	12 1	18 2	36 6	44 8	39700	45800	1358	3	
93	36	"	"	"		42	36	12 1	18 2	36 6	44 8	39700	45800	1358	3	
94	37	"	"	"		42	36	12 1	18 2	36 6	44 8	39700	45800	1358	3	
95	38	"	"	"		42	36	12 1	18 2	36 6	44 8	39700	45800	1358	3	
96	39	"	"	"	x	42	36	12 1	18 2	36 6	44 8	39700	45800	1358	3	
97	40	"	"	"	x	42	36	12 1	18 2	36 6	44 8	39700	45800	1358	3	
98	41	"	"	"	x	42	36	12 1	18 2	36 6	44 8	39700	45800	1358	3	
99	42	"	"	"		42	36	12 1	18 2	36 6	44 8	39700	45800	1358	3	
100	43	"	"	"		42	36	12 1	18 2	36 6	44 8	39700	45800	1358	3	
101	44	"	"	"	x	42	36	12 1	18 2	36 6	44 8	39700	45800	1358	3	
285	4	Odd	Grant	12x18		44	35½	11 0	19 8	34 0	40 2	28125	37500	900	2½	10 Wheel
286	5	"	"	"		44	35½	11 0	19 8	34 0	40 2	28125	37500	900	2½	10 Wheel
290	1	"	Bald.	12x16		38	38	9 8	15 9	35 11	44 6	32625	38100	1050	3	Mogul.
296	45	"	Mason	11x15		34	35	5 0	5 0	20 3	31 6	29900	29900	824	2	6 Wheel
297	3	"	Grant	10x16		44	30	11 0	16 3	29 3	38 0	24643	28750	584	2	

Added Data: Specifications for engines 260-265 (Rhode Island 1886) were: cylinders, 16x20"; drivers, 37"; weight, 71,000 lbs. (per Colorado & Southern Ry. records).

UTAH AND NORTHERN.

CLASSIFICATION	NOS. USED FROM	NOS. USED TO	CAPACITY	LENGTH	ON HAND	NOS. ASSIGNED FROM	NOS. ASSIGNED TO	TOTAL
Pullman Sleepers	....	....	....	....	5			
Officers'	030	031	....	....	2	030	034	5
Coaches	125	143	....	....	19	125	179	55
Coach & Baggage	....	....	....	....	......	720	734	15
Excursion	800	807	....	....	8	800	819	20
Mail	1153	1156	....	....	4	1153	1160	8
Baggage & Express	1407	1411	....	....	5	1407	1416	10
Baggage	1020	1023	....	....	4	1020	1034	15
Caboose	1604	1622	....	....	19	1600	1724	122
Outfit	02575	02576	....	....	2			
"	02580	02580	....	....	1	02575	02624	50
"	02590	02591	....	....	2			
Flat	3700	3700	18,000	24	1			
"	3701	3702	"	25	2			
"	3703	3731	20,000	27	29			
"	3732	3742	24,000	27	11	3700	4189	490
"	3743	3800	28,000	27	58			
"	3801	3802	30,000	27	2			
Coal	9400	9400	18,000	25	1			
"	9401	9402	20,000	25	2			
"	9403	9433	"	27	31			
"	9434	9434	24,000	27	1			
"	9435	9451	20,000	27	17	9400	9699	300
"	9452	9535	24,000	27	84			
"	9536	9548	28,000	27	13			
"	9549	9549	30,000	27	1			
" Dump	9700	9748	40,000	30	49	9700	9799	100
"	....	....	....	....	......	9800	10399	600
Stock	18400	18415	18,000	24	16			
"	18416	18417	"	27	2			
"	18418	18419	20,000	24	2	18490	18699	300
"	18420	18460	"	27	41			
"	18461	18470	24,000	27	10			
Box	25500	25567	18,000	24	68			
"	25570	25633	"	24	64			
"	25634	25650	"	25	17			
"	25651	25654	20,000	24	4			
"	25655	25730	"	26	76			
"	25731	25731	"	27	1	25500	26499	1000
"	25732	25742	24,000	24	11			
"	25743	25756	"	26	14			
"	25757	25758	"	27	2			
"	25759	25762	28,000	27	4			
"	25763	25811	30,000	27	40			
Total	....	....	....	....	754	....	....	3090

SNOW PLOWS — IRON

	LOCATION
Nos. 20, 21	Eagle Rock
22	Butte
23	Logan
24	Spring Hill

FLANGERS

Nos. 11	Eagle Rock
12	Butte
13	Logan

UTAH AND NORTHERN.

NO. OF CAR NEW	OLD	KIND OF CAR	BUILT BY WHOM	WHEN	COST OF CAR	CAPACITY	LENGTH OVER END SILLS	KIND OF HEATER	WHEELS NO. & SIZE
125	3	Coach	O.F.C.Co.	1879	1,900 00	19 Seats	40 2	Stove	8 26
126	4	"	"	1879	1,900 00	19 "	40 2	"	8 26
127	5	"	"	1879	1,900 00	19 "	40 2	"	8 26
128	18	"	"	1878		22 "	40 2	"	8 26
129	9	"	J.&S.			19 "	34 10	"	8 26
130	10	"	"			20 "	34 10	"	8 26
131	13	"	P.P.C.Co.	1882	4,701 68	25 "	42	Baker	8 30
132	15	"	"	1882	4,701 68	25 "	42	"	8 30
133	6	"	"	1882	4,828 25	25 "	42 1	"	8 26
134	7	"	"	1882	4,828 25	25 "	42 1	"	8 26
135	8	"	"	1882	4,828 25	25 "	42 1	"	8 30
136	14	"	O.F.C.Co.	1879	3,500 00	20 "	42 8	Stove	8 30
137	11	"	U.P.Ry.	1880	4,579 23	18 "	33 9	"	8 26
138	12	"	"	1880	4,579 23	18 "	33 9	"	8 26
139	19	"	"	1879		23 "	40 8	"	8 26
140	16	"	"	1883	5,327 08	24 "	42	"	8 26
141	17	"	"	1883	5,327 08	24 "	42	"	8 26
142	20	"	"	1884	5,517 97	23 "	42	Searle	8 30
143	21	"	"	1884	5,517 97	23 "	42	"	8 30
800	30	Exc. Cars	"	1883	*906 00	66 Per's	27		8 26
801	31	"	"	1883	*906 00	66 "	27		8 26
802	32	"	"	1883	*906 00	66 "	27		8 26
803	33	"	"	1883	*906 00	66 "	27		8 26
804	34	"	"	1883		66 "	27		8 26
805	35	"	"	1883		66 "	27		8 26
806	36	"	"	1883		66 "	27		8 26
807	37	"	"	1883		66 "	27		8 26
1153	40	Mail	"	1882	3,067 04		40 2	Baker	8 26
1154	41	"	O.F.C.Co.	1879	1,175 00		40 2	"	8 26
1155	42	"	"	1879	1,175 00		40 2	"	8 26
1156	43	"	"	1879	1,175 00		40 2	"	8 26
1020	54	Bag. Dinkey	U.P.Ry.	1883	1,351 43		28	Stove	8 26
1021	55	"	"	1883	1,351 43		28	"	8 26
1022	56	"	"	1883	1,351 43		28	"	8 26
1023	57	"	"	1883	1,351 43		28	"	8 26
1407	50	Bag. & Exp.	"	1879			35	"	8 26
1408	51	"	O.F.C.Co.	1879	1,175 00		40 2	"	8 26
1409	52	"	"	1879	1,175 00		40 2	"	8 26
1410	53	"	"	1879	1,175 00		40 2	"	8 26
1411	58	"	U.P.Ry.	1883	2,613 03			"	8 26
030	01	Officers'	O.F.C.Co.	1878		1 D.R. 1 Parl'r 10 Bth's	38 6	Baker	8 26
031	02	Pay	U.P.Ry.	1879	3,256 02	4 Bth's 1 Office 1 W.R.	35 3	Stove	8 26

*Cost without trucks

PULLMAN SLEEPING CARS.

NAME OF SLEEPING CAR	GAUGE	ROAD, DIVISION ASSIGNED TO	STYLE OF CAR	DIMENSIONS	CAPACITY	KIND OF HEATER	WHEEL NO. & SIZE
Advance	NG	U&N	OP	42′ 7½x8′ 6	10 Sections	Bak'r	8 30
Argo	"	"	"	42′ 7½x8′ 6	10 Sections	"	8 30
Progress	"	"	"	42′ 7½x8′ 6	10 Sections	"	8 30
Rambler	"	"	"	42′ 7½x8′ 6	10 Sections	"	8 30
Security	"	"	"	42′ 7½x8′ 6	10 Sections	"	8 30

A large group gathered above to be photographed in front of spotlessly maintained U&N no. 13 about 1880, for an occasion now forgotten. (Arthur Petersen Collection) After wandering about the west for a century, the little Baldwin is now preserved at the California State Railroad Museum as Nevada Short Line no. 1 (below; California State Railroad Museum photo).

U&N no. 7 became no. 11 and eventually went to the Sumpter Valley Ry., where it was also no. 11. Out of service and partially scrapped (top), it was rescued by a group of engineering students, reassembled, and placed on display at the University of Idaho at Pocatello. Unfortunately, during the hysteria of a war-time scrap metal drive in 1942 it was cut up for scrap. (Top, Author's Collection; center, C. H. Peake Collection; bottom, Arthur Petersen Collection)

No. 11 in happier days — at Tipton, Oregon, in 1904 on the Sumpter Valley. (Author's Collection, from F. M. Shurtliff)

Backbone of the U&N's motive power fleet in the 1880's were the 23 Brooks moguls purchased in 1881-1882. Pictured above at the Dunkirk works in January 1881 is brand new U&N no. 23 (later no. 80), resplendent in the copious applications of the painters', varnishers', and stripers' art. (G. M. Best Collection) No. 87, seen below at Dillon in the mid-1880's, had been U&N no. 30 originally, and still presents a very original appearance in this view. Other pictures of this class were seen on pages 42, 43, 52 and 57. (Below, Denver Public Library Western History Collection)

Final motive power purchase for the U&N was made almost on the eve of standard gauging — a batch of sturdy 2-8-0 consolidations from the Rhode Island works. As soon as the U&N was converted, these locomotives were quickly transfered to the South Park Division, where they served well for many years (U&N no. 263 still exists as Colorado & Southern no. 60, on display at Idaho Springs, Colorado). Below, no. 261 running on the South Park at Wheeler, still lettered for the U&N (as is the gondola behind it), but having lost the straight stack and long extended smokebox displayed in the builder's photo above in favor of an orthodox diamond stack and short box. (Top, Author's Collection; bottom, Rex Beistle Collection)

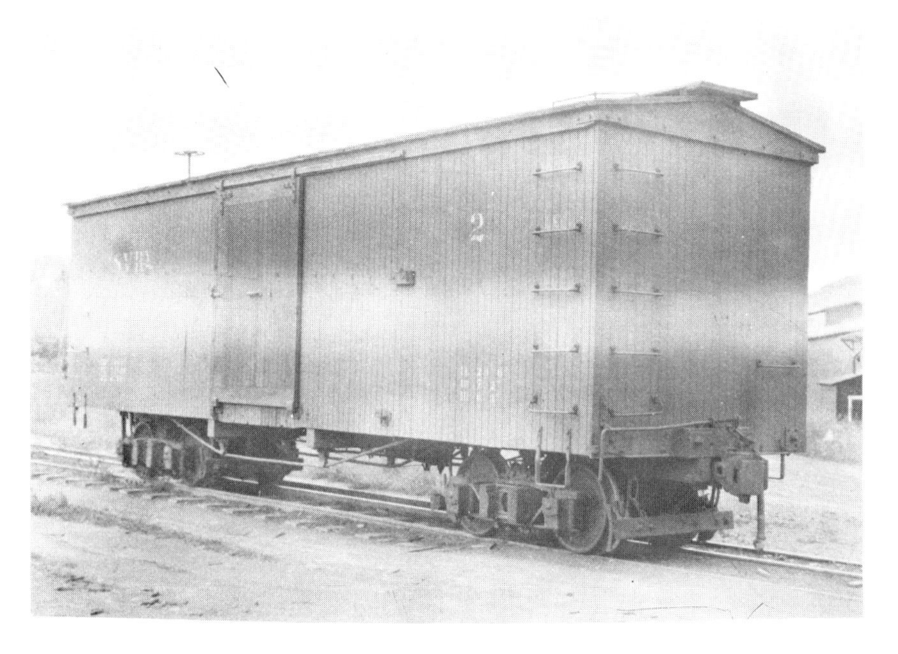

Utah & Northern freight cars were scattered throughout the west after standard gauging. The gondola above went to the Sumpter Valley, and then to the Eureka Nevada, where Ted Wurm photographed it in 1938 — still lettered "S.V. 107." The Sumpter Valley box car no. 2 at left, photographed by Albert Farrow in 1946, had been a U&N insulated box. Sumpter Valley box car no. 1159, whose remains were recorded by John R. Cummings at Whitney, Oregon, in 1964, had been U&N 25792, a 27-foot car of 20,000 lbs. capacity. (All, Author's Collection)

Acknowledgements and Bibliography

Although I had learned first of the Utah Northern many years ago, my interest in the line was renewed later when, as a co-pilot on the "milk run" from Great Falls, Montana to Salt Lake City, I could look down and see portions of the abandoned grade, near the present Union Pacific line that extends north from Ogden to Pocatello, Idaho Falls and Butte. In the mid-1960's, while writing *Rails Sagebrush & Pine*, the story of Oregon's Sumpter Valley Railway, I was able to locate information on the Utah & Northern lines as well as valuable roster material and photographs. The Sumpter Valley had been equipped initially in 1890 with cars and locomotives from the recently standard gauged Utah & Northern.

At this time I had the good fortune to meet the late Arthur Petersen of Pocatello. Art was of invaluable aid in locating historical data and photographs of the line, as well as in driving and hiking over most of the abandoned grade that I had seen from the air. Art was the driving force behind what soon became a project to set down on paper the history of the Utah & Northern.

A great deal of new material was found in the files of the Utah Historical Society. My schedule was such that I could accomplish the necessary research while on Salt Lake City layovers with the airline. Mr. Barry B. Combs was most helpful in locating data and photographs from the Union Pacific Railroad's archives in Omaha.

Robert W. Richardson, the Museum's "Abandoned Lines Reporter," was always able to turn up some tid-bit of knowledge on the Utah & Northern as well as a yellowing file of paperwork to prove his point.

The late Don H. Roberts of Portland did much of the original work in developing the complex locomotive roster, with aid and cooperation from such other pioneers in locomotive archeology as A. L. Lillibridge, Gerald Best and Dr. S. R. Wood. Cornelius W. Hauck located additional information with the assistance of others such as Art Wallace, John Buvinger, Edward Bond and H. L. Goldsmith, and assembled the data into the form in which we have presented it here.

Henry R. Griffiths of Boise was of especial help in locating older views of the Utah & Northern and providing his own excellent comparative views in modern times. Others who assisted in providing photos are noted in the captions.

I am also indebted to artist Mike Pearsall, who took time off from his busy painting schedule to produce the fine watercolor interpretation of a U&N doubleheader reproduced on the dust jacket.

It was Gordon Chappell who had prompted me to begin the task of assembling my scattered notes and formalizing my research, towards preparing a manuscript for a future COLORADO RAIL ANNUAL. Gordon continued to assist in tracking down needed data as well as in preparing the manuscript for submission to the COLORADO RAIL ANNUAL. Editor Cornelius Hauck carried the project on from there, adding other newly discovered material and refining the text for ultimate translation into the finished product presented to you here.

Mallory Hope Ferrell

Bloomington, Minnesota

UTAH & NORTHERN BIBLIOGRAPHY

BOOKS

AMES, Charles Edgar — *Pioneering the Union Pacific*: A Reappraisal of the Builders of the Railroad. Appleton-Century-Crofts, New York, 1969.

ARRINGTON, Leonard J. — *The Great Basin Kingdom*, University of Nebraska Press.

ATHEARN, Robert G. — *Union Pacific Country*, Rand McNally & Co. New York, 1971.

BAILEY, W. F. — *The Story of the First Transcontinental RR*: Its Projectors, Construction and History. The Pittsburgh Printing Co., Pittsburgh, Pa. 1906.

BEAL, Merrill D. — *Intermountain Railroads*: Standard and Narrow Gauge, The Caxton Printers, Ltd., Caldwell, Ida. 1962.

COMBS, Barry B. — *Westward To Promontory*: Building the Union Pacific Across the Plains and Mountains, American West Publishing Co., Palo Alto, Calif. 1969.

DAGGETT, Stuart — *Railroad Reorganization,* Houghton, Mifflin & Co., New York, 1908.

DAVIS, John Patterson — *The U.P. Railway*: A study in railway politics history and economics. The Lakeside Press, R. R. Donnelley & Sons Co., Chicago and S. C. Griggs & Co., Chicago, 1894.

DECKER, Leslie E. — *Railroads, Land, and Politics*: The Taxation of the Railroad Land Grants, 1864-1897. Brown University Press, Providence, R. I., 1964.

DODGE, Grenville M. — *How We Built The Union Pacific Railway*: and other papers and addresses. The Monarch Printing Co., Council Bluffs, Iowa. Reprinted by Sage Books, Denver, Colo. 1965.

FERRELL, Mallory Hope — *Rails, Sagebrush & Pine*: The Sumpter Valley Railway. Golden West Books, San Marino, Calif., 1967.

FOGEL, Robert William — *The Union Pacific Railroad:* A case in Premature Enterprise. The Johns Hopkins Press, Baltimore, Md. 1960.

GALLOWAY, John Debo — *The First Transcontinental Railroad*: Central Pacific — Union Pacific. The Simmons-Boardman Publishing Co., New York, 1950.

GRISWOLD, Wesley S. — *A Work of Giants*: Building the First Transcontinental Railroad. McGraw-Hill Book Co., New York, 1962.

HANEY, Lewis Henry — *A Congressional History of Railways in the United States,* 1850-1887. University of Wisconsin, Madison, Wisc. 1910.

HAZARD, Rowland — *The Credit Mobilier of America.* Pub. by Sidney S. Rider, Providence, R. I., 1881.

HOWARD, Robert West — *The Great Iron Trail*: The story of the First Transcontinental Railroad. G. P. Putnam's Sons, New York, 1962.

KENNAN, George — *E. H. Harriman*: A Biography (2 Vols.) The Riverside Press, Cambridge, Mass. 1922.

McCAGUE, James — *Moguls and Iron Men*: The story of the First Transcontinental Railroad. Harper & Row, New York, 1964.

McCAGUE, James — *When The Rails Ran West.* Garrard Pub. Co., Champaign, Ill. 1967.

MILLER, David E. — *The Golden Spike,* edited by Mr. Miller, Utah State Historical Society, University of Utah Press, Salt Lake City, Ut. 1973. (Chapter VI, "Utah Northern RR, The" by Lawrence G. Lashbrook, covering 1871-78.)

POOR, Henry V. — *Poor's Manual of Railroads,* H. V. and H. W. Poor, New York, 1871-1890.

PACIFIC TRIALS — *Report of the Pacific Railway Commission*: to the U.S. Senate. (Hearings, Transcript) United States Government Printing Office. p. 572-2173. (University of Colorado Business Library, Boulder, Colorado.)

SABIN, Edwin L. — *Building the Pacific Railroad,* J. B. Lippincott Co., Philadelphia, Pa. 1919.

THOMAS, Janet — *This Side of the Mountain,* Harris Pub. Co., Idaho Falls, Ida. 1975.

TROTTMAN, Nelson — *History of the Union Pacific*: A Financial and Economic Survey. The Ronald Press, New York, 1923.

UTLEY, Robert M. — *Golden Spike,* National Park Service, Historical Handbook Series, No. 40, Department of Interior, Washington, D. C. 1969.

WHITE, Henry Kirke — *History of the Union Pacific Railway,* The University of Chicago Press, Chicago, Ill. 1895.

ARTICLES

ATHEARN, Robert G. — *Railroad To A Far Off Country. Montana Magazine* Vol. XVIII, No. 4, Autumn 1968.

COMBS, Barry B. — *The Union Pacific Railroad:* and the Early Settlement of Nebraska, 1868-1880. *Nebraska History* Vol. 50, p. 1-21, Nebraska State Historical Society, 1969.

FARNHAM, Wallace D. — "The Weakened Spring of Government: A Study in 19th Century American History." *The American Historical Review,* Vol. LXVIII, No. 3, April 1963, p. 662-680. The MacMillan Co., New York.

FARNHAM, Wallace D. — "The Pacific Railroad Act of 1862." *Nebraska History,* Vol. 43, p. 141-167, Sept. 1962, Nebraska State Hist. Soc. 1962.

HENRY, Robert S. — "The Railroad Land Grant Legend," Mississippi Valley Historical Review, Sept. 1945.

LEONARD, L. O. — "The First Railroad Entering Montana." *Union Pacific Magazine,* June 1926, Omaha, Nebraska.

SIMMONDS, A. J. — "Cause of Death — Lynching." *Railroads & The Old West* Magazine, Western Frontier Series. Summer, 1974.

NEWSPAPERS AND PERIODICALS

SALT LAKE *HERALD,* Salt Lake City, Utah.

RAILWAY AGE

RAILWAY GAZETTE

OGDEN JUNCTION, Ogden, Utah.

CORINNE DAILY REPORTER, Corinne, Utah.

TAHOE DAILY TRIBUNE, Lake Tahoe, California.

DESERET NEWS, Salt Lake City, Utah.

UTAH REPORTER, Corinne, Utah.

ROCKY MOUNTAIN NEWS, Denver, Colorado.

SALT LAKE TRIBUNE & MINING GAZETTE, Salt Lake City, Utah.

UTAH MINING JOURNAL, Salt Lake City, Utah.

DIARIES

BOURKE, John Gregory — Lt. U.S. Calvary (6th); Aide-de-camp to B. General George Crook, Dept. of the Platte. Original diaries, West Point, N. Y., USMA Library. Microfilm at University of New Mexico Library, Colorado Room, Albuquerque, N. M. (From Dr. Stanley Rhine and Gordon S. Chappell) Vol. 26 1878.

HOGAN, Goudy — Diary of a Utah pioneer of 1848. Original at L.D.S. Church Archives, Salt Lake City, Utah.

PAPERS

YOUNG, John W. — "Railroad Letter File" L. D. S. Church Historian's Office, Salt Lake City, Utah. Letter dated: April 10, 1872 (Utah Northern) Telegrams: June 5, 1872; Nov. 30, 1872 (from Joseph Richardson.) Feb. 26, 1872 (from William B. Preston.) Letter: July 26, 1872 (from Samuel T. Hauser, et al.)

YOUNG, Brigham — "Cash Ledger Books." Vol. 3 (1871-1877) "Utah Northern Account" p. 260. University of Utah Library Archives, Provo, Utah.

UTAH NORTHERN — Articles of Incorporation, August 23, 1871, Utah State Archives, Salt Lake City, Utah.

UTAH IDAHO & MONTANA — Articles of Incorporation, April 13, 1872, Utah State Archives, Salt Lake City, Utah.

UNION PACIFIC — Letterbooks covering Utah & Northern operations, 1880 period. Library, Colorado Railroad Museum, Golden, Colorado.

PUBLISHED REPORTS

Daughters of Utah Pioneers: "Utah Railroads," Kate B. Carter, Nov. 1966, p. 137-192.

Oregon Short Line: "Utah Northern and Utah & Northern:" June 30, 1916, Union Pacific Railroad. Prepared in accordance with I.C.C. Valuation Order No. 20. (Author's Collection.)

Report of the Directors of the Union Pacific Railroad, to the Sect'y of the Interior, 1881, p. 1093-1102: "Utah Northern RR", U.P. RR, Omaha, Neb. (PAM:4537, Utah Hist. Society files)

Timetable: Union Pacific, Employees (various: 1884-1915) Utah State Historical files, Salt Lake City, Utah.

Oregon Historical Quarterly: Vol. XLVLL, No. 3, Sept. 1947, "The Utah & Northern Railway Company; a brief history" by Robert L. Wrigley, Jr.

Utah Historical Quarterly: Vol. 37, Winter 1969, p. 14 "Corinne" by Brigham D. and Betty M. Madsen.

OTHER

PETERSEN, Arthur — Collected letters to the author in reference to the Utah & Northern. 1960-1976.

REEDER, Clarence A., Jr. — *History of Utah's Railroads.* Unpublished PhD dissertation, University of Utah, 1970.

Cornelius W. Hauck

OSL&UN

With the coming of standard gauge to the U&N came a new corporation — the Oregon Short Line & Utah Northern, combining most of the UP properties in Utah, Idaho and Montana. In the late 1880's the narrow gauge was still evident in the photo of the Pocatello yards and roundhouse above *(Idaho Historical Society Collection)*, although minimally — one narrow gauge steamer sandwiched in between the wide gauge power, and a third rail in the yards trackage. In the George H. Sanderson view below *(Collection of Mallory Hope Ferrell)*, the string of standard gauge power can be seen in better detail — older Taunton tenwheelers from the OSL at left, and new Grant and Baldwin eightwheelers for the U&N at right. These were the principal main line power for the two sections of the OSL&UN, but the OSL brought older power to the roster also — witness the two opposite. No. 589 (top) was an 1866 product of Grant and had been UP no. 43, before becoming OSL no. 4 and then OSL&UN 589. OSL&UN no. 368 (below) had been UP 49, then Utah Southern no. 2 and Utah Central no. 15. Another Grant, of 1868 vintage, this engine retained more of its original appearance than the largely rebuilt 589. *(Both, C. H. Peake Collection)*

589
Union Pacific
589

368

With standard gauging of the U&N to Butte came new motive power in the form of a large group of eightwheelers delivered by Baldwin (above) and Grant (below). Subsequently, additional 4-4-0's of similar design came from the Rome Works (New York Locomotive Works) — for the new joint-ownership Montana Union RR in 1887 (top, opposite, at Garrison) and the OSL and U&N system in 1888 (below, at Pocatello). (Upper right, Montana Historical Society Coll.; others, Arthur Petersen Collection from Mallory Hope Ferrell)

4

699
699
699
Union Pacific

Tenwheelers initially made their appearance on the OSL when it was built across southern Idaho. OSL&UN no. 972, shown here at Dillon about 1889, was a Taunton product of 1881 and had earlier been UP 234 and OSL 17. (Beaverhead County Museum Collection) The tenwheeler quickly emerged as preferred power for the merged OSL&UN system, and new larger 4-6-0's arrived from Rhode Island and Cooke. Opposite, top, is near-new no. 1419 on the table at Spring Hill (now Lima), not long after its 1890 delivery from the Rhode Island works. Two others of the series are shown below about 1900, on a freight north of Pocatello. Helper 644 was an 1891 Cooke product and road engine 630 an 1891 Rhode Island; both of these OSL engines were originally OSL&UN 1400-class and were equipped with 51" drivers, marking them as "cut-downs" favored for heavy freight. (Both, Arthur Petersen Collection)

1610

The need for heavier power on the difficult helper assignments up the Monida grade, over the Bitter Root Mountains, became evident in the early 1890's so ten heavy 2-8-0's (Cooke 1890) were transferred from the UP for this service. Here no. 1605 is pictured on the fragile-looking trestle at High Bridge; a couple of brakemen are enjoying the trip back down the hill from rather perilous perches on the back of the tender. Page opposite, UP 1610 is posed on a low trestle in Beaver Canyon; the old narrow gauge grade can be seen behind the engine. (Both views, Arthur Petersen Collection) Below, the same no. 1610 is seen waiting at Monida, between the water tank and depot; a coach is set out at the tail of the wye in the distance. The engine has probably just helped a train up the long grade. (C. H. Peake Collection)

Concurrent with formation of the OSL&UN was the completion of a handsome new depot for Ogden (below, Utah State Historical Society) which served until it was burned down in 1923. Less spectacular but at least as functional was the little frame depot at Willard, Utah, shown here shortly after the change of gauge in 1890. Antique engines continued in branch line service for years; no. 550 shown at top, opposite, at Preston, Idaho, about 1895 was a Norris product of 1867. (Both, Arthur Petersen Collection from Mallory Hope Ferrell) Bottom, eightwheelers still saw some main line use as late as 1905, as is shown by this snowy view of "old Beaver," now Spencer. (C. H. Peake Collection)

550

Thunder and Steam in Beaver Canyon: *A pair of the Union Pacific's mightiest blast smoke to the heavens as they battle the 2.33% grade in Beaver Canyon, climbing toward the crest of the Bitter Root Range at Monida with a heavy Oregon Short Line passenger destined for Butte. Snow and bright sunshine and tall pines provide a contrasting setting for this dramatic 1915 action scene. (Coll. of Henry R. Griffiths)*

Union Pacific
Montana Division

by Cornelius W. Hauck

The Union Pacific's decision to convert the Utah & Northern to standard gauge was prompted by the recognition of two major factors. First, it was apparent that the heavy traffic flowing over the U&N into and out of Montana could more efficiently and expeditiously be handled by a standard gauge line — a factor of increasing urgency with the coming of the standard gauge Northern Pacific as a competitor in the Butte area. And second, freight traffic flow no longer followed the original U&N line to Ogden, but was directed east from Pocatello over the Oregon Short line — supplies and manufactured goods from the east and coal from the UP's Wyoming mines into Montana, and ore and stock and lumber moving eastward — which meant that virtually all freight had to transfer gauge at Pocatello. Thus the original U&N line from McCammon to Ogden was not converted to standard gauge until October 1, 1890 (in large part on an entirely new grade), over three years after the July 24, 1887 conversion of the Butte line.

This fundamental change in the pattern of traffic and service over the Ogden-Pocatello-Butte route can be seen in the passenger schedules of that period also. The July 1890 schedule called for a day express between Pocatello and Butte on about a 10½ hour running time:

#601				#602
1:45 PM	LV	Pocatello	AR	11:45 PM
12:05 AM	AR	Butte	LV	1:00 PM

A "through night express" (part narrow gauge, part standard gauge) was also carded between Ogden and Butte:

#603				#604
6:45 PM	LV	Ogden	AR	5:30 PM
1:00 PM	AR	Butte	LV	7:50 PM

The seeming slowness of this schedule (especially southbound) was not the fault of the narrow gauge connection, but was due primarily to long layovers at Pocatello — 1½ hours northbound, 4 hours southbound; actual running times were 16¾ and 17½ hours respectively. The schedules were so arranged to provide convenient connections with east-west Oregon Short Line trains at Pocatello. Eventually the Ogden-Pocatello line developed greater importance as a route between Utah and the Pacific Northwest rather than Montana. Old relationships established in pioneer days do not die easily, however, and through succeeding decades Salt Lake City and Ogden continued to have commercial ties with western Montana, and these were eventually strengthened when the West developed as an important market for stock and agricultural products from Montana and Idaho. Thus a through Salt Lake-Butte Pullman was a constant in UP passenger service until its demise a decade ago.

A financial step taken on August 1, 1889 was the combining of a number of UP subsidiaries into a single corporate entity — the Oregon Short Line & Utah Northern Railway Co. Not only did this new company include the OSL and U&N in its title, but other UP properties such as the Utah Central and Utah Southern, reaching as far southwest as Frisco, Utah (halfway to present-day Las Vegas). The partially-owned Oregon Railway & Navigation Co. was operated by the OSL&UN under lease. The company was reorganized on February 9, 1897, as simply the Oregon Short Line Railroad, concurrent with the emergence of the UP System from the protracted bankruptcy of the mid-1890's. Beginning with 1,399 miles of track, the OSL&UN and OSL expanded over the years, largely through the construction of branches, until 1903, when the 512 miles of trackage south of Salt Lake City (reaching as far as Caliente, Nevada) were spun off to the San Pedro, Los Angeles & Salt Lake, reducing the total mileage to near 1,500.

Along with corporate consolidation came the consolidation of facilities. Pocatello was clearly the logical operating center for the OSL&UN system, and management lost little time in making it that. A large, 2½ story frame station building had been erected in 1882, and later a private company (which sold out to the OSL in 1902) erected the equally large, frame Pacific Hotel adjacent. Immediately after the July 24, 1887 standard gauging the U&N began moving the repair and shop facilities at Eagle Rock to Pocatello — first the machine shop and forge shop, then the car shop, followed by other facilities — and these formed the nucleus for the extensive OSL&UN and OSL terminal, roundhouse and shop installations that were developed at Pocatello.

Pocatello boomed with the rapid growth of traffic over the OSL&UN in the late 1880's and early 1890's. A temporary peak in traffic and revenues came in 1890-1891, however, and then the OSL&UN was affected by the general depression that gripped the West during the mid-1890's. The Silver Panic crash of 1893 and looming reality of bankruptcy induced the railroad's management to embark on a stringent expense-cutting program headlined in the Pocatello newspaper as "A Spasm of Economy." The article reported that:

> Retrenchment is the order of the day that has been issued from the Union Pacific headquarters, and the next thirty days will show a material reduction in the number of employees of the system . . . The retrenchment order struck Pocatello with force. The shop men went onto the eight hour system first. Then came the new timetable which took effect this week. It pulled off the day train each way on the Utah and Northern between here and Butte, leaving only one train a day each way . . . Then the dispatchers at Pocatello got it in the neck. Four were laid off . . . Every day the section men are being fired by the dozen, until it seems that nothing remains but the section foreman.

Despite the temporary gloom in Pocatello, the traffic from Montana held up relatively well in the 1890's. Although Montana's early mines were oriented towards gold and silver, the emergence of Butte as a copper-mining district after 1882 tended to insulate the State from the worst effects of the silver crash. The value of copper production had exceeded that of silver by 1890, and the production of 56,877,000 pounds of copper in 1892 put Montana ahead of Michigan as the nation's top producer for the first time. Montana metal production, instead of declining, climbed in value:

1884	$14,803,000
1889	36,686,000
1894	38,191,000
1899	68,457,000

Marcus Daly's great Anaconda mine at Butte was in large part responsible for this excellent record in difficult times.

Stock raising provided another steady source of traffic for the OSL&UN. Eastern Montana (the plains) had suffered through a violent boom-bust cycle in 1880-1886 that ended in overgrazing, drought and ruin for many ranchers. But the sheltered valleys of western Montana supported a steady economy of stock raising, and the cattle and sheep came in to summer ranges and went out to market in railroad stock cars. Lumbering provided another gradually growing source of traffic; timbers going up to the Butte mines, and finished lumber going out to metropolitan markets. Agriculture offered still another emerging and attractive generator of revenues, particularly in northern Idaho. Here the rich, volcanic soils in the broad plain of the Snake River valley combined with modern irrigation practices yielded bumper crops of wheat, potatoes, hay, sugar beets and other products.

Thus, when the Union Pacific System emerged from bankruptcy in 1897, under the direction of Edward H. Harriman, the OSL's Montana Division presented an attractive picture, and was included in the forefront of Harriman's plans for upgrading the system. One area needing attention was the motive power roster. When the Oregon Short Line was begun in 1882, it received a motley assortment of about 30 used locomotives from the parent UP; these included a large number of eightwheelers of ancient vintage — two Norris of 1865, a large group of 1866 Grants, and some odds and ends from Hinkley & Williams, Moore & Co. and others — plus an assorted group of Taunton tenwheelers, some old and some new. Six more new Taunton 4-6-0's were obtained in 1883. When the U&N was standard-gauged in 1887, it was equipped with 25 new Baldwin and Grant eightwheelers (nos. 726-735, 746-760, later OSL 300-324). This assorted fleet was inadequate for the burgeoning traffic on the lines, and upon formation of the OSL&UN most of the old power was scrapped or set aside for branch line duty, and 61 new tenwheelers of standardized design were purchased from Rhode Island and Cooke in 1890 and 1891. Numbered 1416 up (later OSL 600 series), the freight versions had drivers of 62″ diameter and some of 51″ (called "cut-downs"), and passenger engines had 69″. These locomotives were standard power for the Montana Division for the entire decade, although later some Cooke 2-8-0's of the 1600-1610 series were borrowed from the UP for helper duty on the Monida grade.

The Harriman administration provided the next motive power upheaval. Between 1899 and 1902 heavier 4-6-0's were added for passenger — 16 from Cooke and 10 from Baldwin, the latter compounds — and the 2-8-0 became the standard freight engine (except for 7 Cooke 4-8-0's). Over 100 consolidations were purchased in the 1898-1908 decade, mostly from Baldwin; 30 of the latter were compounds, all of which were converted to simple (or disposed of) by 1917. The compounds had 16 & 27x30 cylinders; when converted, 21x30, as had 8 Cookes. These were numbered 950-979 and 1000-1004; in 1915 they were renumbered 510-539 and 550-554. Larger were 63 Baldwins and Alcos numbered 1010-1072 (1915, 560-622) with 22x30 cylinders, greater weight (187,000 lbs. on drivers vs 165,000 lbs.) and considerably greater tractive power. All freight was handled by 2-8-0's in the 1900-1915 period, with 2-8-0's and the 4-8-0's used as helpers. As branch lines were expanded in the years before World War I the smaller 2-8-0's (and 4-8-0's) were diverted to these lines, and all traffic north of Idaho Falls (formerly Eagle Rock) was handled by the larger 2-8-0's. Ratings of these engines in 1915 going north ("westward" timetable direction) from Pocatello to Idaho Falls were 1800 tons for the old tenwheelers, 2100 tons for the 21x30 2-8-0's and compounds, and 3000 tons for the larger 560 (former 1010) class. The 560's were rated 1850 tons Idaho Falls to Lima, Montana, with two 560 helpers from Dubois to Monida (on the border at the top of the pass), or 2400 tons with one 560 helper Camas to Dubois and *three* helpers Dubois to Monida. They were again rated 3000 tons from Lima to Dillon, 2100 tons Dillon to Silver Bow with single helpers Dillon-Apex and Divide-Feely. One 560 was rated at 1080 tons Silver Bow to Butte. Going south was not "all down hill" either; a 560 was rated at only 1250 tons from Silver Bow to Dillon, with a helper Silver Bow to Feely and another Glen to Apex; 1250 tons unassisted Dillon to Lima; and 2000 tons Lima to Idaho Falls, with a 560 helper Lima to Monida. The roller-coaster profile of the old U&N provided many opportunities for helper districts, and not a few thrills for engine and train crews from time to time.

Although the U&N had projected many branches and extensions into other parts of Montana, none were ever built. However, the development of Idaho north of Pocatello led to the construction of a profusion of branches there in the 1900-1915 period. Among the earliest and most important were the lines from Blackfoot to Mackay and from Idaho Falls to Rexburg and St. Anthony. The latter line was extended in 1906 to Marysville, just beyond Ashton, and in 1907-08 to West Yellowstone; in 1912-1913 another branch was pushed south from Ashton to Victor. Other shorter branches tapped important agricultural areas.

Pocatello, operational center for the whole Oregon Short Line system, benefited from a continuous stream of capital improvements and expansion projects in the Harriman period. New shop facilities were added in 1902, and ice houses (important for the growing fruit and agricultural traffic) expanded to 12,000 tons capacity — all coming from Market Lake to the north (present-day Roberts). In the next half-dozen years a handsome 35-stall brick roundhouse replaced the old 1883 structure; a new car shop, office building, coal and scrap bins were added; and a new water system installed with a two million gallon reservoir, 26,864 feet of pipe line, and pumping machinery, all costing $110,750. In 1913 15 stalls of the engine house had to be enlarged by 30 feet to accommodate larger engines, and a new all-steel "conveyor-type" coaling station of 900 tons capacity, serving five tracks, replaced the old wooden tower. The following year saw addition of a new concrete, brick and steel "shop plant" including boiler and coach shop of 180x244 feet, a paint shop of 106x187 feet, a wood-working mill, a tin and copper-smith shop, an addition to the power house and various minor buildings. Roundhouse expansion continued in 1916 with the addition of 18 more 96-foot stalls to the existing 35, and in 1917 14 of the old 80-foot stalls were lengthened to 96 feet also, along with the expansion of the coach and boiler shop and the machine shop and construction of a brick plating and upholstery shop.

Biggest event to occur in Pocatello for several decades, however, was the construction of a new passenger depot. The old frame depot of 1882 had long since become inadequate for the tremendous volume of passenger business enjoyed by Pocatello, and it was no longer looked upon as an aesthetically suitable civic monument for the growing city. In fact, it appears to have been regarded as something of a prehistoric eyesore, even though it was only 33 years old. Shortly before its retirement and removal the newspaper published these amusing comments:

OLD DEPOT

Perhaps there is no community in the west that has been damned so much for its depot as has Pocatello, and in these days when it will soon be passing into decline, there is much of amusement, much of railroad history, and considerable of operation woven into the material that forms this dried old structure.

W. H. Bancroft, former general manager, and still vice president of the road, good humoredly referred to the creaky old structure as "the only fireproof building in Idaho," and up to this time, with engines spouting hot cinders over its stained roof a hundred times a day, and with its wooden patchwork and partitions, the expression of the veteran head of the road still remains to be disputed.

Back in those days when Pocatello was beginning to feel its oats as the gateway to a great western empire, and the stakes were being driven to throw steel over the routes that Chief Pocatello had made when he had clear sailing, that old depot was a great institution.

Since that time it has also served as a great institution, as it has attracted attention toward Pocatello. In this later day that attention simmered down to this division point on the Union Pacific system having the worst station in the world. People knew it from Podunk to Yuba Dam.

All of which helped — and the structure still remained fireproof.

But with the passing of the old regime a good many memories undoubtedly cling to the old crib. Many railroaders who got their first clearance ticket in that old structure, and have since grown high in the service, will doubtless smile indulgently at the thought that the old place served its purpose well, and while it was for rather an extended period, it did the business.

But as the splendid new $325,000 structure is beginning to throw its shadows over the yards, and will by the middle of summer be handling thousands of people daily, the after advertising effect of the old station house will become manifest, and passing throngs will recall former conditions, when Pocatello had the worst depot service on earth, and the contrast will be drawn in the magnificent new structure, and eyes will be opened to the public that in all those years of development of the system the heads of the Short Line were clear and saw the advantages of Pocatello, and today have backed up that faith by permanent and pronounced investment.

The final paragraph must set some sort of a record for non-stop, long-winded, undecipherable single sentences, humorous or not. Actually, the old depot was a "complex" of two structures, side by side: the first was a rather handsome three-story affair that housed the telegraph office, express office and baggage room on the first floor, and Idaho Division offices on the second floor; the second, a nondescript two-story frame, housed the ticket office and waiting room on the ground floor and Montana Division offices above. Immediately beyond was the Pacific Hotel, which had a "beanery" on the ground floor, completing the panoply of services offered to the harried traveler.

The new depot, looked forward to with such eager anticipation by Pocatello's citizenry, was dedicated with a grand opening ceremony on August 20, 1915; the structure was bedecked with flags and bunting, and a large parade through downtown Pocatello ended "with Mayor George Williams giving a speech in front of the depot before a crowd of several thousand." It was certainly an impressive and substantial building — of brick, concrete and steel, with stone trim and facing, the cost was said to be $325,000. The three-story center section of 75x90 feet included a 41x86 foot waiting room, and there were two-story wings each of 60x80 feet, plus a heating plant, concourse and platforms, and the like. Little wonder that the new edifice was, as the newspaper put it, "hailed with satisfaction by the people of this city, as well as by the traveling public at large."

Many improvements were made at stations along the line as well. In recognition of its growing importance as well as junction point for the new Yellowstone Branch, Idaho Falls received a fine new one-and-two-story brick and stone depot in 1911, as well as a new freight house. In 1914 McCammon received a new frame depot (the old one was converted into a freight house) and a new interlocking plant at the junction. Also in 1914 Blackfoot gained a new, $27,000 stone depot with steam heat and electric lights, plus a two-stall brick enginehouse with 350,000 gallon steel water tank. A major operational improvement was made in 1917, however, when automatic block signals were installed between Cache Junction, Utah, and McCammon; from Pocatello to Fort Hall (later extended to Idaho Falls); and over the difficult stretch through Beaver Canyon between Spencer and Humphrey.

During the periods of economic stringency and light traffic in the 1890's, only one passenger train was operated each way through to Butte much of the time. By the turn of the century two trains were again in vogue, but only intermittently. For instance, in the spring of 1905 only the "night" train ran through; northbound it left Salt Lake City at 11:45 PM, Pocatello 7:00 AM the next morning, arriving at Butte at 4:00 PM; returning it left Butte at 5:00 PM and reached Salt Lake City at 8:40 AM. The former day train now ran from Salt Lake City only as far as Idaho Falls, and thence up to Rexburg and St. Anthony on that important new branch. The November timetable, however, reinstituted the second Butte train (an arrangement that would now last for over three decades), but the schedule was hardly one designed to be popular in Butte: arrival and departure times were both 2:45 AM! This seemingly zany scheduling was actually dictated by the need to make connections at Pocatello with nos. 1 and 2, the *Overland Limited*, for connections to Chicago. As can be seen in the accompanying timetable reprinting, these schedules were rationalized somewhat by 1911 — in part by making them slower! And in addition to the two Butte and Salt Lake expresses (nos. 1 & 2, 3 & 4), there was now an *Idaho Express* and *Utah Express* (nos. 13-113 and 114-14) on a daytime schedule between Salt Lake City, Pocatello, Idaho Falls and Rexburg-St. Anthony to do much of the local work. By the 1915-1916 period schedules had been refined further; nos. 1 and 2 (now the *Butte Express*) were slightly faster and carried through drawing room sleepers between Salt Lake City and Butte and Ashton (just beyond St. Anthony on the Yellowstone branch), as well as an observation sleeper from Butte to Los Angeles southbound, and a diner. The observation sleeper came north on no. 9, formerly no. 3, now the *Butte Special*. No. 4 became no. 10, the *Salt Lake Special*, on a new daytime schedule, carrying a sleeper (presumably for parlor car service) and diner. Times terminal-to-terminal were as follows in 1916:

9	1		2	10
2:45 PM	11:45 PM	Salt Lake City	8:15 AM	10:10 PM
6:45 AM	4:55 PM	Butte	5:05 PM	7:00 AM

In addition, there was the Salt Lake City-Pocatello-Idaho Falls-Ashton day train, now simply nos. 13 and 14, plus another Salt Lake City-Pocatello night train, nos. 31 and 32. The day train carried a cafe-parlor car both ways, and nos. 9 and 31 going north (timetable "westbound") and nos. 2, 14 and 32 south ("eastbound") carried Salt Lake City-Pocatello Pullmans for Portland, Boise and Buhl via connecting trains.

By 1919 nos. 1 and 2 had become nos. 31 and 32, the *Butte Express*, and 9 and 10 were now 29 and 30, the *Butte and Portland Special* westbound (north) and *Salt Lake Special* eastbound. Both runs offered Pullmans (12 section, drawing room), chair cars and coaches, and dining cars. Old 31 and 32 were now nos. 33 and 34, the *Northwest Express*, and the Salt Lake City-Pocatello run was now extended to Ashton. This "overnight local" handled Portland, Buhl and Ashton sleepers. The day train was now numbered 41 and 42; the old names *Idaho Express* and *Utah Express* were back but the cafe-parlor car was gone. Connecting trains reached out over the branch lines, and important branches like the Idaho Falls-Rexburg-Ashton branch and the OSL's Minidoka-Twin Falls-Buhl branch — had twice-daily service. In addition, summertime saw operation of the deluxe *Yellowstone Special* overnight between Salt Lake City and Yellowstone (West Yellowstone station).

These basic schedules were maintained without significant change all through the twenties. Terminal departure times were adjusted ahead or back minor amounts from time to time, but running times remained virtually unchanged throughout the period. A through Los Angeles-Butte full sleeper was added (although probably most passengers got off or on somewhere en route), but nos. 29 and 30 lost the dining car (meals were taken at Pocatello or Lima, in the depot restaurant). It was a period of stability and predictability.

The twenties were not a period of growth for Montana. Although the population of Silver Bow County (Butte area) increased from 60,300 to 64,800 between 1920 and 1928, Beaverhead County, through which the line passed from Monida to Feely in Deer Lodge Pass, 10 miles from Butte, decreased in population from 7,200 to 5,000 in the period. Copper mining had enjoyed a huge boom during the World War I years; production (virtually all from Silver Bow County) reached 352 million pounds in 1916 and 326 million in 1918. Production was almost halved in the following two years, and plunged to only 48 million pounds in the depression year of 1921. Output quickly bounced back and ranged between 225 and 270 million pounds annually through the 1923-1928 period. Zinc production was even more volatile; from an average of over 100,000 tons annually in 1916-1918 output dropped to 11,600 tons in 1921, with totals ranging from 51,000 to 73,000 in succeeding years. Lead production was somewhat more stable; after many years of low production output jumped in 1918 to 18,500 tons and declined only to 10,183 tons in 1921, thereafter averaging between 15,000 and 20,000 tons through the twenties. However, lead production came from scattered mines all over western Montana and did not provide significant traffic for the Union Pacific. Similarly silver mining (which remained stable) and gold mining (which de-

Time from 1 P. M. to 12:59 Night, Boldface Figures.

UNION PACIFIC—THE OVERLAND ROUTE

OGDEN TO BUTTE AND HELENA. (Idaho Division.)

Pass. A No. 9	Exp. A No. 5	Mls	STATIONS	Ele	Exp. A No. 4	Pass. A No. 10
3 30	**8 00**	....	Lv...**Salt Lake**...Ar	4260	**5 10**	10 50
5 30	**9 50**	0	Lv.....**Ogden**.....Ar	4301	‖ **3 10**	9 15
5 55	**10 15**	9	..Utah Hot Springs..	4275	**2 45**	8 50
6 10	* **10 30**	14	........Willard........	4338	* **2 30**	8 35
6 30	**10 50**	21	.......Brigham........	4313	**2 10**	8 20
6 55	**11 15**	31	......Honeyville......	4274	**1 45**	7 55
7 12	* **11 33**	35	.... Dewey........	4318	* **1 25**	7 40
7 20	·**11 50**	42	...... Collinston	4689	**1 10**	7 25
7 45	**12 30**	49	.... **Cache Junct**....	....	‖ 12 40	7 00
		57	.... Ransom	....		
	1 20	62	.......Cannon.......	....	11 30	
		71	........Card	....		
	2 05	75	.......Garner.......	....	10 45	
	2 25	81	.......Oxford	4766	10 22	
		100	.......Thatcher.......	4818		
		105	.... Arimo	4652		
	4 00	111	.... **McCammon**	4753	8 35	
	‖ 7 00	134	Lv... **Pocatello**...Lv	4466	‖ 7 30	
	* 7 24	146	...... Ross Fork	4450	* 4 35	
	7 50	158	..... **Black Foot**.....	4503	4 10	
	8 15	171	.... Basalt	4577		
	8 45	185	..... Eagle Rock......	4712	3 15	
	9 18	201	.....Market Lake.....	4781	2 40	
	10 00	233	.... Camas........	4822	2 00	
	11 10	252	... **Beaver Canon** ..	6023	1 05	
	11 40	264	........Monida	6807	**12 35**	
	‖ 12 40	280	.........Lima.........	6265	**12 01**	
Mixed A		303	...... Red Rock	5603	**11 00**	Mixed A
4 30	**2 37**	328	.... **Dillon**........	5104	**10 05**	**2 37**
7 00	**3 48**	359	.......**Melrose**.......	5189	**8 55**	12 30
9 40	**5 10**	390	.....**Silver Bow**..Lv	5342	**7 30**	10 15
10 10	**5 30**	397	Ar..... **Butte** Lv	5482	**7 00**	9 45
		470	Ar.... **Helena** Lv	3930	**2 45**	

CACHE VALLEY DISTRICT.

	Ex. A	Mls	STATIONS.	Ele	Pas. A	
	7 45	0	Lv... **Cache Junction** ...Ar	....	7 00	
	8 12	15	............Mendon............	....	6 35	
	8 35	22	............Logan............	....	6 15	
	9 00	30	.... Smithfield	....	5 55	
	9 17	35	.... Richmond	....	5 38	
	9 37	42	............Franklin............	....	5 20	
	10 00	49	Ar........ **Preston**... Lv	....	5 00	

A Daily. B Daily except Sunday. * Stop on Signal. ‖ Meals.

These timetable excerpts illustrate scheduling in the early years of standard gauge operation. Top left, one through train operated Salt Lake City-Butte in 1891 with evening departures and late afternoon arrivals both ways. A local between Ogden and Preston served the old main line, now the Cache Valley branch, and a mixed gave added service Dillon-Butte. By 1895 (right) the single through train now operated on a much faster schedule. There were two through trains by 1906 (bottom), and schedules were arranged to coordinate with east-west OSL trains at Pocatello.

UNION PACIFIC SYSTEM.

OREGON SHORT LINE & UTAH NORTHERN RY. AND CONNECTIONS.

Salt Lake City and Ogden to Butte and Helena.

Mix A No. 22	Exp. A No. 7	Mls	STATIONS	Ele.	Exp. A No. 2	Mix A No. 28
7.00	**5.20**	0	Lv......**Salt Lake City**......Ar	4260	10.10	**7.15**
8.05	**7.05**	37	Lv........... **Ogden**...........Ar	4301	‡ 7.30	**4.00**
8.55	**7.23**	45	........Utah Hot Springs........	4275	7.05	**3.10**
9.40	**7.48**	58	.............Brigham	4313	6.40	**2.20**
10.40	***8.17**	72	.... Dewey	4318	* 6.08	**1.20**
11.25	**8.55**	85	............**Cache Jct**............	4448	5.35	12.30
1.25	**9.58**	118	.... Oxford.............	4766	4.23	10.25
3.00	**10.55**	148	.... **McCammon**	4753	3.15	8.35
4.00	**11.45**	171	Ar......... **Pocatello** Lv	4466	2.20	7.10
	12.30	171	Lv......... **Pocatello** ....Ar	4466	1.15	
	1.16	195	............**Blackfoot**............	4503	**12.30**	
	2.00	221	.... Idaho Falls	4712	**11.42**	
	4.09	288	.........**Beaver Canon**.........	6023	**9.23**	
	4.43	301	...... Monida (Montana)........	6807	**8.48**	
	5.10	316	Ar........... Lima Lv	6265	**8.10**	
	5.15	3 6	Lv........... Lima ....Ar	6265	‡ **7.50**	
	5.54	339	............**Red Rock**	5603	**7.00**	
	6.35	364	..............**Dillon**	5104	**6.00**	
	‡ 7.55	395	.............Melrose	5189	**4.45**	
	9.00	426	Ar........**Silver Bow**........Lv	534	**3.25**	
	9.0	426	Lv. (M. U. Ry.) **Silver Bow**..Ar	5312	**3.20**	
	9.25	433	Ar......(M. U. Ry.)**Butte** . Lv	5482	**3.00**	
	3.30	433	Lv .. (M. C. Ry.)**Butte**.....Ar	5482	10.40	
	6.30	506	Ar.....(M. C. Ry.)**Helena**....Lv	3930	7.30	
	9.05	426	Lv..(M. U. Ry.) **SilverBow**..Ar	3312	8.14	
	9.30	451	.... **Stuart**.............	4995	7.52	
	11.40	459	Ar ....Anaconda..........Lv	5558	9.00	
	10.10	503	.... Deer Lodge...........	4527	7.07	
	10.30	470	Ar..........**Garrison**.........Lv	4338	6.45	
		470	Lv... (N. P. Ry.) **Garrison**. Ar	4338		
		521	Ar....... . **Helena** Lv	3930		

ECHO & PARK CITY RY.

Echo to Park City.

Mix. A No. 126	Mls	STATIONS	Ele	Mix. A No. 125
11.00	0	Lv..................... **Echo** ....Ar	5471	9.15
11.35	5	.......................**Coalville**	5583	8.50
2.00	28	Ar.................. Park City Lv	7000	7.00

* Stop on Signal. ‡ Meals. A Daily. B Daily except Sunday
Time from **1 P. M to 12.59 Night** and **Junction Points Bold Faced Type.**

		The Chi'go-Portl'd Spe'ial No. 5 Daily	The Over'd Lim. No. 1 Daily	Miles from Co.Bluffs	STATIONS (Continued from page 31-32)	Elevation	The Over'd Lim. No. 2 Daily	The Port.-Chic. Sp'l No. 6 Daily		
		10.35	10.20	827	Lv.**Green River**,Wyo(UP) Ar.	1364	**8.55**	**2.25**		
		11.30	11.15	857	Ar.**Granger**..... " " Lv.	1334	**8.03**	**1.30**		
		11.35	11.20	857	Lv.**Granger** ....(OSL) Wyo Ar.	6279	s **8.00**	s **1.30**		
		s12.25	s**12.07**	882	....Opal .... "	6681	s **7.17**	s**12.42**		
		s 2.27	s **2.00**	941	....Cokeville.............. "	6204	s **5.00**	s10.15		
		s 3.25	s **2.50**	972	....Montpelier ....Ida	5951	s **4.05**	s 9.15	Local	
Local		s 4.44	s **4.02**	1019	....Bancroft .... "	....	s **2.25**	s 7.02	No. 12	
No. 11		s 5.30	s **4.50**	1048	....**McCammon** .... "	4762	s **1.20**	s 5.45	Daily	
Daily		s 6.10	s **5.30**	1072	Ar.**Pocatello**.......... "	4466	s**12.40**	s 5.00		
4.05		**11.45**	10.30	0	Lv.**Salt Lake City** ..Utah Ar.	4260	**7.35**	8.30	11.45	
5.15		12.50	11.35	36	Ar.**Ogden**.............. " Lv.	4301	**6.20**	7.30	10.40	
5.20		1.25	**12.20**	0	Lv.**Ogden**.............. " Ar.	4301	‖ **5.55**	7.00	10.35	
f **5.43**		1.44	s**12.38**	9	....Hot Springs .... "	....	f **5.30**	6.40	s10.17	
s **6.01**		2.15	s **1.05**	21	....Brignam.............. "	....	s **5.05**	6.15	s 9.55	
6.55		s 3.25	s **2 05**	49	Ar.**Cache Junction**.. " Lv.	....	s **3.55**	s 5.20	8.55	
		s 5.45	s **4.20**	111	....**McCammon** ...... Ida....	4762	s **1.40**	s 3.15		
		s 6.20	s **5.00**	134	Ar.**Pocatello**.......... "	4466	**12.50**	2.30		
		7.00	**5.55**	1072	Lv.**Pocatello**..........Ida Ar.	4466	11.55	1.50		
		s 7.50	s **6.40**	1096	....Blackfoot .... "	4508	s11.10	s12.59		
		s 8.23	s **7.10**	1113	....Shelley .... "	....	s10.34	s12.25		
		s 8.42	s **7.27**	1121	....**Idaho Falls** .... "	4742	s10.17	s12.10		
		s 9.12	s **7.54**	1139	....Market Lake .... "	4786	s 9.45	s**11.38**		
		s10.07	s **8.53**	1172	....Dubois.............. "	....	s 8.50	s**10.48**		
		s10.42	s **9.28**	1185	....Spencer .... "	....	s 8.23	s**10.20**		
		s11.30	s**10.10**	1202	....Monida .... "	....	s 7.45	s **9.45**		
		s**12.10**	f**10.50**	1217	....Lima ....Mont....	....	s 7.05	s **9.10**		
		s**12.53**	s**11.28**	1240	....Red Rock........... "	5608	s 6.10	s **8.10**		
		s **1.35**	s12.10	1265	....Dillon .... "	5109	s 5.20	s **7.20**		
		s **2.38**	s 1.11	1296	....Melrose............ "	5194	s 4.17	s **6.12**		
		s **3.08**	s 1.36	1306	....Divide.............. "	....	s 3.51	s **5.45**		
		s **3.55**	s 2.25	1327	Ar.**Silver Bow**........ " Lv.	5442	s 3.05	s **5.00**		
		4.15	2.45	1334	Ar.**Butte**.............. " Lv.	5482	2.45	**4.45**		

NEW AND DIRECT ROUTE TO YELLOWSTONE NATIONAL PARK

UNION PACIFIC UNION PACIFIC

OREGON SHORT LINE RAILROAD CO.

Table 66.

GOING WEST						SALT LAKE CITY, OGDEN, BUTTE AND BEYOND				GOING EAST				
Motor	Cache Valley Express	Idaho Express	Butte Express	Butte Express	MILES		ROUTE	TIME	Elevation	Butte Salt Lake Express	Salt Lake Express	Utah Expres	Cache Valley Express	Motor
131- Except Sunday	11- Daily	13- Daily	1- Daily	3- Daily						2- Daily	4- Daily	14- Daily	12- Daily	132- Except Sunday
7.10	4.15	8.00	11.45	2.40	0	Lv. SALT LAKE CITY Utah Ar.	O. S. L.	M	----	10.30	4.55	10.15	11.35	6.55
8.10	5.20	9.00	12.50	3.35	36	Ar. Ogden " Lv.	"	M	----	9.30	3.55	9.15	10.30	5.50
8.25	5.25	9.15	1.15	3.50	0	Lv. Ogden " Ar.	"	M	----	9.15	3.35	9.05	10.20	4.50
* 8.35	* 5.35	* 9.25	------	------	5	Lv. Harrisville " Lv.	"	M	----	------	a	* 8.50	*10.10	* 4.35
8.42	5.42	9.32	* 1.35	------	9	Lv. Hot Springs " Lv.	"	M	----	* 8.58	a	8.40	10.02	4.27
8.51	* 5.50	* 9.38	* 1.45	------	14	Lv. Willard " Lv.	"	M	----	* 8.51	a	8.30	* 9.51	4.15
9.15	6.10	9.55	2.00	4.30	21	Lv. Brigham " Lv.	"	M	----	8.35	3.02	8.15	9.35	3.55
Arrive	* 6.23	*10.10	* 2.20	------	30	Lv. Honeyville " Lv.	"	M	----	* 8.16	a	* 7.55	* 9.15	------
------	* 6.33	*10.17	* 2.30	------	36	Lv. Dewey " Lv.	"	M	----	* 8.07	a	7.46	9.07	------
	6.42	10.25	* 2.40	------	40	Lv. Collinston " Lv.	"	M	----	* 8.00	a	7.37	9.00	------
	7.05	10.55	3.10	5.25	49	Lv. Cache Junction " Lv.	"	M	----	7.40	2.16	7.10	8.40	------
	Arrive	*11.09	* 3.30	------	57	Lv. Trenton " Lv.	"	M	----	* 7.20	a	* 6.51	------	------
	------	*11.20	* 3.40	------	62	Lv. Cornish " Lv.	"	M	----	* 7.10	a	* 6.39	------	------
	------	*11.40	* 4.10	------	71	Lv. Dayton Idaho Lv.	"	M	----	* 6.56	a	* 6.23	------	------
	------	*11.47	* 4.20	------	75	Lv. Carner " Lv.	"	M	----	* 6.48	a	* 6.15	------	------
	------	11.57	4.34	------	81	Lv. Oxford " Lv.	"	M	----	6.37	a	6.03	------	------
	------	*12.02	* 4.40	------	84	Lv. Swan Lake " Lv.	"	M	----	* 6.30	a	* 5.58	------	------
	------	12.22	* 5.05	* 6.48	95	Lv. Downey " Lv.	"	M	----	* 6.10	* 1.03	5.41	------	------
	------	*12.30	* 5.15	------	100	Lv. Virginia " Lv.	"	M	----	* 6.00	a	* 5.32	------	------
	------	*12.40	* 5.24	------	105	Lv. Arimo " Lv.	"	M	----	* 5.52	a	* 5.23	------	------
	113- Daily	12.55	6.00	7.20	111	Lv. McCammon " Lv.	"	M	----	5.40	12.25	5.10	114- Daily	------
		1.45	6.50	8.05	134	Ar. Pocatello " Ar.	"	M	----	4.50	11.35	4.25		------
	2.30	------	8.00	8.45	134	Lv. Pocatello " Ar.	"	M	----	4.00	11.10	------	1.00	------
	* 2.42	------	* 8.13	* 8.58	140	Lv. Tyhee " Lv.	"	M	----	* 3.41	*10.52	------	*12.46	------
	2.52	------	8.23	9.08	146	Lv. Ross Fork " Lv.	"	M	----	* 3.31	10.43	------	12.36	------
	* 3.02	------	* 8.32	* 9.18	151	Lv. Gibson " Lv.	"	M	----	* 3.21	*10.33	------	*12.26	------
	3.15	------	8.48	9.33	158	Lv. Blackfoot " Lv.	"	M	----	3.08	10.20	------	12.12	------
	* 3.27	------	* 8.59	* 9.44	164	Lv. Wapello " Lv.	"	M	----	* 2.53	*10.06	------	*12.01	------
	3.37	------	9.09	* 9.53	170	Lv. Firth " Lv.	"	M	----	* 2.44	9.56	------	11.49	------
	3.51	------	9.22	10.06	176	Lv. Shelley " Lv.	"	M	----	2.33	9.45	------	11.39	------
	4.10	------	9.40	10.25	184	Lv. Idaho Falls " Lv.	"	M	----	2.16	9.28	------	11.20	------
	Arrive	------	* 9.53	*10.38	191	Lv. Payne " Lv.	"	M	----	* 1.56	* 9.12	------	------	------
			*10.02	*10.47	197	Lv. Bassett " Lv.	"	M	----	* 1.49	* 9.01	------	------	------
			10.11	10.56	202	Lv. Market Lake " Lv.	"	M	----	1.39	8.52	------	------	------
			*10.29	*11.14	212	Lv. Hawgood " Lv.	"	M	----	* 1.21	* 8.32			
			*10.38	*11.23	217	Lv. Hamer " Lv.	"	M	----	* 1.13	* 8.22			
			*10.48	*11.33	223	Lv. Camas " Lv.	"	M	----	* 1.04	* 8.12			
			*10.58	*11.43	228	Lv. Jones " Lv.	"	M	----	*12.55	* 8.01			
			11.15	11.59	235	Lv. Dubois " Lv.	"	M	----	12.45	7.45			
			*11.40	*12.25	243	Lv. High Bridge " Lv.	"	M	----	*12.25	* 7.25			
			12.01	12.45	248	Lv. Spencer " Lv.	"	M	----	12.12	7.14			
			*12.35	* 1.20	258	Lv. Humphrey " Lv.	"	M	----	*11.48	* 6.52			
			12.55	1.45	265	Lv. Monida Mont. Lv.	"	M	----	11.35	6.35			
			* 1.08	* 2.02	273	Lv. Williams " Lv.	"	M	----	*11.12	* 6.16			
			1.20	2.15	280	Ar. Lima " Lv.	"	M	----	10.55	6.00			
			1.25	2.20	280	Lv. Lima " Ar.	"	M	----	10.50	5.55			
			1.40	* 2.38	288	Lv. Dell " Lv.	"	M	----	10.29	* 5.35			
			* 1.50	* 2.50	294	Lv. Crab Tree " Lv.	"	M	----	*10.14	* 5.22			
			2.04	3.05	303	Lv. Red Rock " Lv.	"	M	----	9.51	5.02			
			2.13	3.15	307	Lv. Armstead " Lv.	"	M	----	9.39	4.53			
			* 2.22	* 3.27	313	Lv. Crayling " Lv.	"	M	----	* 9.24	* 4.38			
			* 2.37	* 3.42	320	Lv. Barratt's " Lv.	"	M	----	* 9.06	* 4.21			
			2.52	4.05	328	Lv. Dillon " Lv.	"	M	----	8.45	4.05			
			* 3.03	* 4.18	334	Lv. Bond " Lv.	"	M	----	* 8.35	* 3.50			
			3.16	* 4.32	340	Lv. Apex " Lv.	"	M	----	8.25	* 3.38			
			* 3.34	* 4.50	348	Lv. Glen " Lv.	"	M	----	* 7.58	* 3.20			
			* 3.43	* 5.00	352	Lv. Lavon " Lv.	"	M	----	* 7.52	* 3.10			
			3.56	5.15	359	Lv. Melrose " Lv.	"	M	----	7.40	2.58			
			* 4.11	* 5.30	365	Lv. Big Hole " Lv.	"	M	----	* 7.23	* 2.45			
			4.26	5.44	370	Lv. Divide " Lv.	"	M	----	7.11	2.34			
			* 4.38	* 5.55	375	Lv. Woodin " Lv.	"	M	----	* 7.01	* 2.26			
			* 4.56	* 6.15	381	Lv. Feely " Lv.	"	M	----	* 6.48	* 2.13			
			* 5.06	* 6.25	385	Lv. Buxton " Lv	"	M	----	* 6.30	* 2.03			
			5.25	6.40	390	Ar. Silver Bow " Lv.	"	M	----	6.20	1.50			
			5.45	7.00	397	Ar. Butte " Lv	"	M	----	6.00	1.30			
			5.30	9.57	390	Lv. Silver Bow Ar.	B. A. & P.	M	----	12.03	------			
			6.15	10.40	410	Ar. Anaconda " Lv.	"	M	----	11.20	------			
			6.52	8.13	390	Lv. Silver Bow Ar.	N. P.	M	----	12.45	10.00			
			7.50	9.14	423	Ar. Deer Lodge " Lv.	"	M	----	11.34	8.57			
			8.20	9.30	434	Ar. Garrison " Lv.	"	M	----	11.08	8.30			
			1.30	11.35	485	Ar. Helena " Lv.	"	M	----	------	------			
			------	7.30	397	Lv. Butte " Ar.	G. N.	M	----	4.55	10.25			
			------	10.50	470	Ar. Helena " Lv.	"	M	----	1.20	6.30			

THROUGH SLEEPING CAR SERVICE BETWEEN SALT LAKE CITY AND POINTS WEST AND NORTH

WESTBOUND

To Butte, Pullman Standard Sleepers

Lv. SALT LAKE	2.40	11.45
Ar. Butte	7.00	5.45

To Buhl, Pullman Standard Sleepers

Lv. SALT LAKE	11.45	------
Ar. Buhl	1.20	------

To Boise, Pullman Standard Sleepers

Lv. SALT LAKE	2.40	8.00	11.45
Ar. Boise	4.50	11.35	5.00

To San Francisco, Calif., and Ely, Nev., Pullman Standard Sleepers

Lv. SALT LAKE	2.40	C11 45
Lv. Ogden	2.15	4.20
Ar. Cobre	------	9.07
Ar. Ely	------	6.05
Ar. San Francisco	2.08	2.48

To Portland, Pullman Standard Sleepers

Lv. SALT LAKE	11.45	2.40
Lv. Ogden	1.15	3.50
Lv. Pocatello	8.10	8.50
Ar. Portland	11.15	8.00

To Idaho Falls, Pullman Tourist Sleepers

Lv. SALT LAKE	11.45	------
Ar. Idaho Falls	9.35	------

THROUGH SLEEPING CAR SERVICE BETWEEN SALT LAKE CITY AND POINTS WEST AND NORTH

EASTBOUND

From Butte, Pullman Standard Sleepers

Lv. Butte	6.00	1.30
Ar. SALT LAKE	10.30	4.55

From Buhl, Pullman Standard Sleepers

Lv. Buhl	6.35	------
Ar. SALT LAKE	10.30	------

From Boise, Pullman Standard Sleepers

Lv. Boise	2.40	5.45	7.30
Ar. SALT LAKE	4.55	10.30	10.15

From San Francisco, Calif., and Ely, Nev., Pullman Standard Sleepers

Lv. San Francisco	9.00	------
Lv. Ely	------	B 7.30
Ar. Cobre	12.25	12.25
Ar. Ogden	5.35	5.35
Ar. SALT LAKE	6.55	6.55

From Portland, Pullman Standard Sleepers

Lv. Portland	10.00	8.00
Ar. Pocatello	11.15	4.25
Ar. Ogden	3.35	9.15
Ar. SALT LAKE	4.55	10.30

From Idaho Falls, Pullman Tourist Sleepers

Lv. Idaho Falls	2.16	------
Ar. SALT LAKE	10.30	------

* Stops on signal. a Stops to leave passengers from points west and north of Pocatello and east of McCammon. B--Except Sunday. C--Except Saturday. M--Mountain Time.

By 1911 the pattern of service on the Butte line had evolved to a considerable degree. In addition to the two through trains each way, locals were appearing in the timetable to serve emerging local needs, and even off-season (the above is the August schedule) a Pullman was carried between Idaho Falls and Salt Lake City for the new Yellowstone Park trade.

clined steadily from the turn of the century) meant little to the railroad's fortunes. Copper was the important metal, and it came from Butte and Anaconda; in 1927 Silver Bow County produced over 90 percent of Montana's mine output, including copper, lead, zinc, cadmium, sulphur, arsenic, manganese, tellurium and silenium, as well as gold and silver.

While Silver Bow County led Montana in mine output, Beaverhead County led in sale of livestock — nearly $3,500,000-worth in 1927. There was plenty of room in the County for sheep and cattle — there were then only 5,000 people in the entire 5,619 square miles. In the twenties and thirties this created a large volume of traffic for the UP out of Montana — before paved highways and trucks siphoned off the business. In the fall months the regular two scheduled freights each way were insufficient and many stock extras were operated. In fact, retired UP Livestock Agent James Phelps Sr. relates that stock extras would be provided shippers on call for a minimum of twenty cars, and a Livestock Department was maintained for many years to solicit traffic and oversee livestock handling. A growing market in California and the west coast provided a ready market served by the Union Pacific. Peak loadings of livestock in the territory north of Pocatello occurred in the fall after the first frost, when trainloads of feeder cattle and sheep were moved from Montana and Idaho to California feed-lots. In addition to the stock loaded at UP points, as many as 5,000 carloads a year were received by the UP at the Butte-Silver Bow Gateways from the Great Northern, Northern Pacific, Milwaukee and Butte, Anaconda & Pacific.

With greater availability of heavier power during World War I, 2-8-2's and 2-8-8-0's arrived on the line to take over much of the through freight work from the 2-8-0's, while 4-6-2's (particularly of the low-wheeled 3134 class) replaced tenwheelers on many passenger runs. Even with heavier power, helpers were still required as before on the heavy grades, such as the 3% through Beaver Canyon, the short but crooked 2% over Apex Hill each way, and the tough Feely grade. Enginemen on the payroll outnumbered trainmen, as is shown in this summary of expenses in 1927 for the Montana segment *alone*:

CLASS OF EMPLOYES	Number of Employes	Wages Paid	Expended for Improvement
Yardmen	3	$ 7,702.40	$135,169.24
Stationmen	40	75,526.04	
Trainmen	19	56,615.98	
Enginemen	27	71,165.09	
M. P. & M.	50	90,502.30	
Traffic Office	13	28,687.02	
Rental of Office		7,200.00	
M. of W. & S.	280	283,560.53	$135,169.24
Store Dept.	3	4,492.26	
Hospital Dept.	4	2,100.00	
D. C. & H. Dept.	74	81,207.38	

JOINT FACILITIES	Rent	Maintenance	Operation
Silver Bow Station	$ 339.84	$ 25.80	$ 7,451.83
Trackage Silver Bow-Butte	5,009.93	1,442.50	570.72
Butte Pass. Station	5,054.19	510.51	10,194.64
Butte Joint Yard	17,648.79	5,522.03	37,224.04
Engine House and Freight House	6,486.96		

The ratio would seem to imply about 3½ engines on each train. Maintenance of Way and Structures payroll also indicates a line with high requirements for trackwork, bridge work and snow removal. Another high labor input department was the Dining Car and Hotel Department.

The large number of open stations in those days is reflected in the total of 40 stationmen for Montana alone. James Phelps Jr., who was in train service on the line both before and after World War II, provides an approximate accounting of station staffing from Pocatello north in the thirties and forties:

- Fort Hall — agent
- Blackfoot — three tricks around the clock
- Firth — agent
- Shelley, Idaho Falls — three tricks around the clock at both
- Roberts, Hamer, Camas — all had agents at one time
- Dubois — three tricks around the clock
- Spencer, Humphrey — agent, seasonal operator
- Monida — three tricks, later reduced to agent, then to seasonal agency before being closed. Never did have electric lights in the train order signal.
- Lima — three tricks; later closed
- Dell — agent
- Red Rock — agent after Armstead closed
- Armstead — two tricks, 8 to midnight, when the Gilmore & Pittsburgh was operating; site now flooded by the Clark Canyon Dam
- Dillon — three tricks around the clock
- Bond, Melrose, Divide — agents, with three tricks at Melrose during World War II.

For many years Silver Bow was a joint agency staffed by the Northern Pacific, but a few years ago the Union Pacific installed its own agent. In recent years the only open station between Silver Bow and Idaho Falls has been Dillon.

Many of these stations provided coal and water facilities. Phelps recollects that "in steam days we took water going north at Blackfoot, coal and water at Idaho Falls, water at Roberts, coal and water at Dubois, water at Spencer, sometimes at Humphrey, sometimes at Monida, then coal and water at Lima, again at Dillon, and again at Melrose. Supposed to get enough at Melrose and not have to buy any off the Northern Pacific." Reason for the requirement of making the 38 miles into Butte, laying over, and getting back to Melrose before taking coal and water was the fact that the NP owned the engine facilities at Butte and charged the UP "full retail price" for coal. "We could get water at Silver Bow and Butte without much charge, though — nobody gave us the dickens for that." The later use of larger engines with bigger tanks reduced the frequency of water stops somewhat.

Lima had quite a shop in steam days, also, as it was an important helper terminal. Helpers were used from Dubois to Monida (at the top of the grade south of Lima), often cutting off there to drop back to Hamer or to Camas (where there was a wye for turning helpers until taken out later) to help a second train. If not, they would either cut off at Monida and drift down to Lima behind the train they had helped, or stay cut in to Lima. Going south (eastbound) helpers were used from Silver Bow to Feely and Navy to Apex, but in later years a train might be double-headed all the way from Silver Bow to Lima. Occasionally helpers were needed from Lima up to Monida. Passenger trains received a helper going north at Dubois, and in later years the Pacific was taken off at Lima for a Mikado. Subsequently Challengers (3800 class 4-6-6-4's) were used on the passenger run.

From the late twenties through the thirties heavy power on freights were 2-10-2's of the 5000, 5300, 5400 and 5500 classes and 2-8-8-0's of the 3500 and 3600 classes, assisted by Mikados (mostly 2504 class equivalents of USRA light Mikados) in helper duty. Passenger power was now 4-6-2 type of the 2819, 3100 and 3202 classes and somewhat heavier 2860, 2900, 3114 and 3218 classes. These Pacifics all had 77″ drivers, rather highwheeled for this largely mountain run. Frequently in later years 4-8-2's of the 7000 and 7850 classes were substituted; larger engines with 73″ drivers, they could handle nearly twice the tonnage of the lighter Pacifics and 50% more than the heavier Pacifics on the grades. In the forties 3800 class 4-6-6-4 Challengers appeared on the line, and as the steam era waned these engines took over more and more of both the freight and the passenger assignments. In addition, at the end of World War II a group of Norfolk & Western 2-8-8-2 Mallets saw service on the line, to no one's satisfaction — Jim Phelps said "They wouldn't do 25 mph uphill *or* downhill."

Phelps worked on the line during the later steam years and had many interesting experiences. One was a runaway down Feely Grade into Silver Bow six weeks after his return from the Army. "The engineer mishandled the air. I went back over the tops 'clubbing them down' and fortunately we slowed sufficiently that we did not run out onto the NP main at Silver Bow."

On another occasion he was involved in an "unintentional Dutch drop" — a switching maneuver designed to get around a freight car without benefit of a passing siding, by "kicking" the car uphill, then running the engine into the clear as the car rolls back past. "This was an experience I had with the 5067," related Phelps; "I believe it was one of the 2-10-2's that was an oil burner. At any rate, to take the load off our two regular trains during the fall stock rush they put on a local, Idaho Falls to Lima, up on Monday, Wednesday and Friday, and down on Tuesday, Thursday and Saturday. We loaded stock, handled local merchandise, and did the chores. On this day the Agent at Lima instructed us to get one foreign line single deck stock car out of a long string on track 2, a long track at that time. We picked the end of the string out of the siding, kicked the desired car up the main line and shoved the rest back in the siding. A brakeman was at the hand brake, one of the early vertical geared wheel type (most then had staff brakes) — but the chain of the brake caught in the brake step, and he couldn't set the brake as he should. So it started coming back down. I hurried the engine into the clear and lined the main line switch back for the main as the car drifted through it. The other brakeman made a hurried uncoupling ('busted the air' — as we were switching with air), and we chased the car, now behind us, down the hill. We were trying to catch it prior to reaching a derail in the main line which incorporated a little short runaway track that ended in a pile of sand and dirt. This was a split switch sort of derail — trail through it going eastbound (towards Pocatello), but westbound (towards Butte) it had to be lined up for the main, then lined back for the derail. Not only did we catch the car in time — but we had it where we wanted it, a kind of unintentional 'Dutch drop'."

No one wanted to take any longer making a run than necessary, and this meant avoiding doubling a hill whenever possible — particularly the long Monida grade. Creative tonnage accounting could help — as Phelps put it, "I didn't double that hill much in steam days — I carried tonnage 'in my hat' if necessary to get over the hill." He used this technique to advantage one day with a recalcitrant engineer, also. "One time at Pocatello late summer tonnage had piled up, and an extra was called out one morning behind 277, which at that time ran out early in the morning. We had about 1650 tons through west of Idaho Falls, and a little less than 1100 tons was tonnage for our 2-10-2, if I remember rightly; a mallet helper would rate 1250 tons additional. The engineer was mad at me from the trip before, when I had criticized him severely for going down into Lima with a burro crane in the consist at what I thought was excess speed. There wasn't any restriction in the timetable, but I figured he exceeded track speed. So he was out to get even, and was 'doubling the hill' right out of Pocatello. However, I had told him '2100 tons' when actually I only had about 1650. When we got the helper I told that engineer the story. He just shifted his cigar and said 'we'll see'. He about shoved the other engineer over the hill, as the mallet was in good shape."

"That same engineer on the road engine once told me my authority (as conductor) was from the tender back and his was from the tender coupling forward. I think he's the one I set out on the back track at Hamer, and refused to line him out until he got over another one of his mads."

The gradual introduction of heavier motive power during the late twenties and early thirties had no effect on passenger schedules; they remained virtually unchanged from the World War I period. The April 1931 timetable shows the same familiar two-train arrangement:

29	31		30	32
12:30 PM	11:00 PM	Salt Lake City	11:55 PM	7:15 AM
4:50 AM	3:35 PM	Butte	9:05 AM	4:55 PM

In fact, the running time of no. 29 was precisely the same as its predecessor no. 9 back in 1916! And now the only diners were on nos. 31 and 32 between Pocatello and Butte; otherwise passengers enjoyed "meals served in station restaurants." Pullmans (12 section, drawing room standard) were still included on each train, and in addition nos. 29 and 32 carried a 10 section observation through from Butte to Los Angeles.

However, progress soon caught up with the passenger schedule; by 1934 running times had been reduced significantly and the schedules revised to incorporate one overnight train and one day train each way:

29	31		30	32
8:15 PM	7:45 AM	Salt Lake City	11:55 PM	7:00 AM
9:50 AM	9:15 PM	Butte	10:15 AM	6:30 PM

A new feature was a cafe-observation lounge car on each train, Salt Lake City to Butte — no more hurried "beanery" meals. The day train no longer carried a through Pullman, although a Spokane sleeper was in the consist between Salt Lake City and Pocatello. The night train still carried a Pullman, as well as a Boise sleeper from Salt Lake City to Pocatello. In addition there was a local between Salt Lake City and Idaho Falls, and twice daily service to Ashton (although one round trip was now by "motor").

Schedules were further improved until, by 1941, running times averaged around 13 hours Salt Lake City-Butte:

29	31		30	32
8:00 PM	8:00 AM	Salt Lake City	10:30 PM	7:00 AM
12:45 AM	1:10 PM	Pocatello	6:00 PM	2:15 AM
1:30 AM	1:25 AM	Pocatello	5:25 PM	1:30 AM
9:15 AM	9:05 PM	Butte	9:45 AM	6:30 PM

Schedules of this period probably marked the high-point for Salt Lake-Butte service. All trains still carried a "cafe-lounge" car serving meals and refreshments, and the overnight trains (nos. 29 *Butte Special* and 32 *Butte Northwest Express*) carried through standard sleepers between Los Angeles and Butte as well as a tourist sleeper between Salt Lake City and Butte.

This arrangement came to an end in April 1942, when the day train to Butte was taken off, and only the night train remained, now nos. 29 and 30, the *Butte Special*; added local work resulted in slower running time, as shown in this 1943 schedule:

29					30
8:00 PM	LV	Salt Lake City	AR	9:25 AM
11:30 AM	AR	Butte	LV	7:45 PM

The cafe-lounges were gone, and passengers were advised that they could have "breakfast in the Wilbur Cafe in Dillon." The standard sleeper to Los Angeles was succeeded by a modern 6 section, 6 roomette, 4 bedroom car, but this was later removed and a 10 section, 2 compartment, drawing room car substituted. Nos. 31 and 32 continued as Salt Lake City-Pocatello locals, and nos. 33 and 34 were Salt Lake City-Idaho Falls locals; there was still a fair amount of business on the south end of the line. By 1949 the Butte schedule had been accelerated a bit (13½ hours going north, 12¾ south), the tourist sleeper dropped in favor of a 10 section, 3 bedroom car, and a cafe-lounge put back on the run.

During the 1950's the Idaho Falls local was dropped, and the *Butte Special* renumbered 35 and 36, on a somewhat faster schedule:

35				36
7:30 PM	LV	Salt Lake City	AR	7:30 AM
7:30 AM	AR	Butte	LV	7:20 PM

A Salt Lake City-Butte sleeper was included in the consist, a 6 section, 6 roomette, 4 bedroom car; and a club-lounge was carried between Pocatello and Salt Lake City. Nos. 33 and 34 still ran as a Salt Lake City-Pocatello local, scheduled to permit convenient through movement of a Los Angeles-Portland sleeper. Considerable passenger traffic was still seen on the line each summer, when the *Yellowstone Special* tourist train ran between Salt Lake City and West Yellowstone.

The future of passenger travel on the Butte line was no different than that nationwide, however, and the path lay steeply downhill. The remaining Pocatello local went quickly; the once-popular *Yellowstone Special* made it through the mid-sixties; finally, only the *Butte Special* remained. Reduced to a single sleeper, a coach and a few head-end cars, it continued to ply its lonely way between Salt Lake City and Butte until Amtrak Day, May 1, 1971, when finally all passenger service ceased over the one-time Utah Northern — a year short of a century of service.

Freight traffic, of course, still brightens the rails to Butte. While livestock traffic has been lost, other traffic such as forest products (lumber) and agricultural products have continued to come to the line, and new sources of traffic found — the latest being phosphate rock for fertilizer, which now moves over the line in increasing quantity. In fact, unit trains of phosphate rock now move through Silver Bow-Butte for Canada. The coming of diesels greatly changed operating practices on the line, however; helper districts became a thing of the past, and the roundhouse at Dubois and engine terminal at Lima were abandoned. Train and engine crews now run from Pocatello through to Dillon, and then make a "Butte turn" out of Dillon. Each year evidences of the old "glory days" of steam operation on the Montana Division (now the Northwestern District of the Idaho Division) succumb to the relentless march of progress.

Acknowledgments

In gathering the material for this article, three individuals were especially helpful — Clifford H. Peake of Pocatello, James H. Phelps, Jr., of Billings, and the late Arthur Petersen of Pocatello. In addition to providing data, Clifford Peake and Art Petersen made available a great many rare photographs, and Jim Phelps contributed his interesting recollections of his years on the line as brakeman and conductor. Many others assisted also in the search for material, including Rex C. Myers, Henry R. Griffiths, Roger Breeding, A. D. Herrmann, J. H. Phelps Sr., Philip C. Johnson, J. D. Marker, Emil Albrecht, Philip R. Hastings and Warren R. McGee. Thanks are due also to the Montana Historical Society, the Idaho Historical Society, the Utah State Historical Society, the Western History Department of the Denver Public Library and the Union Pacific RR. Considerable material came from the Colorado Railroad Museum Library. Sources included Union Pacific RR reports, schedules and records; the *Official Guide of the Railways* and *Poor's Manuals;* reports of the Montana Department of Agriculture, Labor and Industry; the *Railroad Gazette;* and various other periodicals and newspapers. *Montana, An Uncommon Land* (K. Ross Toole, Univ. of Oklahoma Press: Norman, 1959) and *Union Pacific Country* (Robert G. Athearn, Rand McNally & Co.: Chicago, 1971) provided helpful background. Finally, the many generous contributors of photographs are noted in the captions.

C. W. H.

WESTWARD—SEVENTH SUB-DIVISION—Pocatello and Lima—EASTWARD.

Time Table No. 301

JUNE 20, 1923

Length of Passing Tracks in feet between clearance points, and location of Scales, Water, Fuel, Phones and Turning Stations.	Other Tracks in Feet beyond Clearance Points.	SECOND CLASS 277 Time Freight	FIRST CLASS 29 Passenger	41 Passenger	33 Passenger	31 Passenger	45 Passenger	Distance from Ogden	STATIONS	Distance from Silver Bow	FIRST CLASS 42 Passenger	30 Passenger	34 Passenger	46 Passenger	32 Passenger	278 Time Freight
		Leave Daily	Leave Daily	Leave Daily	Leave Daily	Leave Daily	Leave Daily				Arrive Daily	Arrive Daily	Arrive Daily	Arrive Daily	Arrive Daily	Arrive Daily
	258,400	8.10AM	7.35PM	1.45PM	9.00AM	7.10AM	12.50AM	133.9	DN-R **POCATELLO** H Ca Po — 1.7	256.1	11.00AM	4.30PM	9.00PM	1.40AM	2.55AM	6.20PM
P			7.43	1.52	9.06	7.17	1.00	135.6	IDAHO JCT. — 1.7	254.4	10.52	4.22	8.52	1.30	2.46	
P		8.25	7.49	1.57	9.10	7.22	1.05	137.3	MONTANA JCT. — 1.5	252.7	10.47	4.17	8.47	1.20	2.41	6.05
1,976								138.8	CHUBBUCK — 2.2	251.2						
3,657 P	917	8.40	f 7.56	f 2.04	9.15	f 7.27	**1.12**	141.0	TYHEE — 5.3	249.0	f 10.40	4.11	f 8.41	**1.12**	2.36	5.50
3,670 W	2,112	8.58	s 8.07	s 2.14	9.22	s 7.37	1.20	146.3	D FORT HALL Fh — 5.2	243.7	s 10.30	s 4.04	s 8.33	1.03	2.28	5.30
3,708 P	538	**9.28**	**8.20**	f 2.22	**9.28**	f 7.45	1.27	151.5	GIBSON — 2.4	238.5	f 10.20	3.55	f **8.20**	12.54	2.20	5.15
	520							153.9	YOUNG (Spur) — 4.8	236.1						
11,163 PFYW	18,457	**10.05**	s 8.40	s 2.37	s 9.40	s 8.05	s 1.40	158.7	DN **BLACKFOOT** Bf — 1.4	231.3	s **10.05**	s 3.45	s 8.05	s 12.40	s 2.05	4.50
	8,128							160.1	FACTORY — 4.4	229.9						
3,721 P	1,576	10.20	f 8.50	f 2.47	**9.48**	f 8.15	**1.50**	164.5	WAPELLO — 2.7	225.5	f **9.48**	3.28	f 7.50	12.26	**1.50**	4.30
1,106				f				167.2	KIMBALL — 2.8	222.8	f		f			
3,707 WY	5,614	10.35	s 9.00	s 2.58	9.55	s 8.25	1.59	170.0	D FIRTH Fr — 0.3	220.0	s 9.30	s 3.20	s 7.42	12.18	f 1.39	4.10
								170.3	GOSHEN JCT. — 2.5	219.7						
829				f				172.8	MONROE — 3.3	217.2	f					
5,228	22,054	10.55	s 9.12	s **3.10**	10.05	s 8.38	2.09	176.1	DN SHELLEY Sy — 1.4	213.9	s 9.15	s **3.10**	s 7.32	12.08	s 1.29	3.50
1,100								177.5	MITCHELL — 2.6	212.5						
3,706 P	2,000	11.10	9.18	f 3.18	10.11	8.44	2.15	180.1	COTTON — 3.6	209.9	f 9.00	3.03	f 7.24	12.01AM	1.21	3.35
3,322 P	497	11.25	9.23	**3.24**	10.16	**8.50**	2.20	183.7	BACH — 1.4	206.3	**8.50**	2.58	7.19	11.55PM	1.15	**3.24**
POTFYW	53,379	11.55AM	s 9.35	3.30PM	10.20AM	s 9.00	2.25AM	185.1	DN-R **IDAHO FALLS** Ak — 6.8	204.9	8.45AM	s **2.55**	7.15PM	11.50PM	s 1.12	**2.55**
2,725 P	1,493	12.15PM	f 9.47			f 9.11		191.9	PAYNE — 5.2	198.1		f 2.35			f 12.56	2.12
2,727 P	493	12.35	f 9.55			f 9.19		197.1	BASSETT — 2.6	192.9		f 2.27			f 12.48	1.57
	700					f		199.7	SHEPPARD (Spur) — 2.9	190.3		f				
2,880 PW	3,127	12.55	s 10.05			s 9.30		202.6	D ROBERTS Ar — 5.0	187.4		s 2.18			s 12.40	1.40
2,977 P		**1.15**	10.12			9.38		207.6	TENNO — 5.3	182.4		2.08			12.27	**1.15**
2,708 P		1.30	10.20			f 9.46		212.9	HAWGOOD — 5.1	177.1		f 2.00			12.19	12.55
2,700 P	1,274	**1.53**	f 10.28			s 9.54		218.0	D HAMER Ha — 5.9	172.0		s **1.53**			f 12.11	12.38
2,660 PWY	3,860	2.30	f 10.36			s 10.03		223.9	D CAMAS Ms — 4.9	166.1		s 1.43			f 12.01AM	12.19
2,707 P		2.50	10.44			f 10.11		228.8	JONES — 6.7	161.2		f 1.33			11.52PM	12.01PM
6,499 PYFW	11,893	3.45	s 11.05			s 10.27		235.5	DN-R DUBOIS Bo — 8.0	154.5		s 1.23			s 11.43	11.40AM
2,738 P		4.30	**11.25**			f **10.45**		243.5	HIGH BRIDGE — 5.5	146.5		f 1.06			**11.25**	**10.45**
3,117 WP	4,026	5.15	s 11.40PM			s 11.00		249.0	DN SPENCER Rc — 9.6	141.0		s 12.55			s 11.10	10.05
5,225 WYP	3,171	6.25	f 12.10AM			f 11.30		258.6	HUMPHREY — 6.7	131.4		f 12.35			f 10.50	9.35
3,329 PWY	3,656	7.15	s 12.30			s 11.45AM		265.3	DN MONIDA Mo — 8.6	124.7		s 12.22			s 10.36	9.10
2,792 WP	501	7.50	12.46			f **12.05PM**		273.9	SNOWLINE — 6.6	116.1		f **12.05PM**			10.18	8.30
PTFWY	32,867	8.15PM	1.00AM			12.25PM		■280.5	DN-R **LIMA** Rd	109.5		11.45AM			10.00PM	7.45AM
		Arrive Daily	Arrive Daily	Arrive Daily	Arrive Daily	Arrive Daily	Arrive Daily		(146.6)		Leave Daily	Leave Daily	Leave Daily	Leave Daily	Leave Daily	Leave Daily
		(12.05) 12.0	(5.25) 27.0	(1.45) 29.2	(1.20) 38.4	(5.15) 27.8	(1.35) 32.3		........Time........ ....Average Speed Per Hour........		(2.15) 22.7	(4.45) 30.7	(1.45) 29.2	(1.50) 27.9	(4.55) 29.7	(10.35) 13.8

Westward Trains are Superior to Trains of the Same Class in the Opposite Direction. (See Rule 72)

A portion of the June 20, 1923 Oregon Short Line—UP System employee timetable no. 301 for the Montana Division.

WESTWARD—EIGHTH SUB-DIVISION—Lima and Silver Bow—EASTWARD.

Length of Passing Tracks in feet between clearance points, and location of Scales, Water, Fuel, Phones and Turning Stations.	Other Tracks in Feet beyond Clearance Points.	SECOND CLASS 277 Time Freight Leave Daily	FIRST CLASS 31 Passenger Leave Daily	FIRST CLASS 29 Passenger Leave Daily	Distance from Ogden		Time Table No. 301 JUNE 20, 1923 STATIONS		Distance from Silver Bow	FIRST CLASS 30 Passenger Arrive Daily	FIRST CLASS 32 Passenger Arrive Daily	SECOND CLASS 278 Time Freight Arrive Daily
TFWYP	32,867	9.55PM	12.30PM	1.05AM	280.5	DN-R	LIMA	Rd	109.5	11.40AM	9.55PM	5.45AM
	304		f		285.5		5.0 GOSMAN (Spur)		104.5	f		
2,625 WP	349	10.21	s 12.45	f 1.20	288.6	D	3.1 DELL	De	101.4	s 11.18	s 9.32	5.00
	267				292.3		3.7 McKNIGHT (Spur)		97.7			
2,660 P	236	10.45	f 12.57	f 1.33	294.6		2.3 KIDD		95.4	f 11.02	f 9.18	4.30
2,706 WP	1,564	11.14	s 1.13	f 1.50	303.4	D	8.8 RED ROCK	Dk	86.6	s 10.42	s 9.00	3.50
2,996	3,197	11.32	s 1.25	s 2.05	307.6	DN	4.2 ARMSTEAD	Ad	82.4	s 10.31	s 8.45	3.25
2,654 P	498	11.50PM	f 1.35	f 2.15	313.6		6.0 GRAYLING		76.4	f 10.16	f 8.30	3.00
1,046 P			f	f	316.9		3.3 DALYS		73.1	f	f	
3,421 P	624	12.15AM	f 1.48	f **2.27**	320.7		3.8 BARRATTS		69.3	f 10.03	f 8.15	**2.27**
3,450 TWF	8,659	12.45	s 2.08	s 2.45	328.6	DN	7.9 DILLON	Dn	61.4	s 9.48	s 8.00	1.50
2,082 P	402	**1.15**	f 2.20	f 2.57	335.0	D	6.4 BOND	Kn	55.0	f 9.33	f 7.43	**1.15**
2,606 P	635	1.55	s 2.35	f 3.10	340.9		5.9 APEX		49.1	s 9.23	f 7.33	12.50AM
	450		s 2.54	f 3.30	348.4	D	7.5 GLEN (Spur	Ux	41.6	s 9.03	f 7.09	
2,622 PWY		2.37	2.56	3.32	349.1		0.7 NAVY		40.9	9.01	7.07	11.57PM
2,779 P		2.50	f 3.00	f 3.36	351.8		2.7 LAVON		38.2	f 8.57	f 7.02	11.45
	175		f	f	352.8		1.0 BROWNS (Spur)		37.2	f	f	
3,359 FWP	3,055	3.28	s 3.17	s 3.51	358.8	DN	6.0 MELROSE	Vi	31.2	s 8.45	s 6.50	11.15
2,171 P		**4.01**	f 3.27	f **4.01**	364.7		5.9 QUINN		25.3	f 8.31	f 6.37	10.35
			f	f	365.9		1.2 MAIDEN ROCK		24.1	f	f	
2,285 P	2,648	4.35	s 3.38	s 4.14	370.0	D	4.1 DIVIDE	J	20.0	s 8.21	s 6.27	10.15
3,500 WP		5.05	f 3.48	f 4.26	374.6		4.6 WOODIN		15.4	f 8.11	f 6.17	9.53
	304				378.8		4.2 BEAUDINES (Spur)		11.2			
2,492 YP	1,728	5.45	f 4.01	f 4.41	380.7		1.9 FEELY		9.3	f 8.00	f 6.05	9.30
2,754 P		6.15	f 4.11	f 4.51	384.8		4.1 BUXTON		5.2	f 7.45	f 5.53	8.55
	2,033				386.8		2.0 ENRIGHT (Spur)		3.2			
FYW	17,173	6.45AM	4.25PM	5.05AM	390.0	DN-R	3.2 SILVER BOW	Sb	0.0	7.35AM	5.40PM	8.30PM
		Arrive Daily	Arrive Daily	Arrive Daily			(109.5)			Leave Daily	Leave Daily	Leave Daily
		(8.50) 12.5	(3.55) 28.1	(4.00) 27.5			..........Time.......... ....Average Speed Per Hour..........			(4.05) 27.0	(4.15) 25.5	(9.15) 11.9

Schedules below are for information only. Use Time Table and Rules of Northern Pacific Railway between Silver Bow and Butte.

277	31	29	Distance from Ogden		STATIONS		Distance from Silver Bow	30	32	278
7.50AM	4.30PM	5.05AM	390.0	DN	SILVER BOW	Sb	6.9	7.30AM	5.35PM	7.55PM
8.20AM	4.50PM	5.25AM	396.9	DN	6.9 BUTTE	W	0.0	7.15AM	5.20PM	7.30PM
					(116.4)					

Westward Trains are Superior to Trains of the Same Class in the Opposite Direction. (See Rule 72)

WESTWARD—Yellowstone Branch—EASTWARD.

Time Table No. 301
JUNE 20, 1923

Length of Passing Tracks in feet between clearance points, and location of Scales, Water, Fuel, Phones and Turning Stations.	Other Tracks in Feet beyond Clearance Points.	SECOND CLASS 305 Mixed	SECOND CLASS 303 Mixed	FIRST CLASS 41 Passenger	FIRST CLASS 33 Passenger	FIRST CLASS 45 Passenger	Distance from Idaho Falls		STATIONS		Distance to next station	Distance from Yellowstone	FIRST CLASS 42 Passenger	FIRST CLASS 34 Passenger	FIRST CLASS 46 Passenger	SECOND CLASS 304 Mixed	SECOND CLASS 306 Mixed
		Lv. Monday, Wed., Friday	Lv. Tuesday, Thurs., Sat.	Leave Daily	Leave Daily	Leave Daily							Arrive Daily	Arrive Daily	Arrive Daily	Arr. Monday Wed., Friday	Arr. Tues., Thurs. Sat.
PYFWO	53,379	9.15AM	9.15AM	3.35PM	10.25AM	2.30AM	0.0	DN-R	**IDAHO FALLS**	Ak	3.0	107.1	8.40AM	7.10PM	11.45PM	3.55PM	3.55PM
1,114 PY	997	f 9.25	9.25AM	f **3.42**	10.32		3.0		**ORVIN**		0.7	104.1	f 8.30	6.59		**3.42PM**	f **3.42**
	787			f	f		3.7		ST. LEON (Spur)		3.9	103.4	f	f			
3,017 PW	1,820	9.40AM		s 3.52	s 10.39	2.43	7.6	D	**UCON**	Un	6.2	99.5	s 8.22	s 6.49	11.23		3.30PM
5,082	6,589			s 4.07	s 10.56	2.53	13.8	D	RIGBY	By	4.3	93.3	s 8.10	s 6.37	11.13		
1,876 W				s 4.15	s 11.06	3.01	18.1		LORENZO		2.6	89.0	s 7.56	s 6.23	11.05		
1,433	2,748			s 4.23	s 11.12	3.06	20.7	D	THORNTON	Ho	2.6	86.4	s 7.50	s 6.16	10.59		
1,279				f	f		23.3		WINDER		2.7	83.8	f	f			
3523	3,747			s 4.38	s 11.27	3.16	26.0	D	REXBURG	Rx	3.8	81.1	s 7.40	s 6.06	10.49		
2,626	2,212			s 4.48	s 11.37	3.23	29.8	D	**SUGAR CITY**	Sc	1.1	77.3	s 7.28	s 5.54	10.38		
1,910 YO	11,009						30.9		HART		2.0	76.2					
	386			f	f		32.9		WILFORD (Spur)		2.8	74.2	f	f			
P							35.7		**RHOADES**		1.1	71.4					
6,639 PWY	4,840			s 5.08	s 11.52AM	3.35	36.8	D	ST. ANTHONY	St	1.5	70.3	s 7.15	s 5.40	10.25		
P							38.3		**BELT**		0.9	68.8					
	535			f	f		39.2		TWIN GROVES		3.6	67.9	f	f			
2,212				f **5.25**	f 12.03PM	3.47	42.8		CHESTER		8.2	64.3	f 7.00	f **5.25**	10.13		
2,357 PFWY	13,846			5.45PM	s 12.28	s 4.12	51.0	DN-R	**ASHTON**	Hn	1.5	56.1	6.45AM	s 5.10	s 9.58		
1,702	1,358						52.5		INGLING (Spur)		5.9	54.6					
1,498 PW	312				f 12.45	4.30	58.4		WARM RIVER		5.1	48.7		f 4.45	9.33		
P							63.5		ESTES		3.4	43.6					
1,208 PY	2,093				f 1.20	5.15	66.9		GERRIT		5.7	40.2		f 4.10	8.57		
416 PW					f		72.6		FISHATCH		3.2	34.5		f			
1,292	524				f 1.38	5.45	75.8		ECCLES		4.8	31.3		f 3.52	8.32		
914 P	166				f 1.48	5.57	80.6		ISLAND PARK		4.9	26.5		f 3.42	8.22		
1,553	909				f 1.58	s 6.09	85.5	D	TRUDE	Ru	5.3	21.6		f 3.32	s 8.12		
1,397 WY	2,980				f 2.10	s 6.25	90.8	D	BIG SPRINGS	Bs	6.5	16.3		f 3.20	s 8.00		
1,205 PY	1,477				f **2.45**	7.00	97.3		REAS PASS		9.8	9.8		f **2.45**	7.30		
1,704 PWYF	8,012				3.15PM	7.30AM	107.1	DR	**WEST YELLOWSTONE**	Ws	(107.1)	0.0		2.15PM	7.00PM		
		Arr Monday, Wed., Friday	Arr. Tues., Thurs., Sat.	Arrive Daily	Arrive Daily	Arrive Daily							Leave Daily	Leave Daily	Leave Daily	Lv Monday, Wed., Friday	Lv Tuesday, Thurs., Sat.
		(0.25)	(0.10)	(2.10)	(4.50)	(5.00)			Time				(1.55)	(4.55)	(4.45)	(0.13)	(0.25)
		18.2	18.0	23.8	22.1	21.4			Average Speed Per Hour				26.0	21.8	22.5	13.9	18.2

Westward Trains are Superior to Trains of the Same Class in the Opposite Direction. (See Rule 72)

WESTWARD—Mackay Branch—EASTWARD

Length of Passing Tracks in feet between clearance points, and location of Scales, Water, Fuel, Phones and Turning Stations.	Other Tracks in Feet beyond Clearance Points.	SECOND CLASS 307 Mixed	FIRST CLASS 125 Passenger	Distance from Blackfoot	Time Table No. 301 JUNE 20, 1923 STATIONS	Distance from Mackay	FIRST CLASS 126 Passenger	SECOND CLASS 308 Mixed
		Leave Daily Except Sunday	Leave Daily				Arrive Daily	Arrive Daily Except Sunday
11,163 PFWY	18,457	8.45AM	8.25AM	0.0	DN-R **BLACKFOOT** Bf	85.2	3.25PM	2.15PM
	531	f	f	2.1	2.1 COLLINS	83.1	f	f
				2.6	0.5 GARDNER JCT.	82.6		
504	478	f	f	3.8	1.2 AIKEN	81.4	f	f
1,678	550	s 9.05	s 8.36	5.4	1.6 KEEVER	79.8	s 3.12	s 1.50
				5.6	0.2 THOMAS JCT.	79.6		
P	580	9.10AM	f 8.40	7.1	1.5 **MORELAND JCT.**	78.1	f 3.08	1.40PM
			f	12.5	5.4 FARRIS	72.7	f	
1,732 PW			s 9.05	20.1	7.6 TABER	65.1	s 2.40	
			f	23.5	3.4 KRAUDLIS	61.7	f	
1,291			f 9.25	29.1	5.6 FUREY	56.1	f 2.20	
1,679 P			s 9.37	35.4	6.3 CERRO GRANDE	49.8	s 2.06	
874 W			f 9.56	44.7	9.3 PIONEER	40.5	f 1.45	
1,893 PYWF	4,031		s 10.25	59.1	14.4 D ARCO C	26.1	s 1.15	
407			f 10.36	63.7	4.6 LOST RIVER	21.5	f 1.00	
1,233 P			s 10.47	66.8	3.1 D MOORE Co	18.4	s 12.52	
722			s 11.04	72.6	5.8 DARLINGTON	12.6	s 12.38	
P	542		s 11.17	77.3	4.7 LESLIE	7.9	s 12.26	
	154		f	80.8	3.5 ROTHAS (Spur)	4.4	f	
3,453 PFYW	13,264		11.40AM	85.2	4.4 D-R **MACKAY** My	0.0	12.05PM	
		Arrive Daily Except Sunday	Arrive Daily		(85.2)		Leave Daily	Leave Daily Except Sunday
		(0.25) 17.0	(3.15) 26.2		Time / Average Speed Per Hour		(3.20) 25.5	(0.35) 12.1

WESTWARD—Thomas Branch—EASTWARD

Length of Passing Tracks in feet between clearance points, and location of Scales, Water, Fuel, Phones and Turning Stations.	Other Tracks in Feet beyond Clearance Points.	Distance from Thomas Jct.	Time Table No. 301 JUNE 20, 1923 STATIONS	Distance from End of Track
		0.0	THOMAS JCT.	4.7
1,020		2.5	2.5 TAYLOR	2.2
	731	4.5	2.0 THOMAS	0.2
		4.7	0.2 END OF TRACK	0.0
			(4.07)	

WESTWARD—Gardner Branch—EASTWARD

Length of Passing Tracks in feet between clearance points, and location of Scales, Water, Fuel, Phones and Turning Stations.	Other Tracks in Feet beyond Clearance Points.	Distance from Gardner Jct.	Time Table No. 301 JUNE 20, 1923 STATIONS	Distance from End of Track
		0.0	GARDNER JCT.	7.2
1,296		3.1	3.1 PETERSON	4.1
		7.1	4.0 GARDNER	0.1
		7.2	0.1 END OF TRACK	0.0
			(7.2)	

WESTWARD—Aberdeen Branch—EASTWARD

Length of Passing Tracks in feet between clearance points, and location of Scales, Water, Fuel, Phones and Turning Stations.	Other Tracks in Feet beyond Clearance Points.	SECOND CLASS 307 Mixed	Distance from Moreland Junction	Time Table No. 301 JUNE 20, 1923 STATIONS	Distance from Aberdeen	SECOND CLASS 308 Mixed
		Leave Daily Ex. Sunday				Arrive Daily Ex. Sunday
P	580	9.10AM	0.0	R **MORELAND JCT.**	28.2	1.40PM
620		f 9.16	2.0	2.0 ARMY (Spur)	26.2	f 1.32
1,707		s 9.23	4.3	2.3 ROCKFORD	23.9	s 1.25
1,080		f 9.27	6.0	1.7 LIBERTY	22.2	f 1.15
600		f 9.35	8.4	2.4 VIRDEN (Spur)	19.8	f 1.07
1,703	1,558	s 9.48	10.2	1.8 D PINGREE Pg	18.0	s 1.00
1,685 W		f 10.08	16.5	6.3 SPRINGFIELD	11.7	f 12.35
1,500	2,037	s 10.25	19.7	3.2 D STERLING	8.5	s 12.20
	315	f 10.38	23.6	3.9 STRANG	4.6	f 12.03PM
540		10.45	26.0	2.4 FINGAL	2.2	11.54AM
1,962 Y	4,147	11.00AM	28.2	2.2 D-R **ABERDEEN** Bn	0.0	11.45AM
		Arrive Daily Ex. Sunday		(28.2)		Leave Daily Ex. Sunday
		(1.50) 15.4		Time / Average Speed Per Hour		(1.55) 14.7

Westward trains are superior to trains of the same class in the opposite direction. (See Rule 72.)

WESTWARD—Teton Valley Branch—EASTWARD

Length of Passing Tracks in feet between clearance points, and location of Scales, Water, Fuel, Phones and Turning Stations.	Other Tracks in Feet beyond Clearance Points.	FIRST CLASS 133 Passenger	Distance from Ashton	Time Table No. 301 JUNE 20, 1923 STATIONS	Distance from Victor	FIRST CLASS 134 Passenger
		Leave Daily				Arrive Daily
2,357 PFWY	13,846	12.40PM	0.0	D-R **ASHTON** Hn	45.6	4.50PM
1,107	1,329	s 12.45	1.8	1.8 D MARYSVILLE Va	43.8	s 4.43
1,731		f 12.56	6.0	4.2 GRAINVILLE	39.6	f 4.33
1,238 WP	1,600	s 1.05	8.6	2.6 D DRUMMOND Md	37.0	s 4.27
413		f 1.15	12.8	4.2 FRANCE	32.8	f 4.17
1,730 P		s 1.25	15.8	3.0 LAMONT	29.8	s 4.10
W	473	f 1.37	19.4	3.6 FERRON	26.2	f 4.00
342		f 1.43	22.3	2.9 JUDKINS	23.3	f 3.53
1,184	507	s 1.53	26.2	3.9 FELT	19.4	s 3.43
1,216 PYW	2,998	s 2.03	30.3	4.1 D TETONIA Na	15.3	s 3.33
	489	f 2.10	32.6	2.3 DWIGHT (Spur)	13.0	f 3.27
1,676 P	1,208	s 2.20	37.3	4.7 D DRIGGS Dl	8.3	s 3.17
1,078 YWFP	2,887	2.40PM	45.6	8.3 D-R **VICTOR** VR	0.0	3.00PM
		Arrive Daily		(45.6)		Leave Daily
		(2.00) 22.8		Time / Average Speed Per Hour		(1.50) 24.7

WESTWARD						SEVENTH SUBDIVISION					EASTWARD
Length of sidings in feet between clearance points, location of water, fuel, interlocking plants, turning stations, scales and telephones	SECOND CLASS		FIRST CLASS		Distance from Ogden via Old Main Line	Supplement No. 1 to Time-Table No. 250 April 19, 1938	Distance from Silver Bow via New Main Line	FIRST CLASS		SECOND CLASS	
	333 Mixed Daily	277 Time Freight Daily	31 Passenger Daily	29 Passenger Daily		STATIONS		30 Passenger	32 Passenger	278 Time Freight	334 Mixed
WFTYOP	6.00AM	5.30AM	1.25PM	1.30AM	133.9	DN-R **POCATELLO** H CA PO 3.5	256.8	A 6.10PM	A 1.30AM	A 4.00PM	A 1.20AM
P	6.09	5.39	1.33	1.41	136.7	**MONTANA JCT.** 1.5	253.3	5.55	1.16	2.20	1.00
1,932					138.2	CHUBBUCK 2.2	251.8				
3,669 P	f 6.15	5.45	f 1.38	1.46	140.4	TYHEE 5.3	249.6	f 5.50	1.11	2.13	12.52
3,682 WP	s 6.23	5.53	s 1.44	f 1.55	145.7	D FORT HALL FH 5.3	244.3	f 5.44	f 1.05	2.03	12.42
3,706 P	f 6.31	6.01	f 1.50	2.01	151.0	GIBSON 2.2	239.0	f 5.38	12.59	1.50	12.32
					153.2	YOUNG (Spur) 4.9	236.8				
11,427 WFYOP	s 6.42	6.15	s 2.03	s 2.12	158.1	Block Signals DN **BLACKFOOT** BF 5.9	231.9	s 5.28	s 12.50	1.35	12.20
3,720 P	f 6.51	6.28	f 2.10	f 2.21	164.0	WAPELLO 2.6	226.0	f 5.18	12.34	1.12	12.06AM
	f		f		166.6	KIMBALL 2.8	223.4	f			
3,706 WP	s 7.00	6.39	s 2.17	f 2.28	169.4	D FIRTH FR 0.4	220.6	s 5.11	f 12.27	1.04	11.58PM
Y					169.8	**GOSHEN JCT.** 2.4	220.2				
676	f				172.2	MONROE 3.3	217.8				
5,174 OP	s 7.09	6.48	s 2.27	f 2.35	175.5	DN SHELLEY SY 1.4	214.5	s 5.03	s 12.19	12.54	11.48
					176.9	MITCHELL 2.4	213.1				
3,708 P	f 7.19	6.55	f 2.31	2.39	179.3	COTTON 3.8	210.7	f 4.57	12.13	12.47	11.40
3,324 P	7.23	7.01	2.35	2.43	183.1	BACH 1.4	206.9	4.52	12.08	12.40	11.34
WFTYOP	A 7.30AM	7.15 8.45	s 2.45	s 3.00	184.5	DN-R **IDAHO FALLS** AK 1.3	205.5	s 4.50	s 12.05AM	12.30PM	11.30PM
					185.8	WEST IDAHO FALLS 5.4	204.2	4.31	11.51PM		
2,725 P		9.00	f 2.56	f 3.12	191.2	PAYNE 5.3	198.8	f 4.25	f 11.45	10.55AM	
2,729 P		9.10	f 3.03	f 3.18	196.5	BASSETT 5.5	193.5	f 4.18	f 11.39	10.46	
2,880 WP		9.30	s 3.11	s 3.26	202.0	D ROBERTS AR 5.0	188.0	s 4.11	s 11.33	10.37	
2,762 P		9.40	f 3.18	3.32	207.0	TENNO 5.1	183.0	f 4.02	11.27	10.22	
2,589 P		9.50	f 3.24	3.37	212.1	HAWGOOD 5.4	177.9	f 3.56	11.21	10.13	
2,698 P		10.01	s 3.30	s 3.44	217.5	HAMER 5.6	172.5	s 3.48	f 11.14	10.01	
2,668 YP		10.12	f 3.41	f 3.50	223.1	CAMAS 5.1	166.9	f 3.41	f 11.06	9.42	
2,553 P		10.23	f 3.48	3.56	228.2	JONES 6.7	161.8	f 3.33	11.00	9.33	
5,980 WFYP		11.05	s 4.01	s 4.14	234.9	D DUBOIS BO 8.0	155.1	s 3.25	s 10.52	9.20	
2,676 P		11.25	f 4.12	4.25	242.9	HIGHBRIDGE 5.6	147.1	f 3.13	f 10.40	8.49	
2,782 WP		11.45AM	s 4.25	s 4.38	248.5	Block Signals D SPENCER RC 9.5	141.5	s 3.03	f 10.30	8.36	
2,880 WP		12.15PM	f 4.44	f 4.59	258.0	HUMPHREY 6.7	132.0	f 2.45	f 10.11	8.06	
3,180 YP		12.40	s 4.56	s 5.10	264.7	D MONIDA MO 8.1	125.3	s 2.33	f 10.02	7.45	
2,727 WP		12.55	f 5.09	5.22	272.8	SNOWLINE 7.1	117.2	f 2.21	9.51	7.20	
WFTYP		A 1.15PM	A 5.20PM	A 5.35AM	279.9	DN-R **LIMA** RD	110.1	2.10PM	9.40PM	7.00AM	
						(146.7)		Daily	Daily	Daily	Daily
	(1.30) 34.2	(7.45) 18.8	(3.55) 27.3	(4.05) 25.7	....	Thru Time Average speed per hour		(4.00) 36.5	(3.50) 38.1	(9.00) 16.2	(1.50) 27.7

Westward trains are superior to trains of the same class in the opposite direction

The reproductions on these two pages of the April 19, 1938, employees' timetable no. 250, supplement no. 1, Idaho Division 7th and 8th Subdivisions (as the old Montana Division was now termed) provide both train scheduling and station and mileage data for the line.

WESTWARD					EIGHTH SUBDIVISION				EASTWARD		
Length of sidings in feet between clearance points, location of water, fuel, interlocking plants, turning stations, scales and telephones.	SECOND CLASS	FIRST CLASS		Distance from Ogden via Old Main Line	Supplement No. 1 to Time-Table No. 250 April 10, 1938			Distance from Silver Bow via New Main Line	FIRST CLASS		SECOND CLASS
	277 Time Freight	31 Passenger	29 Passenger						30 Passenger	32 Passenger	278 Time Freight
	Daily	Daily	Daily			STATIONS					
WFTYP	4.15PM	5.30PM	**5.45AM**	279.9	DN-R	**LIMA**	RD	110.1	A **2.00PM**	A 9.30PM	A **5.45AM**
		f		284.9		5.0 GOSMAN (Spur)		105.1	f		
2,563 WP	4.40	s 5.42	s 5.57	288.0	D	3.1 DELL	DE	102.0	s 1.43	f 9.18	3.40
		f		291.7		3.7 McKNIGHT (Spur)		98.3	f	f	
2,571 P	4.55	f 5.48	f 6.03	294.0		2.3 KIDD		96.0	f 1.34	f 9.10	3.21
2,605 WP	5.10	f 5.57	f 6.12	302.8		8.8 RED ROCK		87.2	f 1.21	f 8.58	3.02
2,877 P	5.45	s 6.05	s 6.20	307.0	D	4.2 ARMSTEAD	AD	83.0	s 1.14	f 8.52	2.50
2,651 P	5.57	f 6.15	f 6.30	312.9		5.9 GRAYLING		77.1	f 1.01	f 8.43	2.15
991 P		f	f	316.4		3.5 DALYS		73.6	f	f	
3,421 P	6.12	6.28	f 6.43	320.4		4.0 BARRETTS		69.6	f 12.48	f 8.34	1.50
3,461 WFTP	**6.43** **8.25**	s **6.43**	s 6.57	328.0	DN	7.6 DILLON	DN	62.0	s 12.38	s **8.25**	1.30AM
2,024 P	8.55	f 6.51	f 7.05	334.4		6.4 BOND		55.6	f 12.28	f 8.13	11.50PM
2,429 P	9.25	f 6.59	f 7.13	340.3		5.9 APEX		49.7	f 12.20	f 8.07	11.35
		s	f	347.8		7.5 GLEN (Spur)		42.2	s	f	
2,586 YP	9.50	7.17	7.31	348.7		0.9 NAVY		41.3	12.05	7.50	11.05
2,719 P	10.01	f 7.21	f 7.35	351.7		3.0 LAVON		38.3	f 12.01PM	f 7.46	10.55
		f		352.9		1.2 BROWNS (Spur)		37.1	f	f	
3,256 WFP	**10.40**	s **7.32**	s 7.47	358.9	D	6.0 MELROSE	VI	31.1	s 11.43AM	s **7.32**	**10.40**
2,109 P	11.01	f 7.48	f 7.58	364.9		6.0 QUINN		25.1	f 11.32	f 7.15	9.30
P		f	f	366.0		1.1 MAIDEN ROCK		24.0	f	f	
2,198	11.20	s 8.00	s 8.09	370.1	D	4.1 DIVIDE	J	19.9	s 11.21	s 7.05	9.05
3,454	11.40PM	f 8.05	f 8.15	374.3		4.2 WOODIN		15.7	f 11.13	f 6.59	8.40
				378.9		4.6 BEAUDINES (Spur)		11.1			
2,350 P	12.05AM	f **8.18**	f 8.28	380.7		1.8 FEELY		9.3	f 11.03	f 6.52	**8.18**
1,888 P	12.20	f 8.27	f 8.39	384.6		3.9 BUXTON		5.4	f 10.54	f 6.45	7.55
				386.8		2.2 ENRIGHT (Spur)		3.2			
WFY	A 2.00AM	A 8.40PM	A 8.50AM	390.0	DN-R	3.2 **SILVER BOW**	SB	0.0	10.45AM	6.35PM	7.45PM
						(110.1)			Daily	Daily	Daily
	(9.45) 11.3	(3.10) 34.8	(3.05) 35.7			Thru Time Average speed per hour			(3.15) 33.9	(2.55) 37.8	(10.00) 11.0

Schedules below are for information only. Use time-table and rules of Northern Pacific Railway between Silver Bow and Butte.

	277	31	29	Dist.		Stations		Dist.	30	32	278
	3.00AM	8.45PM	8.55AM	390.0	DN	**SILVER BOW**	SB	7.0	A 10.40AM	A 6.35PM	A 7.10PM
	A 3.30AM	A 9.05PM	A 9.15AM	397.0	DN	7.0 **BUTTE**	BY	0.0	10.25AM	6.20PM	6.45PM
						(117.1)			Daily	Daily	Daily
	(11.15) 10.4	(3.35) 32.7	(3.30) 33.5			Thru Time Average speed per hour			(3.35) 32.7	(3.10) 37.0	(11.00) 10.6

Westward trains are superior to trains of the same class in the opposite direction—See rule 72.

401
401
401

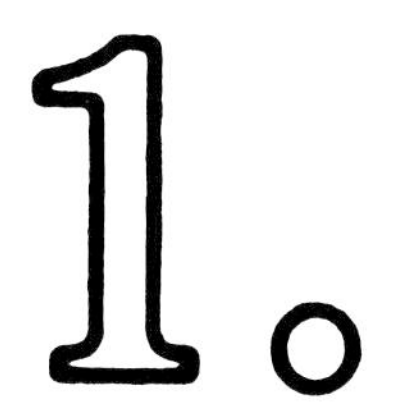

A Series of Photo-Essay Portfolios

Pocatello

Pocatello was the nerve center of the Oregon Short Line system and the principal terminal for the Pocatello-Butte line. Its depot facilities served tens of thousands of passengers and trainmen from trains going east and west, north and south. These facilities — actually, two station buildings and the Pacific Hotel — are shown in 1898 at left, and in 1909 below, with a through flyer smoking up the new striped awnings. The tinder-box frame construction miraculously avoided conflagration for over three decades, giving rise to the eventual claim that the depot was "the only fire-proof building in Idaho." The adjacent roundhouse became the second busiest on the Union Pacific system, and in the early years of the century its turntable still seemed well suited to aging eightwheelers like no. 401. *(Three photos, C. H. Peake Collection)*

The old Pocatello depots are seen clearly here from the top of the water tank, looking west, about 1909. The baker's-dozen cabooses lined up in front attest to the number of freights operating out of Pocatello. Snow or sunshine, George Hessel still met the trains with his trusty horse and wagon to deliver and pick up the U.S. Mail (below). (Both, C. H. Peake Collection)

Cross-compound tenwheelers like the 807 (above, Arthur Petersen Collection) were used on main line passenger trains until bumped by heavier Pacifics. Converted to simple, they turned up on secondary runs, like no. 820 below, waiting at Pocatello in 1913 for the Ashton local. (C. H. Peake Collection)

Center St Viaduct-

High-stepping Atlantics like no. 859, above, appeared in Pocatello on a few fast runs, but the mounds of mail and express being transferred at the depot, below, are an indication of why most schedules were more leisurely. Left above, Engineer George Oliver and Conductor John Freman compare watches as they pose for a photographer, before leaving town with no. 5, a heavy mail and express run. The time is 1913 and the incidence of such long trains at the station day and night has created a traffic problem on Pocatello's streets that the UP sought to alleviate by the construction of a viaduct for Center Street — seen in the background and in the photo below. Although the latter photo dates from about 1912, plenty of horses and wagons are still in evidence, and a pair of Indians are riding a pony bareback in the foreground, accompanied by their dog. (Lower left, Joe Marker; others, C. H. Peake Collection)

A handsome new depot was erected in 1915, in a new, less congested location. Left above, the construction of building and new trackage is well under way in 1914; some of the tracks in the crowded yard scene below have already been moved in a general revamping and expansion. Above, the imposing new structure is dedicated on August 21, 1915, with flags and bunting, parades and speeches. First train to use the new facilities later that day was no. 19, as shown below. (All, C. H. Peake Collection)

The Pocatello station continued to be a busy place into the 1920's, as these views illustrate. The panorama opposite (top) must have seemed impressive to railroad officials and average citizens alike, but the dead engines in the foreground were a harbinger of less prosperous times to come. Still another precursor of change came a few years later, when the first Union Pacific streamliner called at Pocatello. This change would be dramatic indeed. (Upper left and lower right, C. H. Peake Collection; others, Union Pacific Railroad)

SAFETY-FIRST
1ST. STREAMLINE-TRAIN - POCATELLO IDAHO

The Union Pacific's tie treating plant was a busy place in 1925. Green ties were brought in from Montana and other tie-cutting areas, processed in the treating plant, and then brought out into the yard to cool and be stacked for storage and eventual shipment all over the UP system. Little 0-4-0 no. MW001 did the switching for the plant for many years. (Top, Union Pacific Railroad photo from Mallory Hope Ferrell; others, U.S.D.A. Forest Service photos)

A Series of Photo-Essay Portfolios

Branch Lines

With the development of agriculture in the broad valley of the Snake River north of Pocatello, many new branch lines were constructed in the early 1900's. Among the most important was a network of lines leading up to St. Anthony, Ashton, West Yellowstone and Victor; another major line ran to Mackay. The little two-car snow-covered accommodation below is the Mackay Branch train at Blackfoot in 1917; it is pulled by eightwheeler no. 1009, former OSL 400. *(Arthur Petersen Collection)* Traffic sources and density varied greatly over the different branches, but all contributed significantly to the flood of business passing through Pocatello.

Motor Car, Blackfoot, Idaho. 1914
BAGGAGE
470

X1578
1578
UNION PACIFIC

478
2135
UNION PACIFIC

Motive power for the branches was largely inherited main line power, displaced by new heavier engines. McKeen motor cars appeared on the branch lines as early as 1914, as shown above left at Blackfoot. (Joe Marker Collection) The big 560-class 2-8-0's came to the major branch lines after World War I; the 560 itself turned up at West Yellowstone in 1925 (below). Typical power in the 1940's were tenwheelers like the 1578 on passenger and low-wheeled Mikes like the 2135 on freight (opposite), and 2-8-0's like the 525 (bottom) in general service. (All, Arthur Petersen Collection)

The Victor Branch is subject to considerable snow; the 1916 view above shows OSL Rotary 2011 working past MP 9.8, with 4-6-0 no. 1560 and a 4100-series Mogul pushing. At left, 2-8-0 no. 537 is stopped in a particularly deep cut on the branch about 1920. A balmier 1952 view at Victor, below, shows the typical two-car passenger powered by no. 3137, one of the low-wheeled Pacifics favored for such runs. (All, Arthur Petersen Collection)

Yellowstone National Park was a tourist attraction for the original Utah & Northern narrow gauge trains, and as early as 1881 a regular stage service operated from Monida to the Park, about 70 miles. Construction of a Northern Pacific branch right to the north Park entrance at Gardiner in 1903 served both to provide competition for the UP service and to alert the UP to the traffic potential. A branch line had been opened from Idaho Falls to Rexburg and St. Anthony in 1900, and extension of this line towards the Park was begun in 1905-6. West Yellowstone entrance was reached in 1908, and through service begun in the 1909 season. To reach West Yellowstone the line had to cross 6934-foot high Reas Pass, and this section of the route was subject to extreme winter snow conditions. Accordingly, the line was closed each fall and reopened in March; it often took two days for the rotary to fight through the last twenty miles of drifts, some 30 feet deep. In the dramatic view below, the rotary is just coming onto High Bridge, between MP 94 and 95, on one of the annual spring openings many years ago. (C. H. Peake Collection)

Most spectacular of the various branches was the Yellowstone Branch, to West Yellowstone, Montana, via Reas Pass. The view above shows OSL tenwheeler no. 680 at the top of the Pass in 1912. (Arthur Petersen Coll.) Below left, OSL 631 and another 4-6-0 at rear with a work train on the newly constructed High Bridge in 1908. (C. H. Peake Coll.) Idaho Falls' new importance as a branch terminal warranted a new brick and tile station. (J. D. Marker Coll.) Opposite, Warm River Canyon was a scenic feature of the branch. In these 1930 views it is seen from northbound train 45 in the early morning (top) and the first section of southbound no. 46 in the evening. (Both, C. H. Peake Coll.)

President "Teddy" Roosevelt came through Lima on a special, and this tenwheeler was specially decorated by the local Brotherhood of Locomotive Firemen members. Several photos were taken of the locomotive while it was waiting in front of the depot, including one by Mrs. Merrell's Uncle Frank, seen with tripod in the foreground. (W. T. Cheney photo, Mrs. Bonnie Merrell Coll.)

A Series of Photo-Essay Portfolios

Lima

Lima (originally Spring Hill) was situated in a broad valley fifteen miles north of the summit at Monida, and during the years before and after World War I the town was a major helper terminal, boasting a large roundhouse and shops. During this period W. T. Cheney was employed there by the UP as car repairman, foreman and hook operator; and having a proficiency for photography as well he served as sometimes semi-official photographer for the railroad there. Fortunately many of his excellent views of Lima have been preserved by his daughter, Mrs. Bonnie Merrell, and some are reproduced here. Below, one of the earliest is this 1902 panorama of Lima looking northwest; the town is strung out along the railroad (yards are off to the right), with the big schoolhouse beyond and the town race track in the foreground. *(W. T. Cheney photo, Coll. of Mrs. Bonnie Merrell)*

Sometime about 1910-12 Mr. Cheney made a series of photographs of Lima and the railroad's yards. Above, the view looking south from the top of the coal chute, showing turntable, water tower, yards and town; below, a closer view of the water tower (taken from a telephone pole?) looking southwest across the yards tracks and "company houses." (All photos, W. T. Cheney, Coll. of Mrs. Bonnie Merrell)

The views above are looking south-southwest and west-southwest from the coal chute; the large windowless structure is the ice house. Right, looking northeast from the top of the roundhouse; the odd fence apparent here and in several of the other views surrounded the roundhouse area and was said to have been built to keep out strikers during a strike about 1907. (W. T. Cheney, Mrs. Bonnie Merrell Coll.)

4-8-0's like no. 906 above were used on the Monida grade in helper service when this photo was taken about 1905. Standard freight power was represented by 2-8-0 no. 1015 (later UP 565) as pictured at right at Lima about 1910. (Both, Arthur Petersen Coll.)

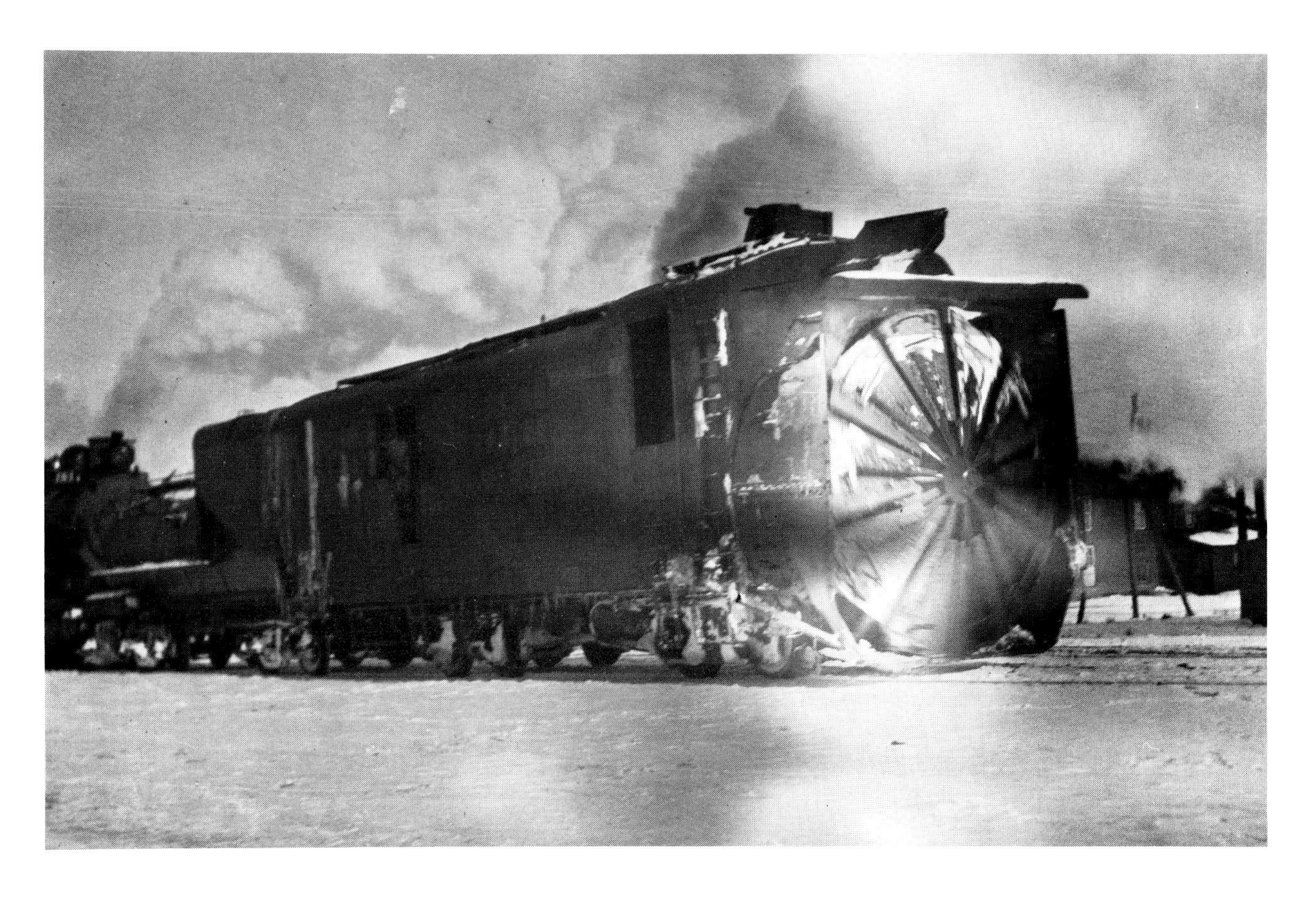

Lima regularly saw the rotary in winter — here (above) in the winter of 1917-18. (W. T. Cheney, Mrs. Bonnie Merrell Coll.) After World War I, mallets like no. 3633 arrived on the line to partially displace the 560-class 2-8-0's. (Don H. Roberts photo)

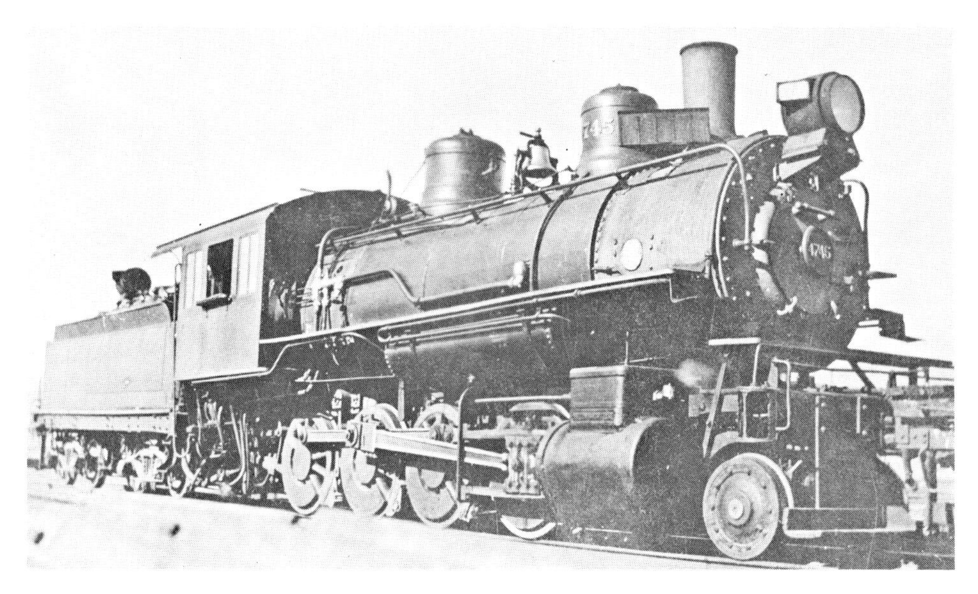

Lima's importance as a helper terminal led to construction of a large brick roundhouse (above). Cheney photographed all of the roundhouse crew about 1917 (opposite) in connection with an award, perhaps for buying war bonds. (All, W. T. Cheney photos) In the twenties old 2-8-0's like no. 4745 turned up as switchers at Lima. (Left, Arthur Petersen Coll.)

579
565

OREGON SHORT LINE

Cheney was on hand for wrecks, and sometimes had a moment free to take photographs. The wreck here illustrated occurred at Barratt's on August 18, 1906, killing the conductor of a freight and injuring ten passengers on no. 10. The freight had pulled into a siding to let the passenger by, but the crew failed to line the switch and the passenger plunged onto the siding and crashed into the caboose. No. 10's tenwheeler and express refrigerator car are shown later at Lima at right. (All, W. T. Cheney photos, Mrs. Bonnie Merrell Coll.)

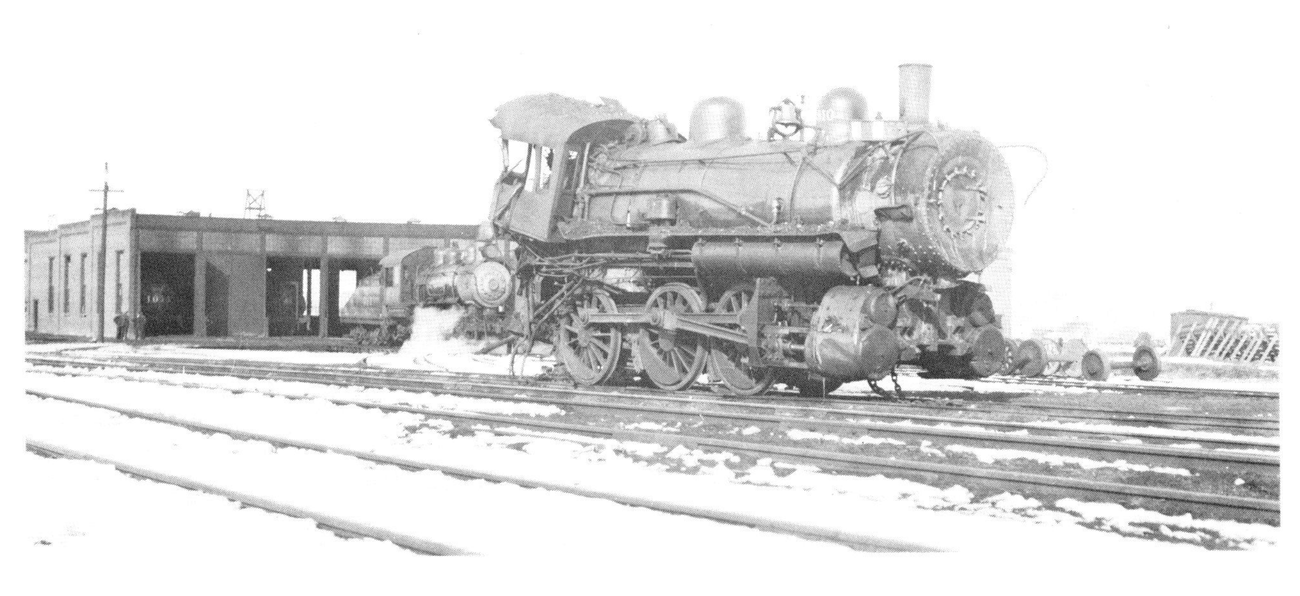

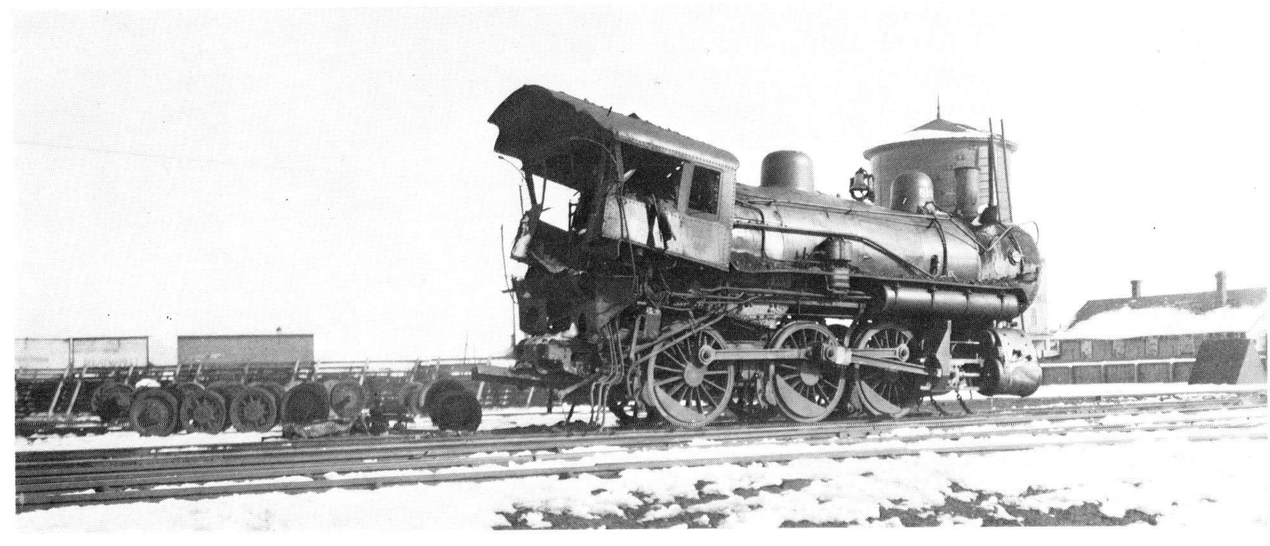

Three views on these pages show the clean-up operations of a freight wreck at Apex around the World War I period. The OSL wrecker was brought up from Pocatello and a Butte, Anaconda & Pacific wrecking train was brought down from Lima where it had been stationed. Another wreck with, for once, some compensations occurred when a stock car filled with watermelons was dumped in the turntable pit, and everyone enjoyed fresh watermelon at the railroad's expense (lower right). (All, W. T. Cheney photos, Mrs. Bonnie Merrell Coll.)

B.A.& P.
TOOL CAR 58

S.P.
Wrecked
Watermelon CAR AT LIMA

A Series of Photo-Essay Portfolios

Over the Line

One of the most important facets of the story of any railroad is that of the trains that operated over the line down through the years. Illustrated in this section are a representation of the trains that ran to Butte between World War I and the 1950's. Perhaps because of the remoteness of the area and ruggedness of the terrain, action photographs of the Butte line, particularly in early years, are quite rare. On the page opposite are two views from about the 1910 period showing passenger trains in scenic Beaver Canyon, while below ten-wheeler 811 was photographed at Melrose in 1914 at the head of train no. 90, a local briefly operated between Butte and Dillon. *(Opposite, top, Henry R. Griffiths Collection; bottom, Montana Historical Society Collection; below, Shira Photo, Arthur Petersen Collection)*

During the 1930's highwheeled 4-6-2's were standard passenger power. Opposite, from top, no. 3120 is stepping along at a good 60 mph clip with train 31, the Butte Express, *nearing Butte on a September afternoon in 1931; the same no. 3120 is seen at the Pocatello engine terminal in March 1935; and no. 3131 is shown leaving Pocatello with no. 31, the* Butte Express, *in November 1936. (Center, Walt Thrall Collection; other two, Otto Perry photos from Denver Public Library Western History Collection) On this page, sister engine 3114 — now considerably modified — pauses at Idaho Falls in May 1947 with train 34. (Arthur Petersen Collection)*

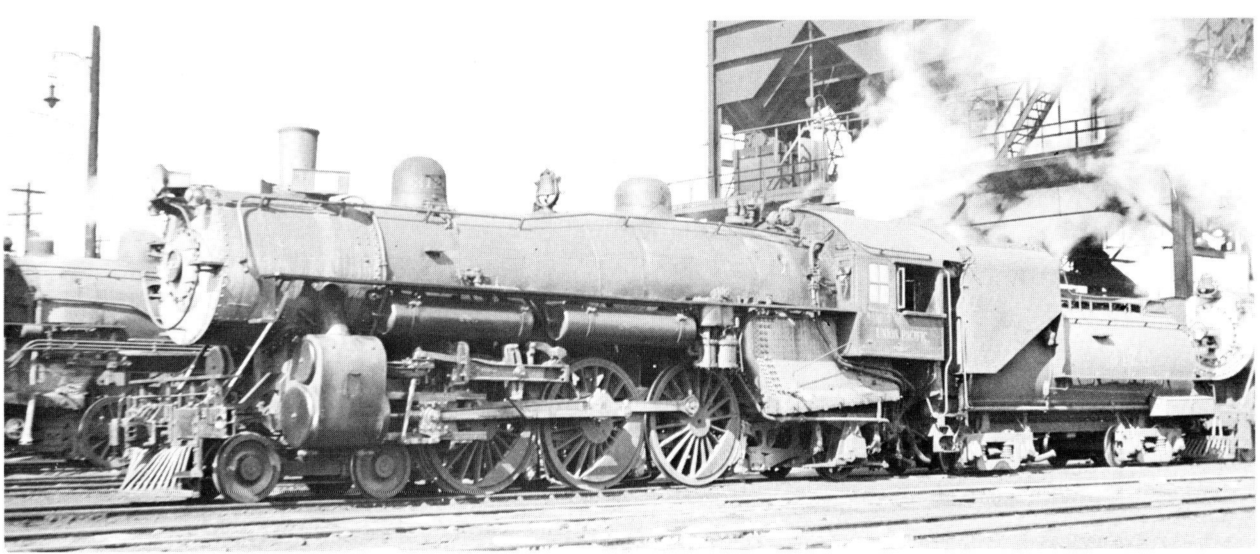

31

Heavier consists for nos. 29 and 30 eventually brought assignment of 4-8-2's to the run, such as no. 7019 at Pocatello in 1940, above. (Arthur Petersen Collection) In June 1949 Otto Perry photographed no. 7867 (below) drifting along near Melrose, Montana, at 35 mph. with train 30 the Butte Special. *(Denver Public Library Western History Collection)*

By 1950, when this mid-summer photograph was made, the Butte Special *rated a 3800-class 4-6-6-4 and business was good.* Here no. 3835 *makes the station stop at Dillon with the eight cars of train 29; it is 5:30 AM, the sun has just peaked over the horizon, and most passengers and Dillonites alike are still sound asleep. Fortunately not our photographer Philip C. Johnson, however, who filmed this handsome panoramic view of the* Special *in its waning glory period.*

Big 2-10-2's arrived on the Butte line around 1930 and were used on through freights until the end of steam. The 5300, first of the class, is shown at top at Butte in 1936 (Harold K. Vollrath Coll.) and at Pocatello in 1946 (Arthur Petersen Coll.) — with a change in headlight position in the interim. 3500 and 3600-class 2-8-8-0 articulateds were also used in main line service — such as the 3507 below, at Pocatello in 1947. Upper right, no. 3633 is seen coming into Ft. Hall, Idaho, in 1928 with a westbound freight, in a view that implies carefully manicured, class I railroading. (Both photos, Arthur Petersen Coll.) Bottom right, no. 3500 storms along near Glen, Montana, with the twenty cars of scheduled time freight no. 256 in the spring of 1947. (Warren R. McGee photo)

1468

In the latter days of steam, modern power arrived on the line in the form of 3800-class 4-6-6-4 articulateds. Above, Henry R. Griffiths photographed no. 3832 threading the upper part of Beaver Canyon in July 1951 with the 21 cars of train 277. The 3821 is at Pocatello in 1950 in the rail-level view at left by Arthur Petersen. Below, Otto Perry (Denver Public Library, Western History Dept.) found nos. 3833 and 3834 shoving train 277 up the hill near Spencer in 1949.

In this dramatic view by Henry R. Griffiths, 4-6-6-4 no. 3836 is battling up the 2.33% grade in the heart of Beaver Canyon with train 277 on May 30, 1948. This section of the line up the south side of the Bitter Root Mountains is probably the most spectacularly scenic of any part of the old Utah & Northern route.

RATING OF STEAM LOCOMOTIVES IN FREIGHT SERVICE IN TONS OF 2000 POUNDS

Total weight of train exclusive of locomotive and tender, which the different classes of locomotives will haul in each direction between stations named, under favorable weather conditions. A deduction of ten per cent may be made for time freight trains.

TYPE OF LOCOMOTIVE			NUMBERS Inclusive	Granger to Kemmerer	** Kemmerer to Montpelier	Montpelier to McCammon	Pocatello to McCammon	McCammon to Montpelier	** Montpelier to Kemmerer	Kemmerer to Granger	Pocatello to Idaho Falls	Idaho Falls to Lima	Lima to Dillon	Dillon to Silver Bow	Silver Bow to Butte	Butte to Silver Bow	Silver Bow to Dillon	Dillon to Lima	Lima to Idaho Falls
C 57	22 / 31	190 191	201 to 358 560 to 622	2060	3350	2850	2060	1500	2100	3100	3450	*2530	4000	3200	1080	4650	*1300	1500	*2500
FEF 77 FEF 80	24½ / 32 25 / 32	266 266	800 to 819 820 to 844	3300	5000	4540	2950	2130	3050	5000									
MacA 57	23¾ / 30	206 210	1900 to 1949 2000 to 2034	2400	3800	3250	2400	1700	2400	3525	3800	*2850	4250	*3600	1200	5250	*1500	1650	*2850
MacA 63	26 / 28	214 216	2504 to 2532	2500	4050	3450	2525	1800	2500	3750	4250	*3050	4350	*3800	1300	5850	*1600	1850	*3050
MacA 63	26 / 30	220	2535 to 2554	2600	4200	3575	2600	1900	2600	3900	4335	*3200	4400	*3900	1350	5970	*1650	1940	*3200
MacA 63	26 / 28	228	2555 to 2564	2550	4110	3500	2540	1860	2540	3820	4250	*3130	4370	*3820	1325	5850	*1625	1900	*3150
P 77	22 / 28	135 143 149 150	2819 to 2859 3100 to 3113 3160 3202 to 3217	1630	2560	2140	1390	900	1450	2900	2340	*1560	2700	*2310	610	3230	*780	1000	*1540
P 77	25 / 28	163 165 167 184 193	2860 to 2899 2900 to 2911 3114 to 3181 3218 to 3227	2060	3350	2850	2060	1500	2100	3100	3390	*2280	3900	*3060	890	4550	*1140	1320	*2260
SA-C 59	23-23 / 30	475D	3500 to 3569								7900	*4250	7000	*5650	2150	8000	*3180	3500	*5310
MC 57	25-39 / 32	485	3600 to 3674								8000	*4980	7350	*6120	2550	8000	*3240	4110	*5780
CSA 69	22-22 / 32	400 394 407	3800 to 3809 3810 to 3814 3815 to 3839	4600	5000	5000	4600	3700	4600	5000	7900	*4150	7000	*5550	2050	8000	*3080	3400	*5210
4-6-6-4 69	3 / 4 / 5 — 21-21 / 32	404 407 406	3930 to 3949 3950 to 3969 3975 to 3999	4600	5000	5000	4600	3700	4600	5000									
4-8-8-4 68	1 / 2 — 23¾-23¾ / 32	540 545	4000 to 4019 4020 to 4024	8000	8000	8000	6500	4800	6800	8000									
TTT 63	29½ / 30	290 311	5000 to 5089 5300 to 5318 5400 to 5414 5500 to 5529	3350	5000	4750	3350	2600	3600	5000	5600	*4100	5000	*4800	1730	7600	*2120	2450	*4120
MT 73	29 / 28	256	7000 to 7039 7850 to 7869	2650	4250	3625	2650	1950	2650	4000	4340	*3170	4350	*3850	1300	5950	*1620	1925	*3175
UP 67	27 / 31-32	368 372	9000 to 9087	4600	5000	5000	4600	3700	4600	5000									

EXPLANATION

C Consolidation
P Pacific
MC Mallet
MacA MacArthur
MT Mountain

TTT 2-10-2
C-SA Challenger
SA-C Mallet SA

UP 4-6-6-4
UP 4-8-8-4
FEF 4-8-4

Example: Consolidation locomotive having 57-inch drivers, cylinders 22-inch diameter and 30-inch stroke and weighing 191,000 pounds on drivers:

C 57 $\frac{22}{30}$ 191

*With helpers.
**With helpers between Nugget and Kemmerer.
McCammon to Pocatello—car limit.
Idaho Falls to Pocatello—car limit.

A Series of Photo-Essay Portfolios

Butte

Butte emerged both as the northern terminus of the Montana Division and as a major source of traffic for the line. Because the Union Pacific did not have its own facilities at Butte, but rented from the Northern Pacific (a result of having spun off the Butte-Garrison line to the Montana Union), Butte never had the appearance of a major UP terminal. In days of steam, however, the presence of many UP engines at the Northern Pacific engine house attested to Butte's importance to the UP. The chart at left (reprinted from the August 1949 UP timetable for the Division) lists the power used on the line and tonnage ratings. Below, this August 1917 view across part of Butte towards the busy Neversweat and Anaconda mines provides something of the flavor of Butte during those days of mining prosperity. *(University of Washington Libraries Collection)*

X5315
5315

X5307
5307

Heavy power on the Butte line included 2-10-2's like those at left, both at the engine house — no. 5315 in March 1936 (top, Don H. Roberts photo), and no. 5307 a few years later, with a center-mounted headlight (Museum Collection). 2-8-2's were also common, particularly in helper and local freight work. No. 2552 above (Museum Collection) clearly shows its USRA parentage, while the 2522 below (Robert Graham photo) has more of a Harriman-era appearance.

29
UNION PACIFIC
3119

62 32
2862
UNION PACIFIC
2862

For many years passenger trains were powered by 4-6-2's such as those shown on these pages. Top opposite, Don Roberts found no. 3119 sitting placidly by the depot one March day in 1936, at the head of train 29. Below, Otto Perry photographed no. 2862 with train 32, the Butte-Salt Lake Express, *in August 1938 as it was loading at the station. (Both, Denver Public Library Western History Dept.) On this page, nos. 3114, 3115 and 3131 are all at the engine terminal in the 1930's, after bringing in train 29. The 3131 has clearly encountered some snow in the coming. (Robert Graham, Museum Collection)*

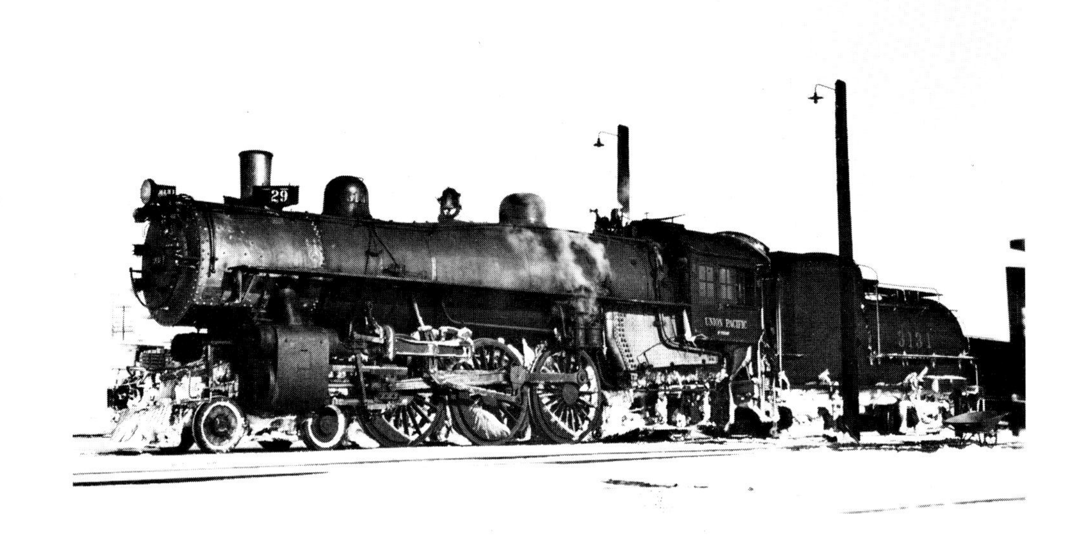

Philip R. Hastings had the good fortune to ride the Butte Special *in October 1968, and took these excellent photographs while waiting for the train's departure. Above, the train was already made up and waiting at the station when the westbound Northern Pacific* North Coast Limited *stopped to discharge passengers, a few of whom would transfer to UP train 36. Below, 2½ hours still remained before train time; the two* **E9's** *waited with a baggage, sleeper* American View, *and two coaches. The sleeper was unusual: the two end open sections had been converted to a mini-buffet, with a galley on one side and a dining table with four chairs on the other, making the car a 6 roomette, 4 bedroom, 4 section cafe sleeper.*

An approaching snow squall, below, threw a shadow over the station, but the E9's and old NP freight house beyond were still in sunlight. As dusk arrived, left, the platform lights and car lights were turned on, and the Butte Special *would soon be loading for its 7:30 PM departure for Salt Lake City. (Four photos, Philip R. Hastings)*

While waiting for the Butte Special *to leave, Phil Hastings explored the yards and found the old engine house populated by four UP units being readied for a night run to Pocatello — a GP20, GP9B, GP9 and a GP30. (Both, Philip R. Hastings)*

Heading into the sunset: although the Butte Special *still had nearly six years of continued operation ahead of it when Philip C. Johnson made this panoramic view in 1965, its days were clearly numbered and the scene somehow seems prophetic. The last rays of the setting sun bathe the train in fading light as it approaches Silver Bow, having just switched off the Northern Pacific main line (foreground) and onto UP tracks for the night's run across the forbidding mountain fastness ahead.*

"Outward Bound from Leadore" is the title of this dramatic photograph made by J. Foster Adams on August 22, 1912. The short mixed train is charging out of Leadore towards the steep grades of Bannock Pass behind 2-8-0 no. 13, a Pennsy hand-me-down, and 2-8-2 no. 10, one of the pair of Baldwin Mikes that would see nearly 30 years of service as the G&P's principal freight power. Adams was a talented postcard photographer in the Pacific Northwest who took many outstanding railroad action photos — including a number of the G&P — in a day when very few were doing so. (Collection of Rocky Mountain Railroad Club)

the implausible

Gilmore & Pittsburgh

Northern Pacific subsidiary, Union Pacific tributary

by Rex C. Myers

" 'Tis a dull week without its Railroad Inspiration," a Salmon, Idaho, newspaper editor observed during the first decade of the Twentieth Century. For the editor, for the town, for farmers, ranchers and miners spread along the bottom of the Lemhi Valley or scattered across the broad expanses of Horse Prairie, inspiration came in the form of the Gilmore & Pittsburgh Railroad. Linking Armstead, Montana, with Gilmore and Salmon, Idaho, this 120 mile railroad served as a Northern Pacific-controlled, Oregon Short Line feeder from 1910 until its abandonment in 1939. Its history is a study in short line frustration and deficit operation.

Edgar C. Ross of Pittsburgh, Pennsylvania, began developing lead and silver mines along Horse Shoe Gulch, near the headwaters of the Lemhi River, in 1902. Before long a community sprang up, and boomers for the district secured a post office under the name Gilmore. For three years Ross shipped ore by wagon to the nearest railroad connection at Dubois, Idaho, where the Oregon Short Line started the concentrates on their way to Pittsburgh smelters. Word soon spread of the rich deposits tucked away in Horse Shoe Gulch and eastern investors began looking to potential profits in the far off Lemhi Valley.

Other eyes gazed at the Rocky Mountains and beyond. In a last spurt of transcontinental railroad building, the Chicago, Milwaukee & St. Paul looked to the Pacific Coast, as did the Chicago & Northwestern, the Burlington Road and others. To the north the Great Northern and the Northern Pacific eyed Pacific ports further south than the Columbia River — a lucrative California market and competition with the Southern Pacific. Front men, investors, speculators and survey crews shared the mountain valleys of Idaho and Montana during the summer while untold local editors cogitated the possibilities and potential year around.

In the middle — at least in the minds of Salmon and Gilmore residents — lay their valley. Editorial speculation in Salmon's *Lemhi Herald* ran rampant. At one point the editor identified ten potential entrants in the race to build into the Lemhi country:

1. The Chicago, Burlington & Quincy — "going via Salmon to the coast."
2. An electric interurban line from Idaho Falls through Salmon to Butte, Montana "a go."
3. A Butte to Boise line — "still a most lively issue."
4. An Oregon Short Line extension — "coming our way."
5. A Denver-Seattle railroad with "at least a branch" to Salmon.
6. The Chicago & Northwestern — which "must have this route for its coast extension."
7. Salmon-Boise-Coos Bay Railroad — "a great road, flatteringly alluded to."
8. The Butte, Salmon, Thunder Mountain and San Francisco road — "which will open the mineral empire and cross all the other roads."

9. Northern Pacific — whose officials "undoubtedly aim to build into Salmon."
10. The Gilmore & Pittsburgh Railroad — "to be the grandest scenic route in the world."

When the puff and editorial dust had settled the Lemhi Valley had but one railroad. Yet in the dreaming years before the Gilmore & Pittsburgh's construction, illusions of grandeur sparked local optimism and warmed the hopes of businessmen and ranchers from Horse Shoe Gulch to Salmon.

> Salmon is to become the only great city and great railroad center of this great northwest. It will be the chief supplying center and distributing point between the Pacific and the Missouri River, the grand emporium and convention center of Idaho, where north and south will shake hands, and where east and west will change cars if they want to go anywhere. It will be the biggest hotel city in the West and by reason of its abundant water power will vie with all competitors as a manufacturing center.

Dreams. But in the Eastern financial centers, concrete plans developed to bring trains to the Lemhi Valley and rail service closer to Edgar Ross's mines. On February 20, 1907, four Pennsylvania businessmen and W. F. Stone of Junction, Idaho, formed The Gilmore & Pittsburgh Railroad Company, Ltd. Stone, C. H. McCracken, J. H. Crehan, and Robert B. Little each invested $100.00 and their support toward the goal. W. A. McCutcheon invested too — $69,600 in cash for controlling interest in the company.

McCutcheon envisioned a standard gauge line from the Oregon Short Line at Armstead where Horse Prairie Creek joined the Beaverhead River, west through the prairie, south over 7,672 foot Bannock Pass, and into Idaho. On striking the Lemhi River, the Pittsburgh businessman proposed to divide the railroad: one branch to head north and west toward Salmon; the second, to follow the river southeast to Gilmore's mines, where McCutcheon also had financial interests.

Armstead had revenue potential the easterner liked. Harry Armstead shipped regularly from his Silver Fissure Mine at Polaris to the OSL. He spurred development of a town at the shipping point, named it after himself, and helped get a post office established a month before the G&P idea reached the incorporation stage. McCutcheon planned to intercept Armstead's ore shipments some fifteen or twenty miles up Horse Prairie Creek and share that traffic, in addition to revenues Lemhi Valley would generate.

When it came to future revenues, Salmon and Lemhi residents proved not the least bit

modest in their estimations. With unabashed boosterism they bombarded McCutcheon — or any railroad man who appeared interested — with petitions and letters, tonnage surveys, and a $300,000 annual gross revenue prediction for any railroad constructed into their region. Horse Prairie residents also pointed to livestock shipped out of their valley each year, suggesting the Gilmore & Pittsburgh might enjoy all or part of that traffic.

Optimistic, yes; but McCutcheon also knew the realities of railroad construction. He incorporated the G & P at $2,000,000 and knew it would take more to build the line — perhaps twice that amount. He needed financial assistance and turned to the Oregon Short Line, the Great Northern and the Northern Pacific for possible help. Each road investigated the potential.

Northern Pacific surveyors joined those of

Armstead was named for Silver Fissure Mine owner Harry Armstead, shown at left with his two Police Dogs, Prinz and Doley; the town is shown below from the new G&P track, with a corner of the UP depot at right. (Both, Beaverhead County Museum Coll.) An earlier view of Armstead is at right, with snowcapped peaks beyond. (Collection of Rose Corum)

the G & P in the field during the summers of 1907 and 1908 to explore the possibilities. Earlier surveys in the 1850's and 1870's revealed river route potential for a railroad along the Salmon, to the Snake, the Columbia and the Pacific. In the early 1900's the Northern Pacific had two difficult Continental Divide crossings at 5,800 foot Mullan Pass west of Helena, and the 6,375 foot Homestake crossing near Butte. Perhaps the grade through Horse Prairie and the Lemhi Valley would prove easier; so the survey crews went out to check.

Northern Pacific officials did not find the results of the survey encouraging. Bannock Pass failed to offer substantial grade improvements, and the Salmon River Canyon's rugged confines — the River of No Return — promised to frustrate construction crews at every turn. Still those nagging traffic predictions from Lemhi Valley residents and the solicitations of W. A. McCutcheon persisted.

Without public fanfare, the Northern Pacific directors agreed in early 1909 to provide financial and material backing for the Gilmore & Pittsburgh. If McCutcheon completed the railroad, and if revenues justified, the NP planned to extend its branch line from Twin Bridges, Montana, southwest along the Beaverhead River, through Dillon, to Armstead — thus draining off traffic from the Oregon Short Line.

To Montana and Idaho residents the source of funding remained obscured — the Gilmore & Pittsburgh became a "Mystery Road;" but McCutcheon commenced construction immediately. On February 13, 1909, he filed a right-of-way with the U.S. Land Office in Helena: Armstead to Gilmore and Salmon. Lemhi Valley would get its railroad.

Within a month the Chicago contracting firm of MacArthur Brothers had the bid for grading,

Before the coming of the G&P, Harry Armstead's Silver Fissure Mine hauled their ore from Polaris to Armstead over primitive roads with this "road train," powered by a huge steam tractor — a product of the Pitts Co., Buffalo. In the view above the rig is being driven past Gray's Roadhouse at Mill Point, in Grasshopper Valley, by engineer Fred Woodside. (Beaverhead County Museum Collection) Below, the raw new trackage of the G&P leads west down Railroad Canyon. (Rose Corum Collection)

bridge work, and track laying. On March 15 John Duffy stepped off the train in Dillon and opened a bank account in the name of MacArthur Brothers. April 1st, 1000 teams entered the field, and subcontractors began to push work all along the way. Residents in Beaverhead and Lemhi Counties awoke to the realities of railroad construction.

Armstead boomed as an "end of track" town. In 1907 it had a post office and a siding. By the time snow left the ground in 1909, the town sported three general stores, a hotel, two barber shops, a blacksmith, several restaurants, numerous real estate agents and "all the usual businesses found in such a place." Such a place, and such people. Before long James Blair and Van Purdam had the Horse Prairie Club operating day and night. It hindered railroad construction and encouraged a "dangerous element" Beaverhead County Commissioners soon decided — license revoked. Then John Gelhaus appeared before the district judge. Armstead now had a stable population of 180, not counting transients; he argued the town needed a saloon — new license issued.

In August, Joe Nevin killed Shattuck Doyle at Armstead's Merry Widow Resort after an evening of dancing, drinking, and whoring. Nevin stole a horse from the Gilmore & Pittsburgh stable, left $15 for his girl friend — in a Dillon jail on prostitution charges — and fled. In disgust the local judge fined all "inmates" of the Merry Widow $25.00, and closed the place temporarily. Then subcontractor Frank Brown raped the thirteen year old daughter of an employee. By the time of Brown's trial and conviction in mid-November, Dillon residents did not care if they ever heard of the Gilmore & Pittsburgh again. But the mood soon changed.

W. A. McCutcheon appeared in Dillon on November 26. His railroad, he announced, would be extended from Armstead to Dillon early the following spring. Reporters covering the construction in Horse Prairie soon discovered two Northern Pacific locomotives and a string of NP box cars assisting with the work. Did it mean the NP would join the Gilmore & Pittsburgh at Dillon? McCutcheon did not say, but he suggested the Dillon Commercial Club secure a right-of-way between its town and Twin Bridges — just in case. Suddenly Dillon took an interest in the new railroad. Their enthusiasm blossomed with the flowers of spring.

Through the fall and winter of 1909-1910, construction and track laying proceeded westward from Armstead. Using a mechanical excavator, contractors turned dirt from the broad plains of Horse Prairie and Lemhi Valley. Successive horse-drawn dump wagons pulled under the conveyor, loaded, then deposited the fill on the grade. For major cuts — like the Desmond Cut west of Grant — crews drilled and blasted.

Gradually gandy dancers laid their 70 pound rail up Horse Prairie Creek to the west past Grant, Brenner and Donovan; then south. They made a wide 12° loop at Divide Creek and climbed toward the ridge of Bannock Pass on a 2.8 per cent grade; first with a three mile switchback, then a modest trestle over Divide Creek. Next came Wyno station, and finally a 600 foot, untimbered, curved tunnel at the Continental Divide, 7,575 feet above sea level.

By the new year — 1910 — Northern Pacific work engines had nudged construction down a winding, switchbacked course along the sage slopes of Canyon Creek, past Keefe and newly constructed cattle pens at the mouth of Cruik Creek, through Railroad Canyon, and down to the floor of the broad Lemhi Valley. On January 18 the first train reached Leadore, the junction point on the Lemhi River where branches left for Gilmore and Salmon. Grading and track laying continued: south 18 miles past Purcell to Gilmore; and then 48 miles northwest along the valley to Maier, Lemhi, Tendoy, Baker and Salmon.

On April 25, 1910, construction crews reached Salmon and by September, Gilmore. Done — 118 miles of track, 367,091 ties, 291 culverts, 51 pile bridges, four miles of snow fence. The Gilmore & Pittsburgh had become a reality. Salmon set May 18 as the official day of celebration. "The day will be filled with banquet and dancing," the paper said. "Dancing will continue for two days without intermission, everybody rag, . . . and everybody will be supposed to enjoy himself according to the varying turn of his sweet will." Town fathers invited ex-President Theodore Roosevelt and Democratic stalwart William Jennings Bryan to attend. They declined, but Idaho Governor James H. Brady and former Montana Governor B. F. White headed the program. F. B. Sharkey, the first settler in the Lemhi District, received the honor of driving a $600 golden "last spike" to commemorate the occasion; railroad president McCutcheon received a four foot long key to the City of Salmon, while young and old alike celebrated with an elaborate banquet put on by the Salmon City Commercial Club. Indeed, everybody went "rag."

Despite the driving of the gold spike at Salmon, the construction of the G&P was not finished when the merrymaking took place. For one thing, the drilling of the tunnel at the top of Bannock Pass was not yet completed. In order to hasten construction while this task was still uncompleted, the contractors had built a steep temporary track over the top of the pass, using still more switchbacks. Several of the road's surveying party had ridden over from Armstead in McCutcheon's private car, on the special to the gold spike ceremony, and one of them, E. B. Skeels, described the crossing of Bannock Pass in his memoirs:

> While Mr. McCutcheon was in the observation end of the car I showed Mr. Bacon [the Chief Engineer] some pictures I had taken of the Salmon River Canyon. While we were looking at the pictures . . . the train came to a sudden, jolting stop. We rushed outside to see what had happened and found that the engine had derailed on the skeleton track approaching the summit of Bannock Pass. The tunnel at the summit had not been completed and switchbacks on each side of the summit were in use . . . the rerailing of the engine on the skeleton track was a difficult and slow job.

The interest in the Salmon River Canyon photos was because Skeels and his party had been exploring and surveying the wild Salmon and Snake Rivers for an extension of the G&P line on a "water level grade" to the Columbia River and the coast. The undertaking was an arduous and dangerous one, and had to be done in boats over long stretches of white water — and proved in vain, as no one has ever attempted to run a railroad line through those forbidding canyons.

As his agent and general manager, W. A. McCutcheon selected W. N. Bichler who had managed G&P affairs during construction. On May 30 Bichler announced regular passenger schedules: leave Armstead Monday, Wednesday and Friday at 8:00 AM and arrive at Salmon that evening; leave Salmon alternate days (except Sundays) and arrive in Armstead in time to connect with the Oregon Short Line northbound. The established fare: Salmon or Gilmore to Leadore, $3.00; between the two Idaho termini and Armstead — $6.00 one way.

True to his promise, W. A. McCutcheon looked toward Dillon during the early months of 1910. In February, G&P attorney John R. Wheeler sent word to the community that he would be in town on the 16th and wanted to talk to businessmen and ranchers about the G&P extension to Dillon. Local interest in the new railroad revived immediately.

Wheeler walked into the packed Beaverhead Club rooms on the appointed night with a simple message. If Dillon residents pledged to help finance the purchase of land and the construction of a depot, the Gilmore & Pittsburgh would be into town before snow flew in the fall. Would they? Yes! — to the tune of $10,000 the local ranchers and townspeople stepped forward. All subscriptions specified completion of the line to Dillon before payment; but if Wheeler, Bichler, and the G&P could deliver, Dillon would do likewise.

The attorney left Beaverhead County for Pittsburgh the next day. Within two weeks he returned optimistic as ever. March 16th he proudly told the *Dillon Examiner* he had just signed papers for the purchase of 60 acres on the city's eastern edge. J. E. Morse and John F. Bishop sold the land through the Dillon Realty Company at an announced price of $37,500. The property, Wheeler explained, would provide sites for a depot, round house and switching yard. He left the date for construction to the discretion of the G&P engineering department.

Anxiously, Dillon residents waited . . . and waited . . . and waited. Railroad President W. A. McCutcheon announced unequivocably that his line would not extend down the Salmon River Canyon to the west, but he said nothing about Dillon or Twin Bridges.

Three factors dampened G&P enthusiasm. First, heavy costs involved in completing the line to Gilmore and Salmon drained company coffers and taxed the financial interest of its benefactor, the Northern Pacific. NP officials also began to get an inkling during those early months of operation that annual gross revenues would not approach the $300,000 figure Lemhi Valley residents foresaw.

Most important and debilitating, legal complications arose in securing right-of-way to the railroad's acreage adjacent to Dillon. Beaverhead County's leading ranching operation, the Poindexter and Orr Live Stock Company, owned 6.6 acres of land the railroad needed. Likewise, sheepman C. C. Cornell held another 5.5 acres which thwarted access to proposed yard and depot sites. Both parties refused to sell, so the Gilmore & Pittsburgh began the long process of condemnation.

Anticipating a successful suit, McCutcheon and Northern Pacific officials negotiated a joint trackage agreement with the Oregon Short Line giving the G&P running rights from Armstead to a point two miles south of Dillon. There Gilmore & Pittsburgh workmen inserted a switch and a short side track, awaiting only the outcome of the suit to push on into Dillon.

Initial appraisals for the Poindexter and Orr and the Cornell land left G&P officials aghast: $12,875.00 for property and damages to the ranch company; $11,500.00 to Cornell. The railroad appealed and the process dragged on through 1911 and into the next year.

On February 5, 1912, a jury trial on the matter came before District Judge L. L. Callaway. For a week, Dillon residents followed arguments and counter arguments between railroad and property owners. The verdict came in February 9 — original assessments were, indeed, too high: Poindexter and Orr deserved only

Above, the G&P tracklaying train approaches the Lemhi Valley from the mouth of the Junction Road Canyon — subsequently called Railroad Canyon. The snow and bitter cold must have made the job difficult. The logical objective was the established town of Junction (below), in the Lemhi Valley, but the railroad chose to bypass it a mile south and establish the new town of Leadore. Right, the railroad's engineers work on the plans. (Collection of John K. Yearian)

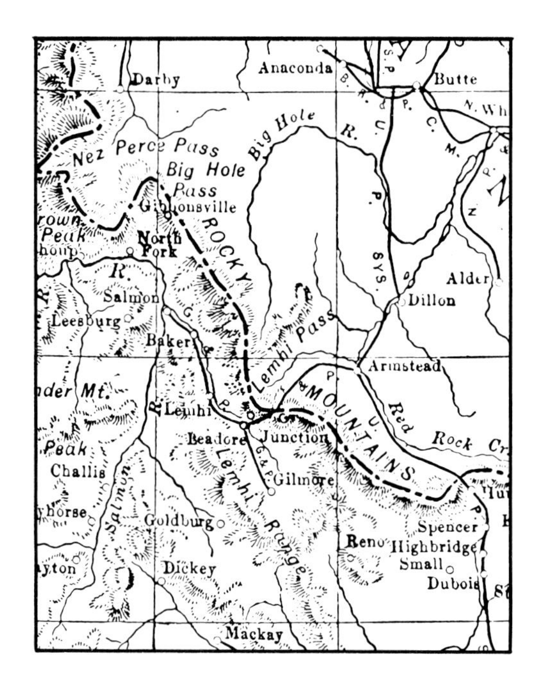

The Gilmore & Pittsburgh's line began at Armstead, Montana, on the Union Pacific and went southwest across the Continental Divide at Bannock Pass to Leadore, where the line branched to reach its two termini — Salmon (to the north) and Gilmore (to the south), in Idaho's Lemhi Valley — as shown on the small inset map above. Armstead and Leadore were destined from the outset to be the major terminals on the line. A track diagram for the Armstead yards is shown on this page, while the Leadore layout is shown on the page adjacent. (Track diagrams by John Buvinger)

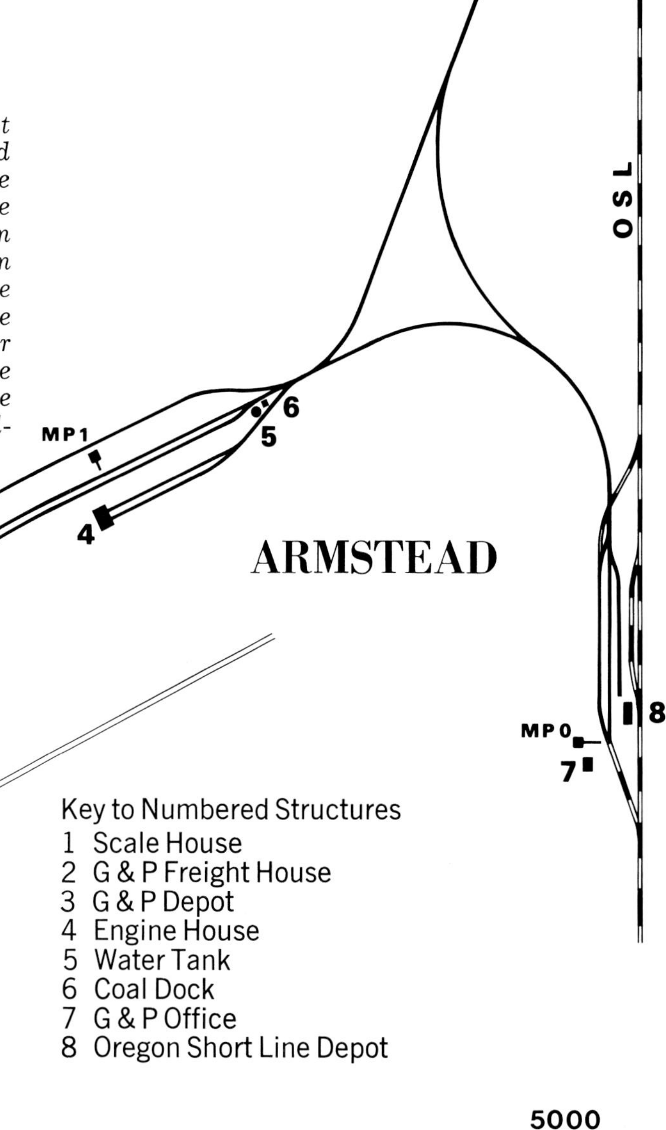

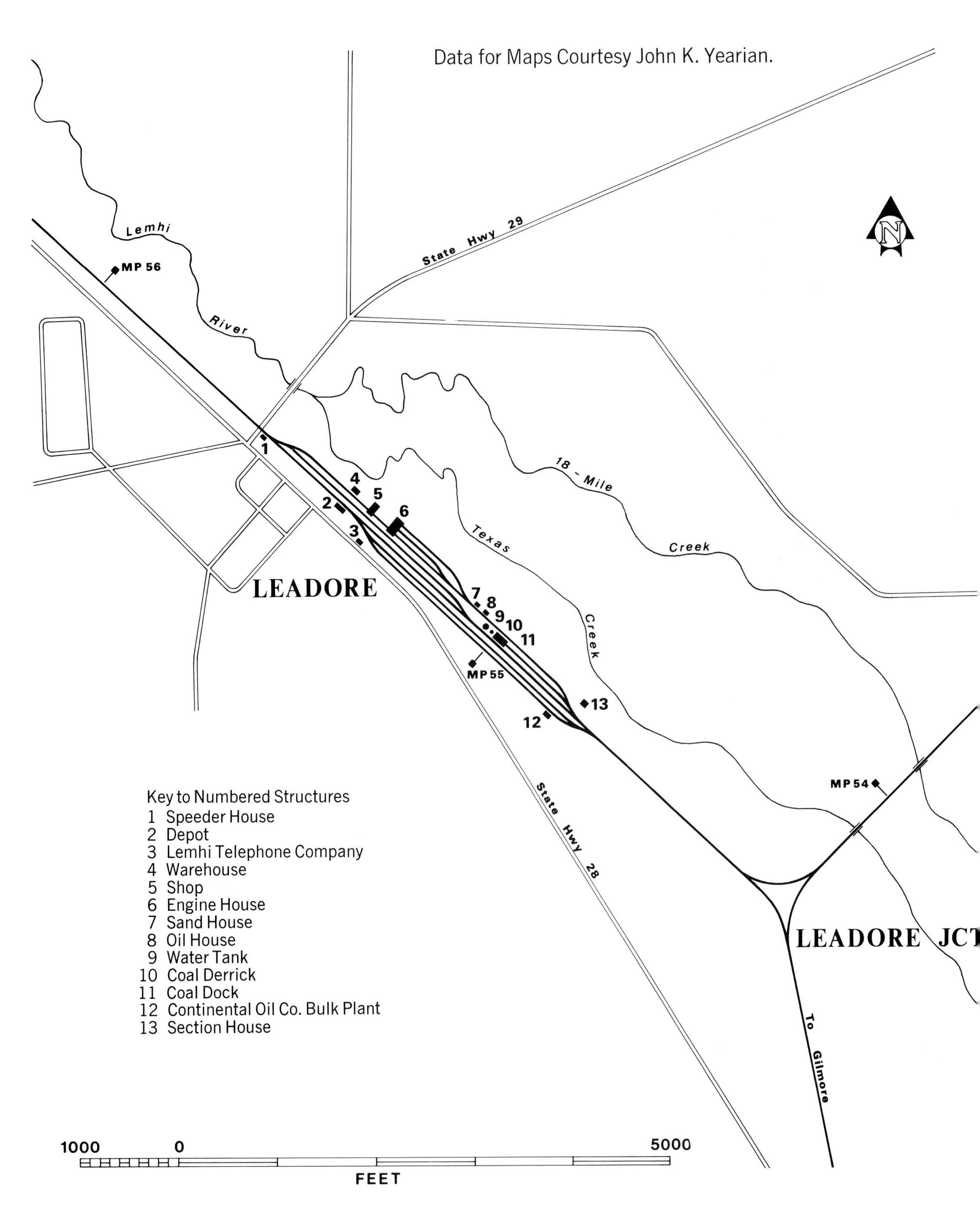

Data for Maps Courtesy John K. Yearian.
Lemhi
River
MP 56
State Hwy 29
18 - Mile
Creek
Texas
Creek
LEADORE
1
2
3
4
5
6
7
8
9
10
11
12
13
MP 55
State Hwy 28
MP 54
LEADORE JCT
To Gilmore
Key to Numbered Structures
1 Speeder House
2 Depot
3 Lemhi Telephone Company
4 Warehouse
5 Shop
6 Engine House
7 Sand House
8 Oil House
9 Water Tank
10 Coal Derrick
11 Coal Dock
12 Continental Oil Co. Bulk Plant
13 Section House
1000
0
5000
FEET
JB 80

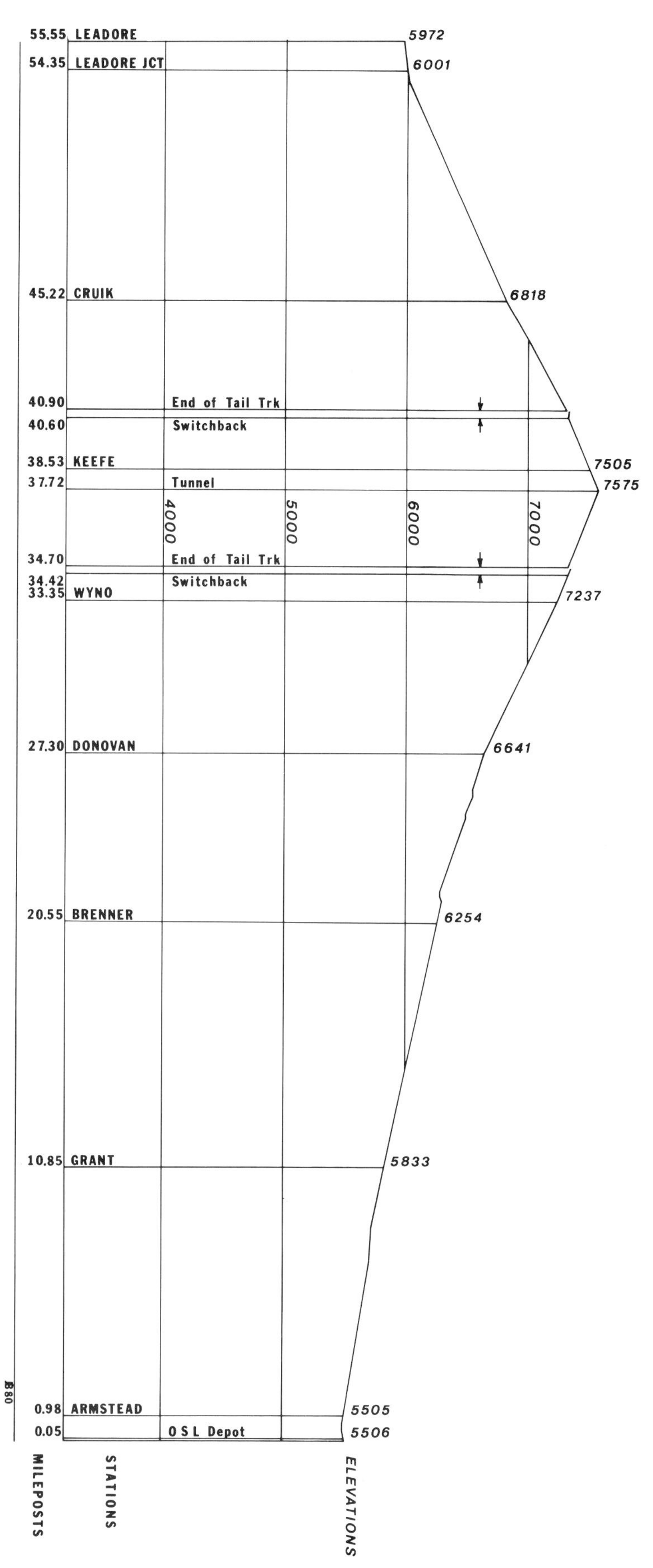

The track profile on this page indicates graphically one of the Gilmore & Pittsburgh's major problems: the whole line was on virtually continuous heavy grades. The heart of the problems lay in the Bannock Pass crossing, shown in detail at right: in addition to the tunnel at the 7575 foot level, it was found necessary to employ a single switchback on each side of the Pass to scale the steep slopes; and to permit operation of the rotary plow through the deep snows that beset the line each winter, it was then necessary to install a wye at each switchback. The layout reveals that the rotary was normally operated from Armstead to open the line. (Track diagrams by John Buvinger)

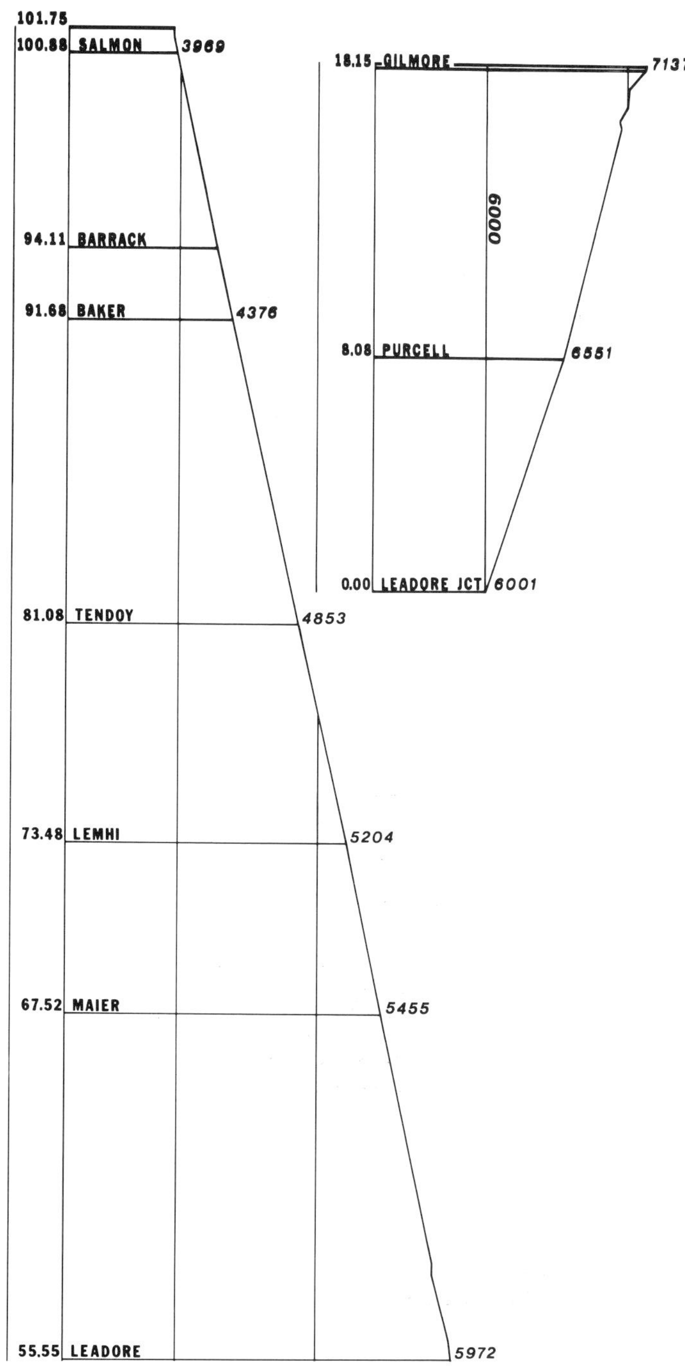

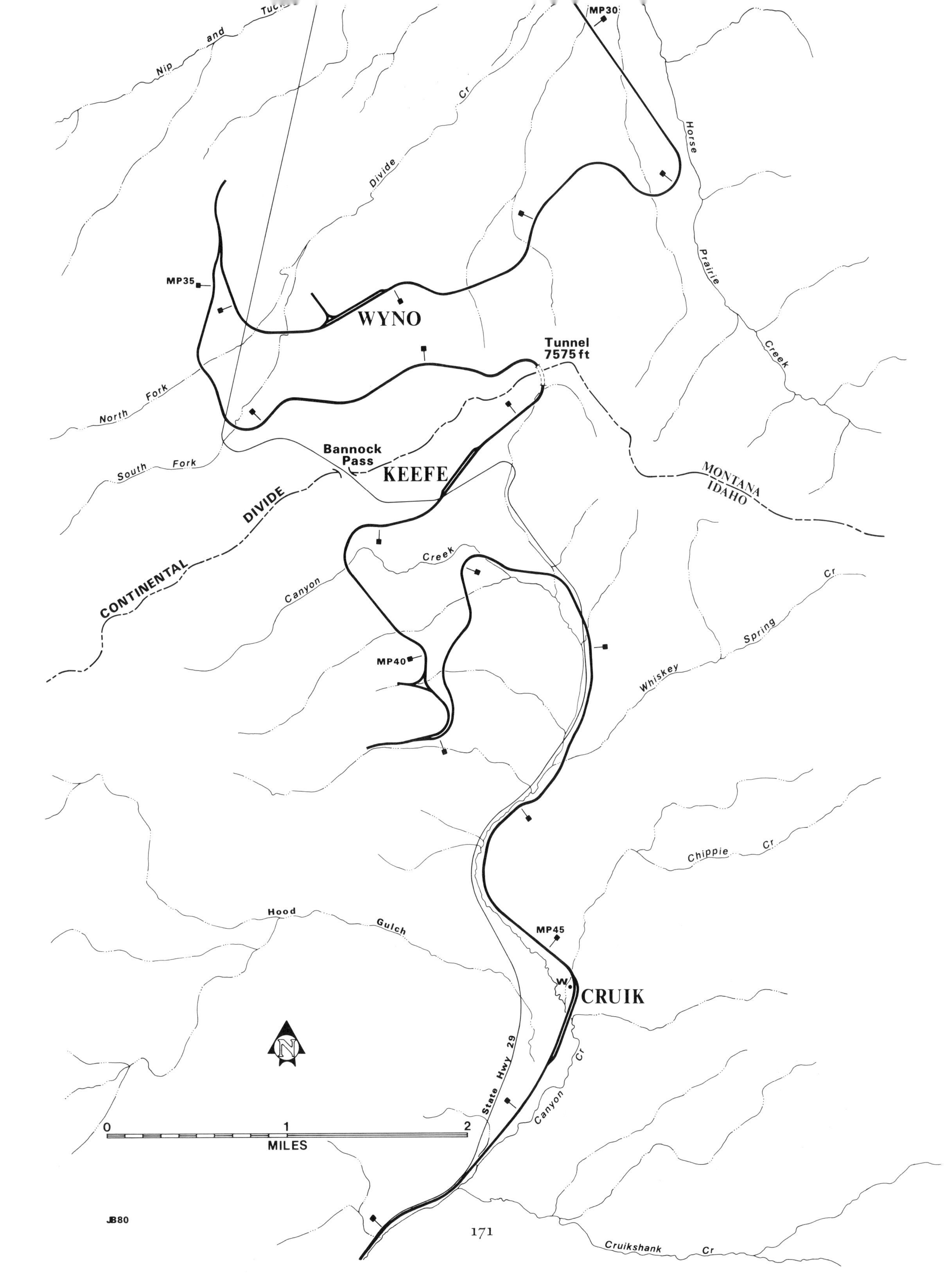

Nip and Tuck
MP30
Divide Cr
Horse Prairie Creek
MP35
WYNO
Tunnel
7575 ft
North Fork
South Fork
Bannock
Pass
KEEFE
MONTANA
IDAHO
CONTINENTAL DIVIDE
Canyon Creek
MP40
Whiskey Spring Cr
Chippie Cr
Hood Gulch
MP45
W
CRUIK
N
State Hwy 29
Canyon Cr
0
1
2
MILES
JB80
Cruikshank Cr

With the building of a new railroad, everyone concerned has his picture taken. Above, one group poses on the pilot of no. 11 (left) and another on the back platform of the coach (right). Below, this group photo made in August 1911 includes such important persons as (left to right, numbered 1-8) T. A. Bacon, G&P Chief Engineer; E. C. Ross, President, Ally Mining Co.; J. A. Crehan, Asst. Sec.-Treas., Pittsburgh Idaho Mining Co.; W. A. McCutcheon, President of the G&P; Mr. Boomer, the contractor; "Uncle Dudley" — W. N. Bichler, the road's General Manager; and A. S. Ross, President, and J. E. Walker, Superintendent of the Pittsburgh Idaho Mining Co. (James Mansfield Coll.)

These two photos were apparently made during construction; the two trains appear to be delayed by some unseen impediment. The fresh, undulating track seems bereft of ballast and must have provided a roller-coaster ride. The passenger cars in the first train show unmistakable Pennsylvania Railroad heritage, and the second train is powered by an ex-PRR tenwheeler, no. 14. (James Mansfield Coll.)

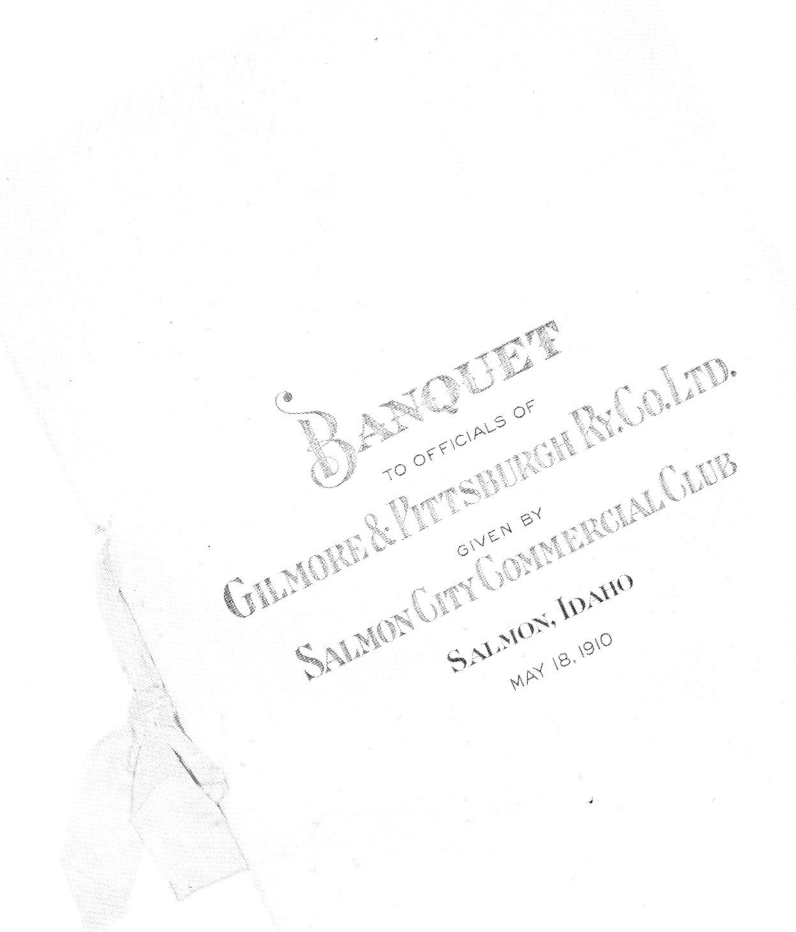

The railroad reached Salmon in May, 1910 and a grand gold spike ceremony was held on the 18th, followed by a banquet and program arranged by the Salmon City Commercial Club. A natty menu and souvenir program, reproduced here in part, was struck to commemorate the event. (John K. Yearian Coll.)

MENU

SHENON HOTEL, CATERE

Consomme en Tasse

Sweet Pickles — Olives

COLD

Dinde a l' Americane — Jambo

Gelee Canneberge — Salade Choux

Veau

Salade Pomme De Terre

Creme Pomme De Terre

Pain — Beurre

GLACE

Salmon Ice Cream — G. & P. Ice Cream

Chocolate — Amande — Nouget

Gateau Assortis

American Fromage

Orange — Banana — Pommes

Noix Assortis — Cafe Noir

PROGRAM

N. I. ANDREWS, TOASTMASTER
F. J. COWEN, VICE TOASTMASTER

Address of Welcome — President of the Club, W. J. BROWN

Response — President G. & P. Ry. Co., Ltd., W. A. MCCUTCHEON

Vocal Solo, "A May Morning," *L. Denza* — MRS. CARL

OUR STATE — GOVERNOR JAS. H. BRADY

OUR SISTER STATE — EX-GOV. B. F. WHITE

Violin Solo — Melody in F, *Rubenstein* — MRS. BISCOE

OUR COUNTY — Chairman of the Board, W. F. STONE

OUR CITY — Mayor F. C. MILLER

Vocal Solo — "Sweet Mignonette," *Tours* — MRS. PHELPS

THE COMING OF THE RAILROAD, THE OPPORTUNITY OF THE TOWN — ATTY. J. R. WHEELER

Euphonium Solo, Waltz, "Josephine," *Kryl* — DR. RICHARDSON

THE PRODIGAL'S RETURN — REV. C. A. EDWARDS

PIONEER DAYS — M. M. MCPHERSON

$8,228.00, and costs; C. C. Cornell, $4,800.00 plus fees. On March 8, 1912, the Gilmore & Pittsburgh settled the claims, but corporate enthusiasm for a Dillon terminal had vanished.

When the Beaverhead Commercial Club proudly announced its success in securing a right-of-way to Twin Bridges, rumors of impending construction bubbled briefly, only to die. The railroad lost interest in Dillon, and Dillon lost interest in the railroad. Neither ever resurfaced during the entire operation of the Gilmore & Pittsburgh. Construction never began on the 60 acres; no G&P engine ever exercised running rights on the OSL track between Armstead and the lonely switch two miles outside of Dillon.

The Northern Pacific served as the G&P's secret benefactor from 1909 to 1913. Newspaper sleuths discovered NP equipment during construction, but official confirmation of the Northern Pacific's involvement did not surface until four years later. In the interim, the parent company became deeply involved. To finance construction, the NP advanced $4,812,181.17 to W. A. McCutcheon's company. By the time trains linked Salmon with Armstead, interest on the loan brought the total to $5,806,814.70.

Very quickly McCutcheon realized ore from the Silver Fissure at Polaris, concentrates from Snow Shoe Gulch mines at Gilmore, livestock from Lemhi County, and passengers all along the way, would not produce revenues sufficient to repay the Northern Pacific's investment. Worse yet, when the link with the NP at Twin Bridges failed to develop, it became obvious the benefactor could expect nothing in the way of reward for its assistance. The Oregon Short Line received 99% of the Gilmore & Pittsburgh traffic, provided both passenger and freight connections as well as car supply, and demanded a beneficial traffic division with the smaller line — 31% for out-bound; 37% for in-bound.

Northern Pacific Directors demanded resolution of the financial crisis facing the Gilmore & Pittsburgh, and in 1913 the two sides reached agreement. G&P returned some materials to the NP, scrapped out four locomotives used primarily during construction, and thus managed to secure credits in the amount of $104,579.17. On June 1, 1913, the short line also issued $4,000,000 in $500,000 promissory notes to the Northern Pacific; and as a final measure, transferred all capital stock to its benefactor — worth $2,000,000 par value. Beginning July 1, 1913, The Gilmore & Pittsburgh Railroad Company, Ltd., became a Northern Pacific subsidiary — an Oregon Short Line feeder, but an NP progeny.

W. N. Bichler continued as superintendent of the Gilmore & Pittsburgh. He occupied the position from the time gandy dancers spiked the first rail in place until salvage crews pulled the last tie plate; and W. N. Bichler ran a frugal railroad. The $300,000 gross revenue estimate haunted his every move.

Had Gilmore & Pittsburgh operations reached the $300,000 figure, the line could have operated and paid off its contracted debt. Not once during its entire life did revenues reach that magic number; seldom did they average 50% of that figure. Some years gross revenues were 30% or even less. The G&P paid little on its bonded debt, and never issued a single dividend. Some years operating expenses even exceeded revenues. When this occurred, Bichler had no alternative but to petition the Northern Pacific for cash advances to meet payrolls and expenses. Good years — when net income exceeded operating expenses — kept advances minimal, but still they mounted.

If a time card came in and Bichler thought an employee began work too early or took too long to complete a task, back came the modification:

> Your time slip shows reported for duty 5:00 a.m. Hereafter report for duty at 5:45 a.m. 5:45 a.m. to 6:15 a.m. is ample time for you to get . . . ready to load passengers, baggage, mail and express and get out of Salmon on time.
>
> Referring to your time slip April 27, item two hours repairing brake hanger . . . This time has been reduced to 30 minutes. It should not have taken you any longer than that to repair a brake of that kind.

World War I increased prices for agricultural produce and brought a few good years to the Gilmore & Pittsburgh. Net operating income hit $18,604 in 1915, $17,915 the following year, and an all-time high of $60,886 in 1917. Then it began to fall. Bichler approached the Northern Pacific for more cash advances, and the transcontinental benefactor began to look for ways to cut expenses even further.

Scheduling on the Gilmore & Pittsburgh was simple and varied little. The following condensed timetable published in February 1913 reflects the original three-times-a-week scheduling:

5	1				2	4
	a 8:00 AM	LV	Armstead	AR	1:00 PM	
b 5:55 AM	11:50 AM	AR	Leadore	LV	9:40 AM	3:00 PM
6:50 AM	1:25 PM	AR	Gilmore	LV	b 7:40 AM	a 2:00 PM
	3:00 PM	AR	Salmon	LV	b 7:00 AM	

a: Mon-Wed-Fri　　b: Tue-Thu-Sat

All were steam-powered mixed trains; nos. 1 and 2 ran through from Armstead to Salmon, while the Gilmore branch had a stub run from Leadore to provide a connection from Armstead. Travel from Salmon to Gilmore could be accomplished (if desired) on Tuesdays and Thursdays by waiting over 28 hours at Leadore. By January 1915 the eastbound sched-

The driving of the golden spike, marking completion of the line to Salmon, was done on May 18, 1910, amid much celebrating. A special was run from Armstead (seen at upper left about to leave) to bring in dignitaries for the occasion; nearly-new 2-8-2 no. 11 did the honors. A large turnout of local people provided an enthusiastic audience as the various important personages (such as the unidentified gentleman at left) drove home the precious spike. It might be noted from the photo above that some of the track was merely laid on the grass, without benefit of any grading whatsoever. (Top left, W. R. McGee Coll.; bottom left, John K. Yearian Coll.; others, James Mansfield Coll.)

The view at right, showing Tenwheeler no. 14 with a lengthy varnish at the Armstead depot, conveys a deceptive note of main line importance; the train was probably being run in connection with the line's opening, and may have been one of the longest passenger trains to operate over the road. (John K. Yearian Coll.) In comparison to the handsome stone and timber passenger facilities at right, the general office was modest (below). The two-story Gordon Hotel, behind it, offered a refuge for passengers who had to wait overnight for their connections. The station at Brenner (bottom), some 20 miles west, was merely an old boxcar body. (Both, James Mansfield Coll.)

The substantial stone-and-timber construction of the road's principal stations is clearly shown in these two views of the station at Leadore, where the Salmon and Gilmore lines diverged. (Top, James Mansfield Collection; below, J. Foster Adams, Collection of Rocky Mountain Railroad Club)

ule had been set back a half hour, now leaving Salmon at 6:30 AM and arriving in Armstead at 12:30 PM. That October the schedule was lengthened 15 minutes westbound (to arrive at Salmon at 3:15 PM) and 30 minutes eastbound (leaving Salmon at 6:00 AM).

A drastic revision in the schedule occurred in February 1919, when no. 1 was moved back to a 5:30 AM departure from Armstead, arriving in Salmon at 12:30 PM — still on Mondays, Wednesdays and Fridays. No. 2 now left Salmon eastbound at 5:30 AM, arriving in Armstead at noon. A stub run connected with no. 1 to Gilmore, reaching that town at 11:05 AM; it returned at 11:50, reaching Leadore an hour later. *No* connection was run on the alternate days for no. 2; Gilmoreans now faced a 20 hour layover in Leadore if they wanted to go *anywhere* by train.

The scheduling retrenchment mirrored the financial plight of the railroad. Although operating revenues continued to climb to new highs in 1917 ($193,000) and 1919 ($194,000), so did operating expenses. Revenues were off slightly in 1918, and for the first time since 1913 the road failed to cover its operating expenses. But 1919 was worse by far — even though revenues recovered, such influences as inflation and a bad winter ballooned costs by some 42% and the line suffered a $69,000 deficit. Despite another good increase in revenues in 1920 — to $223,458, the highest yet — the year still ended in red ink. And then the worst two years in the road's history followed in 1921-22: in part the result of a national economic recession, G&P revenues were cut in half, but expenses changed little. The result was a combined loss, out-of-pocket, for the two years of over a quarter of a million dollars.

The railroad had purchased a 1918 model Brill railbus, and this was placed into service initially on the profitless Leadore-Gilmore run, instead of a steam train. It provided passenger, mail and express, and less-than-carload freight service, and steam had to be called upon only when there was sufficient carload business to warrant a run. Operation of the railbus was soon extended to the Salmon-Leadore run as well, with the Brill providing six-day-a-week service between the towns. Mail and passengers were transferred alternate days between the railbus and the steam mixed at Leadore, and in addition on Tuesdays, Thursdays and Saturdays the bus continued up the Gilmore branch, thereby offering thrice weekly service between that town and Salmon. Sure, there had been days of long trains of ore cars from Gilmore, but those days had passed.

With the schedule of no. 1 returned to an 8:00 AM departure from Armstead, and the railbus making its daily round trip between Leadore and Salmon, the G&P timetable looked like this by July 1922:

MOTOR	1				2	MOTOR
	a 8:00 AM	LV	Armstead	AR	12:54 PM	
	12:05 PM	AR	Leadore	LV	8:51 AM	
b 10:10 AM		LV	Gilmore	AR	10:05 AM	
11:20 AM	12:35	LV	Leadore	AR	8:45 AM	8:45 AM
1:50 PM	3:05 PM	AR	Salmon	LV	b 6:15 AM	a 6:15 AM

a: Mon-Wed-Fri b: Tue-Thu-Sat

This schedule was continued for a decade with no significant change (inexplicably, running time for no. 1 from Armstead to Leadore was *cut* by *two minutes* in 1929). Speeds were certainly moderate; the Armstead-Leadore segment was negotiated at an average speed (for the 55 miles) of about 13½ mph by the mixed, while the Brill railcar covered the 45.3 mile Leadore-Salmon stretch at an 18 mph clip.

When the railbus proved adequate, Bichler looked at idle rolling stock and decided it had become superfluous. In 1920 he "sold" several passenger and combination cars, along with many box cars, flatcars and gondolas to the NP. He also returned Schenectady built locomotive no. 17 (NP no. 1288). The fiscal implications of the action resulted in a $660,000 "credit" for the G&P, and one of the few concrete financial returns the Northern Pacific enjoyed from its Lemhi Valley offspring.

Residents of Horse Prairie, Leadore, Gilmore and Salmon who had once welcomed the Gilmore & Pittsburgh with enthusiasm began to wane in their interest. Motor cars and trucks became the new infatuation. During the 1920's increasingly better roads developed, linking the Lemhi Valley with other parts of Idaho and southwestern Montana.

While it seems clear that passenger travel on the G&P was modest in volume during the twenties, nevertheless there is evidence that the Union Pacific promoted travel over the line! A fat, timetable-size folder in the Colorado Railroad Museum collection, issued by the UP in 1926 and titled *Utah-Idaho Outings*, publicized attractions in the area for the sportsman and outdoorsman. One such attraction was the Salmon River Gorge. The folder extolled the "Salmon River region, a vast wilderness of mountains, lakes and streams . . . traversed by the mighty Salmon River. For the adventuresome . . . a thrilling trip down the Salmon by boat is offered beginning at Salmon City and ending at Lewiston, Idaho . . . 350 miles away." The trips were run by a Captain Henry Gueleke of Salmon City; four to six trips were run each season, using large flat double-bottom scows about 32 feet long and 8 feet wide. The trip took from 12 to 20 days "according to the desires of the party", and a new boat was required for each trip. And oh yes! "The journey by train is to Armstead, Montana, via the Union

Pacific System, thence by the Gilmore and Pittsburgh Railroad over the Continental Divide to Salmon City." This may be as close as the G&P ever came to being a part of a major passenger travel promotion.

Despite dismal revenue prospects, made worse by the complete closure of Gilmore mines in the late 1920's, the decade represented a halcyon era for the G&P. Alternate days, later every day, railbus 650 left Salmon for Leadore and returned, carrying passengers, small loads of freight and mail. From Leadore a mixed train ran to Armstead to pick up livestock or deliver box cars of freight. Short trains and picturesque surroundings typified branch line operations throughout the nation during the optimistic years following World War I.

Yes, Bichler ran a frugal railroad. From his Armstead office he oversaw every phase of the line's operation. In the spring, as frost came out of the ground, ties had to be replaced and the usual repairs made. Flooding along the Lemhi often damaged roadbed or washed it away altogether, hampering service and revenue. Summer brought scattered traffic; some from the mines, some from Salmon residents who wanted to visit Dillon for a friendly game of baseball, or head to Idaho Falls, maybe Butte, for big city shopping. In autumn, long stock trains wound their way out of the Lemhi Valley to market — twenty cars or more full of cattle and sheep.

With winter in the mountains came Bichler's real challenges. Fireman B. J. Waugh remembered those twenty below zero mornings, the wind whipping snow across the track at fifty or sixty miles an hour. Again and again the ex-NP rotary came out; chewed through drifts at Desmond Cut, spewed snow along the Continental Divide, took a breather through the tunnel, worked down to Leadore, labored upgrade opening track to Gilmore. Shifts were long, coal ran short, and on occasion the only food available had to be grubbed from ranchers along the way. Waugh later remembered one of these "adventures" when he was about 20 and worked on the rotary in the winter, about 1920:

> I can tell you about one trip that I will never forget. I was fireman on the rotary snow plow. We had some warm weather, it thawed, then turned down below zero. We left Leadore to plow out the mountain between Leadore and Armstead. General Manager W. N. Bichler was on the train following the rotary and after we plowed out the mountain they set the rotary out at a siding or passing track called Brenner, named after a man who owned a large stock ranch. Mr. Bichler said 'I will call Mr. Brenner and make arrangements' for Alfred Rosendahl [sic], who was running the rotary, and myself to eat at the Brenner ranch. That was some time around 3 AM. I had used about 15 tons of coal firing this rotary and had had nothing to eat in the past 12 hours. We laid down in the rotary on solid boiler plate and tried to get some rest. I had a wash basin for a pillow, covered with my jumper. We decided about 9 AM to walk to the Brenner ranch, which was at least a half mile away, and the snow was knee deep and we were very hungry when we arrived.
>
> Mr. Brenner came out on his porch and said 'what's wanted here' and 'who are you fellows.' I being a young fellow and full of pep said 'we are on the rotary snow plow and want to eat. Mr. Bichler said he would call you.' Mr. Brenner said 'he has not called me and made any arrangements for you to eat here. You fellows come back at noon.' Here we are, nearly starved. Guess Mr. Bichler went to bed when he got home. Back to the rotary, and then back to the ranch. Again Mr. Brenner came out and said 'you fellows go back to the rear and you will find a cook shack, back there, and go in and eat.' I would say there were eight cowboys eating and did they look us over — guess they thought we had never eaten before in our lives. We went back that evening for dinner and breakfast the next morning.
>
> During the lay over I asked Rosendahl 'have you called Mr. Bichler about coal. I have it all in the fire box banked against the flue sheet.' He said 'no, I have not.' So that just suited me, I went to the phone which was located in a little booth, the operator said 'who do you want,' and I said 'I want to talk to Mr. Bichler.' On came Mr. Bichler and I said 'I have no coal left.' I said, 'have a car of coal on number one and some section men to coal this rotary.' He said 'are you refusing to coal the rotary?' and I said 'yes.' Of course I was burned up about the whole condition that existed. My father was working there also. Mr. Bichler went to him and said, 'Alex, if you hadn't been so loyal to this company I would fire that kid of yours and black ball him on every railroad in the U.S.A.'

Working in such snow and cold was often dangerous, as the following experience of Waugh's points out:

> They had a big track gang working a couple miles west of a station named Tendoy, which is an Indian name. One night we had a heavy, wet snowfall and the next morning it cleared off and the sun reflecting off that new snow would just blind a person. A man by the name of Kelly was the foreman in charge of the track work, and he got on a small motor car and started to the place the

70

225

These remarkable action photos of G&P mixed trains starting east out of Leadore were made in 1912 by J. Foster Adams. Top left, 2-8-2's nos. 10 and 11 on July 23; bottom left, a similar consist on August 27; and on this page, nos. 10 and 11 at the same point in May. These two locomotives quickly became the mainstay of the G&P's roster. (Collection of the Rocky Mountain Railroad Club)

On this page we see the G&P mixed preparing to depart from Leadore. In the busy May 13, 1912, scene above, no. 11 holds down the main line run while Tenwheeler no. 14, behind, is probably waiting with the Gilmore branch train. No. 11 is again on the point in the quieter August view below. On the page opposite are two views of G&P mixed trains starting the impressive climb up the west side of Bannock Pass; the first train (top) has 2-8-2 no. 10 and ten cars, while the second consists of eight cars pulled by no. 11. The photographer recorded the date of August 24, 1912, for both, which would imply special dispatching for the benefit of the photographer. (J. Foster Adams, Rocky Mountain Railroad Club Collection)

72 G. & P. R. R. TRAIN IN BANNOCK PASS NEAR LEADORE, IDAHO

work was being performed. During the night a telephone pole had fallen on the track and Kelly, blinded by the snow, hit the pole and of course it derailed his car and he hit his head on something and was knocked out. So Mr. Bichler gave us orders to switch out Kelly's car and start for Armstead so we could get him on the Union Pacific and to the hospital at Butte, Montana. Mr. Bichler said 'stop at my residence and pick me up.' By this time there was a wind blowing at least 50 or 60 miles per hour and about 20 below zero. I had on a blizzard cap with the ear flaps pulled down over my ears which made it difficult to hear. He said 'is Kelly dead,' and I said 'yes' as I thought he said is Kelly *in bed*. He went to Kelly's car but Kelly was still alive, so did I get another dressing down from Mr. Bichler. As it turned out, Kelly died of his injuries in the Butte hospital.

Although he left the G&P in 1922, Waugh still had clear recollections 55 years later of his days with the road and the idiosyncrasies of the engines he fired there:

I was firing a locomotive for a man by the name of Otto Dorman. He was a man that never hooked an engine up to keep from working back pressure, and that throws work on the fireman. One day we were going along and I noticed Dorman was dozing so I, being a young man, went over and put my foot on the boiler head and hooked the engine up where it belonged — you do this by moving the Johnson Bar to proper position to avoid back pressure. In a couple minutes Dorman woke up and stuck his head out the cab window and said to me in a gruff voice: 'this is the first time that you have had a fire in her since you have been on the job.' He let the Johnson Bar down where he had it and I let the steam drop back 15 lbs., so you can see the friction between he and I for that trip.

No. 14 I fired many times. It was a tenwheeler, had about 70 inch drivers built for speed, and a narrow, long firebox. Believe me, if you wanted to get along with that engine you hardly ever left the fire box door. One just had to fire the engine very light, and if you didn't, you only built up clinkers. I am speaking about while the engine was working. The engine would not stand to be slugged, and if you fed the coal to her lightly, she would steam well.

The no. 10 and no. 11 had much wider fire boxes. One time when the 10 and 11 were in back shop for heavy repairs — flue, side sheets, and etc. — the G&P leased two engines from the OSL, or Union Pacific. I do not remember the numbers, but they were in pretty good shape.

No. 14, the ex-Pennsylvania RR 4-6-0, was deemed expendable after the Brill railbus took over the Salmon and Gilmore runs, leaving only nos. 10 and 11, the 2-8-2's. Earlier, when extra motive power had been needed, it was brought over from the Northern Pacific; but as Waugh indicates, after 1920 it was found simpler to rent power from the Union Pacific, even though the G&P engines were still sent over to the NP shops at Livingston for work.

Never numbering more than thirty-five or forty, the G&P work force exhibited a cohesive camaraderie which would endure beyond the line's abandonment. A half century later, G&P employees maintained contact with one another, anxious to remember the line's operation and share experiences with anyone willing to listen. Today the roster is anything but complete, yet a few names survive. Engineers like Otto Dorman, Jack Haines, Harold Robison and Lee Vorges ran nos. 10 and 11 on their infrequent trips. Firemen, brakemen and conductors included men like Andy Burnham, Bernard J. Waugh and John K. Yearian. Yearian was on the line for seventeen years, beginning in 1921. After firing for two years, he drew the job of operating the Brill railbus no. 650, which was then operated six days a week from Salmon to Leadore and return, a 90 mile run; on three days the run was extended to Gilmore, an extra 36 miles. When the B-7 gas electric car was put on the Armstead-Salmon run, a 200 mile round trip daily except Sunday, Yearian was made engineer on that run and held the job until the line was abandoned. Similarly, men like Alfred Rosedell did multiple duty as work required, including running the rotary plow when Montana and Idaho winters demanded its use. To keep equipment and track in operating trim, foremen Kelly and Jerry Rhyn stayed busy year around, as did Master Mechanic/Maintenance Supervisor E. R. Lambert, and repairmen Al Rosendahl and Joe Steel. Armstead clerk Lawrence McGivine and his Salmon counterpart Vern Chandler handled ticket sales, plus the necessary bills of lading and ever-present forms. Shirley Johnson oversaw the telephone company end of G&P operations, further linking Armstead and Salmon.

There were others: Frank Hayes, Clem Zaak, Terry McRea, Bob and Ken Plumb, Frank Proulx, Buck Reddington, Charlie Noble, Mike and Bob Gourtney, Floyd Whittiker, Jim Givens, William Hill, and Robert Lambert.

Even for a generation caught up in the expansion of auto and truck transportation, it was a memorable era to bustle and jostle along the Lemhi River as the railbus "galloped" down the track; to see heavy black smoke in the valley or on the pass and know it meant "train coming;" exciting times in Leadore and Armstead cafes when "hot box, smoking" got you

Above, 2-8-2 no. 11 stands in front of the G&P engine house along with some assorted freight cars; an air of newness is evident, and all the trackage is not yet completed. (James Mansfield Coll.) Below, a source of revenue from the Lemhi Valley — loading wool at Tendoy, between Leadore and Salmon. (Rose Corum Coll.)

So that W. N. Bichler (and other officials) could commute back and forth over the G&P without the necessity of calling out an engine, crew and business car, the railroad converted a Ford Model T touring car into an officials' railcar — apparently by merely removing the fenders and fitting railroad wheels instead of auto wheels. Above, on a balmy day Bichler (in dark suit) and passenger enjoy a spin over the line with the top down. Below we see the proper attire for cold weather — Bichler (left, with pipe) and passenger (a Mr. Stout) are bundled up in huge fur coats, and the Ford's top is up and sidecurtains buttoned into place. Right, a Mr. Hill from Minneapolis poses similarly bundled up alongside the Ford, which wears a slightly droopy Pantasote radiator cover to keep it from freezing up. (All, James Mansfield Collection)

a well-done steak, and "running orders with two, blanket the headlights" meant a hearty breakfast of pancakes and eggs over.

Depression hit the nation in 1929, only to worsen. A deteriorating economic picture gave the Gilmore & Pittsburgh's parent company cause for reflection. NP directors looked at an investment which had never paid returns, a branch line which generated no traffic, and totaled up $47,700 in cash advances. The NP could ill afford the beneficence. To make matters worse, the U.S. Post Office threatened cancellation of the mail contract unless G&P service improved — and nothing less than daily round-trip runs between Salmon and Armstead would suffice. Such a cancellation would mean a loss of $8,607 annually when net operating income already ran into the red $10,000 a year and more.

After consultation with Bichler, NP officials suggested — insisted — the Gilmore & Pittsburgh continue to operate only "so long as earnings were sufficient to pay expenses" — no more cash advances. Bichler acquiesced and began the most austere operation possible. To handle l.c.l. freight and passenger traffic, and meet U.S. Mail schedules, he secured gas-electric car B-7 from the Northern Pacific for $26,000, in monthly payments of $276.80. Requiring only an engineer and conductor, the gas-electric made daily (except Sunday) trips between Salmon and Armstead — round trip. During winter and after 1937 on a permanent basis, sleighs, automobiles or trucks provided tri-weekly service from Leadore to Gilmore, relieving aging Brill no. 650 of the task.

The gas electric car could make the run over Bannock Pass in an hour less time than the steam mixed, and this permitted a new scheduling requiring just one car for a daily round trip:

1:25 PM	LV	Armstead	AR	12:45 PM
4:25	LV	Leadore	LV	9:30 AM
6:50 PM	AR	Salmon	LV	7:00 AM

In addition to this daily-except-Sunday service, the little Brill railbus still ran to Gilmore on Tuesdays, Thursdays and Saturdays, now making a direct connection from Salmon with the eastbound motor:

9:35 AM	LV	Leadore	AR	12:20 PM
10:50 AM	AR	Gilmore	LV	11:05 AM

These schedules were, of course, "weather permitting," and in the winter frequent snows and high winds still required constant use of the rotary plow and a steam locomotive. Old timers like John Yearian remember it as a constant problem, with the rotary in use "every day" through the heart of the winter. In particular, the wind would fill in the cuts going over the pass from one day to the next. It was an expensive problem, even the way the G&P did it with minimum crews — two engineers, two firemen and a conductor. A watchman was stationed near the tunnel during the winter to check on the condition of the line and call the shop at Leadore if the rotary would be needed that day. The switchbacks made the job more difficult also, for the rotary had to be turned on the wye at each of the switchbacks so that it would always be working forwards.

Bichler's "go it alone" policy seemed to reap rewards in 1934 and 1935. For the first time in several years the railroad operated in the black — but the improvement was illusory. During the Depression, the Civilian Conservation Corps moved men and equipment into the Lemhi Valley over Gilmore & Pittsburgh rails providing a temporary boost in revenues. Before long the G&P returned to deficit operations.

In truth, Bichler only forestalled the complete demise of the railroad he managed. He effected his greatest savings in two particular areas — he did not pay state and local taxes (amounting to $29,357 from 1932 to 1939), and he spent little money for maintenance on equipment or right-of-way. The respective governments did not hurry the Gilmore & Pittsburgh for back taxes; but the roadbed and equipment deteriorated rapidly.

The G&P operated on a shoe string. Where once thirty-five employees turned in time cards each week, now only twenty-five or fewer drew pay. Rolling stock fell to the bare minimum. The gas-electric and the Brill railbus provided most service. Baldwin locomotives nos. 10 and 11 handled heavier traffic as needed. Additional rolling stock included three passenger cars (coaches) and a like number of combination cars, ten box cars, nine flat cars, two refrigerator cars, two gondolas for coal and 19 miscellaneous service and freight cars, including the rotary plow.

Physically the Gilmore & Pittsburgh deteriorated while the condition of roads in and out of the Lemhi Valley improved. Highway discussions occupied the agenda of most Salmon City Council and Chamber of Commerce meetings throughout the period from 1932 to 1938. With federal and state monies, crews gravelled and improved both U.S. Highway 93 to Darby, and Idaho 28 through Leadore and Gilmore. During the winter of 1937-1938, the Highway Department kept Gibbon's Pass open for the first time, marking the creation of an all-season highway to Salmon. Rubber-tired competition for the railroad poured over these highways into the Lemhi Valley.

By 1938, Salmon had daily scheduled bus service north to Missoula and south to Mackay and Idaho's principal cities. Three regular truck

Shown above is the second depot erected at Armstead by the Union Pacific, while Salmon's Main Street is shown below about 1929. (Top, Beaverhead County Museum Coll.; below, John A. Elliott Coll.) Right: at some early date a big slide ran in Desman Cut, about five miles west of Grant, and passengers were forced to transfer on foot over the rubble from one stub-run train to the other until the line could be cleared. (James Mansfield Collection)

With the acquisition of Northern Pacific gas-electric car B7 (above) steam was relegated to on-call (and intermittent) freight duty, and the B7 carried the mail, express, passengers and even a bit of local freight on a daily Salmon-Armstead round trip. Andy Burnham was the conductor and John K. Yearian the engineer. In this 1933 view at the Salmon depot, Ken Yearian is standing in the doorway and his young son Calvin is by the steps. (John K. Yearian Collection) Below, little Brill bus no. 650 arrived on the line about 1918, and alternated with the mixed train on runs between Leadore and Salmon or Gilmore. Posing here with the car in 1940 are Harold Jones of Butte and Wilbur Hall of Livingston. (W. R. McGee Photo)

lines operated between Salmon and Missoula, a fourth ran south to Idaho Falls, and another joined Butte and Salmon, paralleling the Gilmore & Pittsburgh for its entire length. Private operators also did "considerable hauling." Commercial truckers consciously undercut the railroad's freight rates, diverting a good portion of its traffic. Bichler stated, and Federal officials later agreed, that if the G&P instituted truck-competitive rates the trucks "would simply reduce their rates further." In addition, the Gilmore & Pittsburgh's less than carload rate of 96.5 cents per hundred pounds exceeded parcel post costs in some cases. As a result, much of the wool, livestock, ore, potatoes and other agricultural produce — not to mention passengers and incoming finished goods — which might have travelled by rail, went by truck.

As the 1930's wore on, it became obvious the Gilmore & Pittsburgh's days were numbered Then, on June 5, 1938, a short mixed train worked its way up Horse Prairie Creek in the morning, the locomotive rumbling across a modest bridge oblivious to its fire-weakened condition. Suddenly the structure gave way and the tender and trailing box car settled into the creek. No one ever discovered the cause of the fire, but the G&P could ill afford the cost of repairing the damage, the lost service time for the locomotive and the delayed schedules. In many ways the accident provided an omen of things to come.

December 14, 1938, W. N. Bichler made the announcement he had managed to forestall since 1932:

> Effective May 1, 1939, the Gilmore and Pittsburgh Railroad company will discontinue operations of the railroad between Armstead, Montana and Salmon, Idaho because on that date the company will be without funds to continue operations.

To make the act official Bichler and the Northern Pacific filed an abandonment notice with the Interstate Commerce Commission.

Suddenly Lemhi Valley residents again became interested in the railroad. During Christmas holidays the Salmon City Council, the Chamber of Commerce, the County Commissioners, the Rotarians and the livestock growers all met with Bichler to discuss his plans. To each group the superintendent patiently explained that when the frost came out of the ground, the roadbed would need repairs; but in their present state, railroad funds would be exhausted by May 1. Continued operation could not be maintained. Each meeting adjourned without any "definite plan of action" on the part of the respective groups. All agreed, however, that railroad service must be retained.

On the other side of the Divide, Dillon residents, secure in their Oregon Short Line connection, paid so little attention to Bichler's announced decision that notice of the pending abandonment did not even appear in the local newspaper. Similarly, Montana's Board of Railroad Commissioners decided not to protest the proposed abandonment — let the Idaho Public Utilities Commission and the I.C.C. fight the battle and decide the case.

Lemhi County hired Tom Jones of Pocatello as a special attorney to protect its interests. Jones offered several plans of action. Initially, he indicated he would seek to have the Northern Pacific guarantee the continued operation of the line. If that failed, the attorney was ready to ask the Union Pacific's Oregon Short Line to absorb the G&P as a branch. Should neither of these queries prove fruitful, Jones readied necessary paperwork to secure an injunction and prevent abandonment until the I.C.C. heard the case and made a decision. In the meantime, Jones urged everyone to patronize the railroad in every way possible and increase revenues so money would be available for operating expenses and repairs.

Both the Northern Pacific and the Union Pacific quickly shunned Jones' propositions. B. W. Scandrett, Vice President of the NP stated unequivocally that his line "would not put any more money into the Gilmore & Pittsburgh." L. H. Anderson, Idaho counsel for the Union Pacific said the UP was "not interested" in acquiring the railroad or operating it as a branch line. Undaunted, Jones appeared before District Court Judge Guy Stevens seeking an injunction against Bichler's proposed abandonment, pending an I.C.C. hearing scheduled for May 31, 1939, in Salmon. Judge Stevens set a May 4 date for arguments on the proposed injunction.

True to his word, unmoved by pending hearings, Bichler ran the last Gilmore & Pittsburgh train out of Salmon on April 30, 1939. May 1, the line ceased operation although legal haggling continued for almost a year. Amid all the momentary alarm and confusion, postal officials proved more realistic in their outlook, for on May 1, mail service from Armstead continued uninterrupted, *via* truck.

When the I.C.C. met May 31 and June 1, 1939, in Salmon, a battery of Northern Pacific experts assembled to make three points: 1) the Gilmore & Pittsburgh had never operated at a profit — in fact the line incurred a career corporate deficit of $6,021,093.00; 2) in B. W. Scandrett's words, traffic potential in the Lemhi Valley was insufficient to sustain any railroad — the line could not be made to pay "if it got all the business in Lemhi County"; 3) roadbed and equipment required extensive and costly repairs — well beyond G&P means.

On the final point, the Northern Pacific went to great lengths to demonstrate its case. Late in April 1939 G&P Maintenance Supervisor E. R. Lambert accompanied NP Division Engineer D. C. Rysnesburger and his counterpart from the Chicago, Milwaukee, St. Paul & Pacific Railway on a tour of the line. The three men estimated it would cost $174,145 to repair the roadbed and adjacent facilities: 89,788 ties and 18 sets of switch ties needed replacing; forty bridges and sixty-three timber culverts needed repair. Another $10,500 to $11,500 was needed to make repairs on one of the two remaining locomotives, to overhaul the gas-electric (in continuous operation since 1932), and to fix the rotary plow.

Even had the money been available, additional complications prevented equipment repairs. The G&P did not have the facilities necessary to fix the firebox or renew tires and axles on the locomotive; work had to be performed at the NP's Livingston shops and this would take about forty-five days. The railroad could not continue to operate during that period, however, because derailments occurred with such frequency that the company needed one locomotive to rerail the other. The Gilmore & Pittsburgh could overhaul the gas-electric car; yet while doing so, no piece of equipment could make round trips between Salmon and Armstead in the sixteen hours required by law to keep the U.S. Mail contract. Northern Pacific spokesmen concluded their arguments pointing to the fact that if all repairs and maintenance could be performed, the G&P would still need at least $68,884 annually to insure continued safe operation.

On March 22, 1940, the Interstate Commerce Commission acquiesced to the realities of the Gilmore & Pittsburgh's situation. Abandonment granted. The Salmon *Recorder Herald* sighed an editorial sigh and conceded a fact which Northern Pacific officials recognized some years before: "The official abandonment of the G&P will have little or no effect upon the community life of Lemhi county."

Now the process begun in 1909 reversed. Company officials estimated the salvage worth of the Gilmore & Pittsburgh at $180,000. Before long, work locomotives and dismantling crews backed their way from Salmon and Gilmore to Leadore; up Railroad Canyon and the switchback; through the tunnel; down the other switchback; along Horse Prairie Creek. By January 1, 1941, all but a few hundred feet of track adjacent to the Oregon Short Line depot in Armstead had been removed.

Finished with their tasks, locomotives no. 10 and no. 11 retired to Butte where they waited out World War II scrap metal drives, only to succumb to cutting torches in 1945. The Northern Pacific returned dismantling and scrapping proceeds to its treasury; absorbed the Lemhi Valley Telephone Company's line, which the Gilmore & Pittsburgh had constructed to further break down the isolation of the Salmon River country. The NP assumed title to the 60+ acres of land its profitless progeny had acquired in Dillon. April 10, 1946, The Gilmore & Pittsburgh Railroad Company, Ltd. was dissolved.

Gone — the G&P, the Mystery Road, the Get-out & Push, Lemhi Valley's Railroad. Today Clark Canyon Reservoir covers the site of Armstead where the Northern Pacific branch line fed 99% of its traffic into the OSL. An all-weather highway rushes modern travelers past the vestiges of a right-of-way hidden along the willow-filled bed of Horse Prairie Creek. Near Grant, the grade breaks briefly from the valley floor, clinging to the barren hillsides, slipping past old Desmond Cut, and turning south toward Bannock Pass. A discerning eye can find the route along the ridge, and an adventurer can enter the timberless tunnel from the west and explore to its collapsed eastern portal. Along a grass and sage-choked right-of-way the roadbed descends Railroad Canyon and moves across the flat to Leadore where a remodeled combination car and a few scattered outbuildings indicate a railroad once passed that way. The streets of Gilmore and the mines along Horse Shoe Gulch are as deserted as the railroad built to serve them. To the north, several decades of spring floods and new generations of willows and brush hide all that remains of the railroad's path toward Salmon.

The Gilmore & Pittsburgh never reached Dillon, never extended down the River of No Return toward the Pacific, never met its parent line at Twin Bridges, never paid a dime. Its history provides a study in short line frustration and deficit operation; but, ah, 'tis a dull week without its railroad inspiration.

Hotel at Gilmore, 1975. (Idaho Hist. Society)

The Gilmore & Pittsburgh Railroad Company, Ltd.
Financial Statement
1914-1940

Year	Operating Revenues	Operating Expenses	Net Operating Income	Deductions[1] Interest &	Net Income
1914	$120,994	$115,664	$ 6,000	$445,178	$443,817[D]
1915	117,724	93,713	18,604	240,000	211,107[D]
1916	140,955	117,787	17,915	240,000	209,216[D]
1917	193,009	135,971	60,886	240,000	161,669[D]
1918	164,111	166,512	9,588[D]	246,391	227,025[D]
1919	194,243	236,511	69,693[D]	241,946	244,870[D]
1920	223,458	257,103	19,303[D]	217,559	196,496[D]
1921	102,693	232,652	120,018[D]	209,785	354,087[D]
1922	119,979	234,370	132,706[D]	203,319	334,069[D]
1923	138,343	156,237	36,257[D]	201,900	236,895[D]
1924	119,910	149,527	46,986[D]	201,950	247,962[D]
1925	139,763	124,713	5,136	201,948	206,439[D]
1926	170,062	132,312	14,164	201,909	183,532[D]
1927	157,670	126,069	8,078	201,909	188,627[D]
1928	155,642	124,021	12,670	201,775	185,651[D]
1929	122,585	116,645	12,162[D]	200,400	209,021[D]
1930	95,777	107,237	27,838[D]	200,401	226,635[D]
1931	84,731	78,787	9,523[D]	200,465	209,206[D]
1932	63,062	69,643	21,241[D]	201,162	221,728[D]
1933	68,802	68,154	12,704[D]	201,162	213,188[D]
1934	77,334	68,316	4,717	201,162	205,202[D]
1935	95,605	72,506	10,876	201,162	189,955[D]
1936	98,972	88,041	2,257[D]	201,162	202,762[D]
1937	92,756	88,101	7,647[D]	201,162	208,210[D]
1938	81,890	88,535	20,103[D]	201,162	220,658[D]
1939[2]	25,395	38,229	2,483[D]	201,439	223,432[D]
1940	No Statement;	Abandoned:	Mar. 22, 1940.		

NOTES:

1) Includes taxes and interest on eight $500,000 notes given to the Northern Pacific Railway Company in 1913.
2) January 1 to April 30, 1939, inclusive.
D) Deficit.

SOURCES:

U.S. Interstate Commerce Commission. *Finance Reports*, Vol. 239 (January-April, 1940), p. 242.
Moody's Manual of Investments, American and Foreign: Railroad Securities, 1928-1941.
Northern Pacific Railway Company. ______________ to B. W. Scandrett, February 8, 1935. Gilmore & Pittsburgh File, 358-1.

FORM 459
THE GILMORE AND PITTSBURGH RAILROAD COMPANY, LTD.
EXPEDITED FREIGHT SERVICE

Salmon Ida 1/19 192 8

MR. O H Ross

TO THE GILMORE AND PITTSBURGH RAILROAD COMPANY, LTD. DR.

FOR TRANSPORTATION OF Bx WEIGHT 45 LBS. $ 1 13
ON W. B. FROM NO. WH DATE 1-19 19 28
CHARGES ADVANCED TO EX. CO. AT St Louis $ 3 50
FROM TRANSPORTATION FROM
CONSIGNOR TOTAL CHARGES $ 4 63
RECEIVED PAYMENT J J Moore AGENT

Acknowledgments

Information on the Gilmore & Pittsburgh is as scattered and sparse as the remaining ties along the abandoned right-of-way. But as the ties were important, so were the sources that made the G&P story come together. The first word in thanks has to go to John Kenneth Yearian of Salmon, Idaho, who shared memories, maps, and photographs, then filled in numerous details and answered countless questions. The late James Mansfield of Grant, Montana, and B. J. Waugh of Rialto, California, remembered the lines in personal terms sharing tangible and intangible memories.

Credit for providing photographs should be widely shared. In addition to those mentioned above, Rose Corum and the Lemhi County Historical Society provided some; Warren R. McGee of Livingston, Montana, took numerous photographs during the last years of G&P operation and shared them. R. H. Kindig and the Rocky Mountain Railroad Club provided the Adams pictures, while Walter Ainsworth and the Beaverhead County Museum provided other shots. John Buvinger drew maps which appear in this story, often relying on detailed information Kenneth Yearian provided. Finally, the list of people who helped compile locomotive data includes: G. M. Best, Harold Goldsmith, Don Roberts, Ivan Saunders, L. P. Schrenk, and Thomas T. Taber.

Published information on the Gilmore & Pittsburgh is equally scattered. Salmon's two newspapers, *The Lemhi Herald* and *The Idaho Recorder* detailed much of the construction period and provided a generally complete running commentary of operations during the history of the line. *The Dillon Tribune* did likewise from the Montana side. Articles of incorporation and annual reports are in the Montana Secretary of State's offices; the Interstate Commerce Commission, *Financial Reports,* Vol. 239 (January-April, 1940) contains an excellent financial history with many operational details; the Northern Pacific Railway Company's *Annual Reports* from 1913 to 1941 and the Gilmore & Pittsburgh File (358-1) in the NP Archives provide financial and operational details. *Moody's Manual of Investments* for the period is likewise helpful. The Montana Historical Society Library, Helena provided two valuable unpublished manuscripts — the first is Thomas T. Taber's history of the "Short Lines of the Treasure State" which contains an excellent overview of G&P history, and the second is E. B. Skeels' account of the surveying of the G&P route.

Outside-braced wooden ore car no. 300 lasted the entire life of the railroad, arch bar trucks and all (top). These cars were identical to the NP 50,000 series. Below, gas electric car B7 still carried its original Northern Pacific lettering even after the G&P was abandoned. (Both, Warren R. McGee photos) Page opposite, a G&P "expedited freight service" receipt. (Rose Corum Collection)

The rare early view of the Armstead enginehouse above shows ex-PRR 2-8-0 no. 13 when it was briefly numbered 17. No explanation of the derelict saddle-tankers is available. Center, the long string of ore cars was obtained in anticipation of much traffic from local mines. (Both, James Mansfield Collection) Bottom, NP Y-4 2-8-0 no. 1293 was a sister of no. 1288, which served for a time as G&P no. 17. (Harold Vollrath Collection)

Locomotive Roster

G&P NO.	TYPE	BUILDER	CONST. NO.	DATE BLT.	DATE ACQ.	NOTES
10	2-8-2	Baldwin	32667	2/08	1909	Orig. Missouri River & Northwestern no. 10; sold to American Iron & Metal Co. 7/1940; to Duliene Scrap Co. late 1945; scrapped 1946. (See Note B)
11	2-8-2	Baldwin	32668	2/08	1909	Orig. Missouri River & Northwestern no. 11; sold to American Iron & Metal Co. 7/1940; to Duliene Scrap Co. late 1945; scrapped 1946.
12	2-8-0	Rome (N.Y. Loco. Wks.)	448	1889	9/28/09	Orig. Western New York & Pennsylvania no. 113, then 161; to PRR 6287, then SI&E 632. (See Note A) Retired 1913 and scrapped at Armstead.
13	2-8-0	Baldwin	10567	1/90	9/28/09	Orig. Western New York & Pennsylvania no. 163; to PRR 6289, then SI&E 586. Scrapped at Armstead 12/1920.
14	4-6-0	Baldwin	17289	12/99	8/28/09	Orig. Western New York & Pennsylvania no. 136; to PRR 6272, then SI&E 707. Scrapped at Leadore 8/31/34.
15	2-8-0	Baldwin	13182	1/93	1909	Orig. PRR no. 1602, then Monongahela RR 203 (1903); to SI&E. Retired 1913 and scrapped at Armstead.
16	2-8-0	Juniata	114	7/92	1909	Orig. PRR no. 1524, then Monongahela RR 204 (10/03); to SI&E. Retired 1913 and scrapped at Armstead.
17	2-8-0	Schenectady	27355	5/03	1910	Orig. Northern Pacific no. 1288; returned to NP 7/1916. (See Note C)
650	Bus	Brill		c1918	c1918	Purchased new as inspection car; later used for revenue service. Scrapped at Armstead, 1940.
B-7	Motor	General Electric		1931	1932	Orig. Northern Pacific no. B-7. Gas-electric, combination body. Returned to NP 1940.

Note A: Nos. 12-16 were former Pennsylvania RR locomotives purchased from the Southern Iron & Equipment Co. 2-8-0's were all PRR class H3a or equivalent, with 20x24″ cylinders, 50″ drivers and approximately 65 tons engine weight. The 4-6-0 had 67″ drivers and 18x26″ cylinders.

Note B: Nos. 10 and 11 were built new for the Missouri River & Northwestern RR, which went bankrupt and was sold under foreclosure on January 12, 1909; the two locomotives were then resold to the G&P. They had 20x28″ cylinders, 48″ drivers, and weighed about 85 tons.

Note C: NP Class Y-4, 22x30″ cylinders and 63″ drivers. Other engines of this class were used under lease or rental.

4-6-0 no. 14 is shown above at Leadore in August 1912, in this J. Foster Adams view (Rocky Mountain Railroad Club Collection), while 2-8-0 no. 13 is shown below in 1909 while still at the Southern Iron & Equipment Company's yard, before delivery to the G&P (Museum Collection). Both Baldwins were originally built for the Western New York & Pennsylvania, and the Tenwheeler was less than ten years old when it was obtained by the G&P.

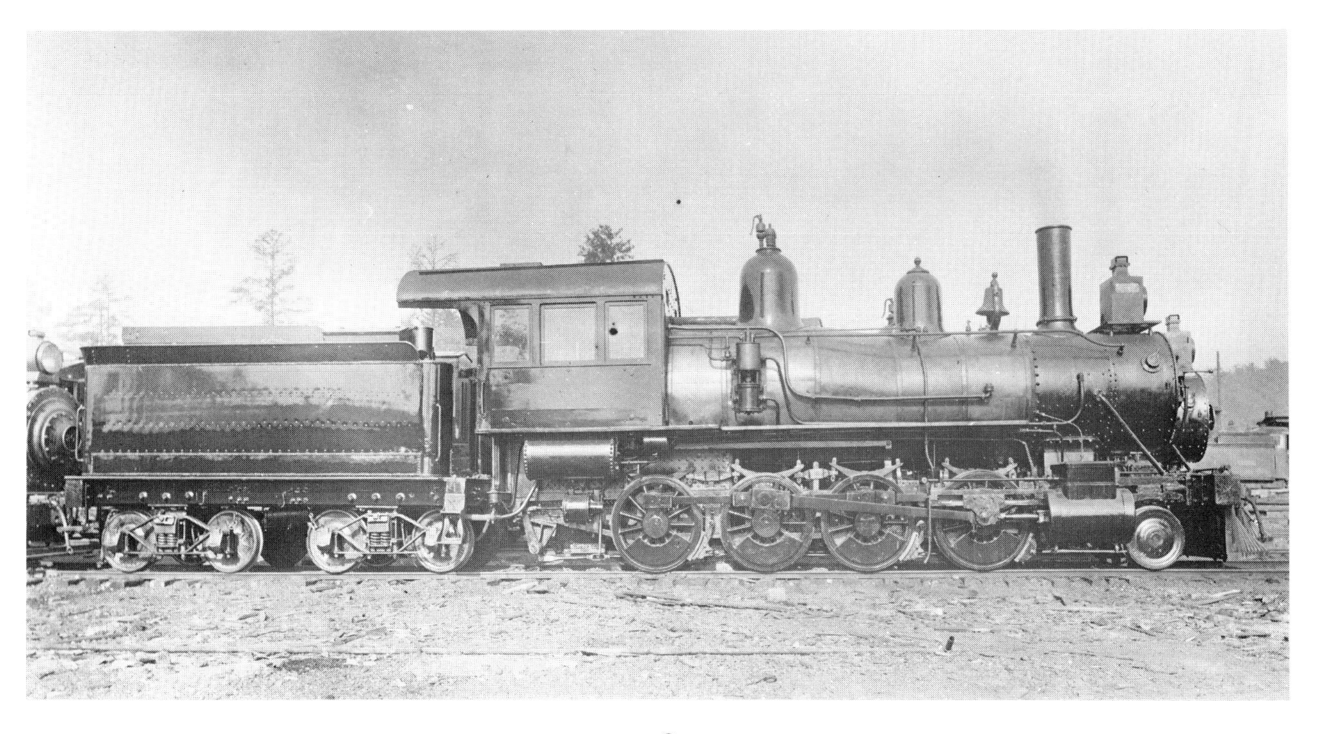

Nos. 10 and 11, two low-wheeled Baldwin 2-8-2's that had been built for the ill-fated Missouri River & Northwestern and resold when still virtually new to the G&P, quickly became the principal power for the railroad, and remained so for 30 years. Above, no. 10 at Leadore in 1912 (J. Foster Adams photo, Rocky Mountain Railroad Club Collection); below, no. 10 in the 1930's at the NP's Livingston shops (Don Roberts photo). Only visible changes are headlight and larger tender tank.

wrecks

The G&P had its share of wrecks, although the record does not indicate many of any severity. One typical wreck that occurred a few years before the line's demise is shown here. No. 11 was westbound about three miles out of Armstead when it went through a bridge that had been burnt out partially — the result of the bridge crew's leaving a fire unattended. Top, the crew has started to work; the engine has been propped up with a bridge timber, and rails removed preparatory to installing a shoo-fly. Center, with shoo-fly completed the crew can begin salvage operations. Bottom, the no. 11 has been removed and the tender and gondola are being fished out of the creek. The locomotive had almost reached solid ground when the wreck occurred, and rolled back into the ditched tender, smashing the cab (the engine crew jumped). (All, James Mansfield Collection)

All we know about the wreck above was that it occurred 4 miles west of Grant and that the engine "turned over shortly after [the] Golden Spike [ceremony]" — probably due to new soft track. Below, a car has turned over ½ mile from the tunnel on the Idaho side of Bannock Pass, and Engineer Yearian has brought up the salvage crew with 4-6-0 no. 14. Several cars of rails were involved in the mishap. (John K. Yearian Collection)

floods

Water was a periodic source of trouble to the G&P, and sometimes threatened this rare, archaic wooden Howe truss bridge three miles east of Salmon. (John K. Yearian Collection) Below, a flood in the same area on another occasion created havoc with the roadbed. (James Mansfield Collection)

snow

Winter was no time to be working on the G&P. If the memories of oldtimers can be trusted (and modern experience indicates they can), winters were endless and filled with deep snow, raging blizzards and biting cold. Below, a train powered by nos. 11 and 17 has stopped at the tank at Cruik amid the numbing cold and snow, while Conductor Boyle (center) speaks to the engineer of no. 17 about the impossibility of seeing signals through the escaping steam. The immensity of (a) the icicles on the water tank and (b) the fur coat on the bystander (right) testify to the level of the temperature. (All photos, James Mansfield Collection)

Snowfall was no more than an ordinary north country problem in the Lemhi Valley, and little Brill bus no. 650 managed to ply its way between Salmon and Gilmore on winter days such as that at right. But Bannock Pass was another matter, and it was quickly found necessary to have a rotary snow plow ready at all times to keep the line open in winter. The two lower views show the rotary cleaning out the tracks in front of the G&P depot at Armstead while the view at far right finds the rotary idling adjacent to the UP tracks at Armstead with a G&P mixed train waiting behind it alongside the UP depot. (All photos, James Mansfield Collection)

Above, the rotary tears into a light drift of snow somewhere west of Armstead on December 16, 1919 (James Mansfield Coll.), while below the whole outfit pauses for water at some other unrecorded location in the open country (J. D. Marker Coll.). Page opposite, the rotary eats its way through some deeper stuff with the help of no. 10 pushing. (Two photos, John A. Elliott Collection) The photo of the snow cut near the top of Bannock Pass (bottom) provides some idea of the snow depths encountered. (James Mansfield Collection)

The views on these two pages were all taken by J. Foster Adams and, according to his inscription, were "between Leadore and Gilmore on the G&P Ry., during the snow blockade of January and February, 1916". In this instance borrowed Northern Pacific 2-8-0 no. 1287 provided motive power for what must have been a thorough workout for the rotary and the crew, if these photos are an indication. (Rocky Mountain Railroad Club Collection)

abandonment

After service was discontinued in 1940, little time was lost in pulling up the rails and writing finis to the G&P story. By mid-September the scrappers had already retreated from Salmon, shipping the rails out four cars at a time. Here, on October 22, a rather weary no. 10 has tied up briefly at the tank at Cruik, a gon and four flats of steel in tow, while the crew is eating in the outfit train's kitchen car to the left. The journey to Armstead will be resumed shortly. (Warren R. McGee photo)

The rails come up. Left below, the dismantlers were working along the river valley near Lemhi, between Salmon and Leadore, in late September. Left above, the scrappers' rig had reached this point a few miles east of Leadore by October 22. A winch mounted on the first flat car was powered by steam from the engine (no. 11); four rails were pulled onto the flat cars at a time, and after two pulls (eight rail lengths) the train was moved again. Above, no. 11, festooned with pipe and hoses, works the scrapping train, while no. 10 — stopped at the tank at Cruik — hauls out the steel. By Christmas the scrapping crew was entering Armstead, and the G&P was a relic of the past. (All photos, Warren R. McGee)

As the rails came up, the G&P terminal at Armstead acquired a desolate appearance (top, opposite. W. R. McGee photo). Even the site disappeared after 1961, when Clark Canyon Dam was constructed; the old Oregon Short Line depot was removed to a nearby ranch, where it remained in 1977 (center). An old G&P coach saw many years of use at Leadore (bottom) as an adjunct to a motel. This page: a tangible reminder of the G&P is the tunnel and grade on Bannock Pass. These views show the west portal and approaching grade, looking almost north, as they appeared in 1977. (Four views by the author)